What people are saying about …

The Fresh Life Series

"I'm touched and blessed by Lenya and Penny's heart for His kingdom."

Kay Arthur, Bible teacher and
author of many best-selling Bible studies

"What a great way for women to learn to study the Bible: interesting stories, thought-provoking questions, and a life-changing approach to applying Scripture. Lenya and Penny provide a great method so women can succeed and grow spiritually in a short period of time. Kudos!"

Franklin Graham, president and CEO of Billy Graham
Evangelistic Association and Samaritan's Purse

"Skip and Lenya Heitzig have been friends of my wife, Cathe, and I for more than twenty years. Lenya loves to study God's Word and teach it to women in a way that is both exciting and accessible. I trust her latest book will be a blessing to you."

Greg Laurie, pastor and evangelist of Harvest Ministries

"Lenya and Penny's love for the Lord and knowledge of His Word uniquely equips them to help other women discover the pathway to God through these in-depth Bible studies."

Kay Smith, wife of Chuck Smith (Calvary Chapel)

"The Fresh Life Series is an insightful and in-depth look at God's Word. Through these Bible studies Lenya Heitzig and Penny Rose lead women to deeper intimacy with God."

K. P. Yohannan, president of Gospel for Asia

"Lenya and Penny have created another wonderful Bible study series that invites participants to spend time in God's Word and then see the Word come to fruition in their lives. What a blessing! These studies are perfect for small groups or personal daily devotions."

Robin Lee Hatcher, women's event speaker
and award-winning author

Live Relationally

The Fresh Life Series

A
20-Minutes-a-Day
Study

Live Relationally

Lessons from the Women of Genesis

Lenya Heitzig & Penny Rose

David C Cook®

transforming lives together

LIVE RELATIONALLY
Published by David C Cook
4050 Lee Vance View
Colorado Springs, CO 80918 U.S.A.

David C Cook Distribution Canada
55 Woodslee Avenue, Paris, Ontario, Canada N3L 3E5

David C Cook U.K., Kingsway Communications
Eastbourne, East Sussex BN23 6NT, England

The graphic circle C logo is a registered trademark of David C Cook.

The Web site addresses recommended throughout this book are offered as a resource
to you. These Web sites are not intended in any way to be or imply an endorsement
on the part of David C Cook, nor do we vouch for their content.

All Scripture quotations, unless otherwise indicated, are from the New King James Version.
Copyright © 1982 by Thomas Nelson, Inc. Used by permission. All rights reserved. Scripture
quotations marked NIV are taken from the *Holy Bible, New International Version*®. NIV®. Copyright
© 1973, 1978, 1984 by International Bible Society. Used by permission of Zondervan. All rights
reserved. Scripture quotations marked NLT are taken from the *Holy Bible, New Living Translation*,
copyright © 1996, 2004. Used by permission of Tyndale House Publishers, Inc., Wheaton, Illinois
60189. All rights reserved. Scripture quotations marked KJV are taken from the King James Version
of the Bible. (Public Domain.) Italics in Scripture have been added by the authors for emphasis.

Additional material provided by Misty Foster and Christy Willis.

ISBN 978-1-4347-6748-6
eISBN 978-1-4347-0026-1

© 2009 Lenya Heitzig and Penny Rose
Published in association with William K. Jensen Literary Agency
119 Bampton Court, Eugene, OR 97404

The Team: Terry Behimer, Karen Lee-Thorp, Amy Kiechlin,
Sarah Schultz, Jaci Schneider, Caitlyn York, and Susan Vannaman
Cover/Interior Design: ThinkPen Design, Greg Jackson

Printed in the United States of America

First Edition 2009

6 7 8 9 10 11 12

082913

With Gratitude

We've grown to admire the women highlighted in *Live Relationally: Lessons from the Women of Genesis* because they found triumph in the midst of tragedy. Many of these women would have remained obscure if not for their relationships with famous and sometimes infamous men. Whether facing infertility, insecurities, intimidation, or marital instability, most left a legacy of faith for modern women to follow.

We've encountered many of their contemporary counterparts whose faith served as beacons of hope as we wrote this book. Although you may never know their stories of triumph, the heavenly Father does. Thanks to Karlie Row, Sandy Schweitzer, Lisa Dahlquist, Vonda Curtis, Odessa McClain, Karen Puccini, Lorraine Lamar, Nel Thurston, and Larissa Lusko.

Contents

Lesson Nine

Lesson Ten

Introduction

LIVE RELATIONALLY

Ask a woman to tell you a little bit about herself, and more than likely you'll hear something like this: "I'm the middle child. I'm married to Joe, who's an architect. And I'm the mother of three girls." While men identify themselves occupationally, women tend to define themselves relationally. That's probably because God created us to be life-givers and nurturers. Therefore, what women value most are people. Little girls cling to baby dolls and love to play house, looking forward to their future families. Young women read romance novels and dream of marrying Prince Charming. Grown-up women, embarking on their own relational ups and downs, realize that life is more complicated than make-believe.

Thankfully, God illustrated the complexity of human relationships throughout the Bible. Like their modern counterparts, the women of Genesis lived, loved, and learned about life from the roles they played and the relationships they cherished. In this study we'll see these first women run the gamut of relationships as wives, mothers, sisters, and friends. We'll learn from their successes and failures how to *Live Relationally*.

THE WOMEN

If we asked you to name your favorite Bible character, would you name a woman? Most likely you would not. To a great extent women in the Bible were faint figures somewhere in the background. But let's not mistake unnoticed for unimportant. By spotlighting them, we see the integral part they played in God's story.

Women were not an afterthought, nor were they secondary to God's plan. They were equal to man in creation and dominion. God made both Adam *and* Eve in His image. Eve was "a helper comparable to [Adam]" (Gen. 2:18). The Hebrew word for woman (*ishshah*) is the feminine form of man (*ish*). Herbert Lockyer said, "Eve, then, was Adam's second self and differed from him in sex only, not in nature."[1]

Though time separates us by millennia, their experiences are as modern as *Desperate*

Author: Moses

Audience: People of Israel

Theme: Relationships

Timeline: Probably written between 1450 and 1410 BC

Setting: The area known as the Middle East

Scripture: "It is not good that man should be alone" (Gen. 2:18).

Housewives. We'll see these women experience emotions ranging from lust to love, anger to anxiety, and helplessness to hope. We'll read about experiences that are common to all humanity, including death, marriage, divorce, rape, and family tragedy. We'll meet women from various backgrounds: slaves and owners, Hebrews and foreigners, saints and sinners. Their stories will shock us, inspire us, and draw us closer to God.

THE LESSONS

Genesis is the book of beginnings. In other words, it is the book of firsts. In it we see everything for the first time, from families to nations. The lives of earth's first inhabitants teach us invaluable lessons:

- We'll discover the first temptation with Adam and Eve and witness its grave consequences.
- The first matriarch, Sarah, teaches us the beauty of faithfulness and that God keeps His promises even if it takes a long time.
- Through Hagar we'll see the beginning of the Arabs and discover that sometimes you can do the right thing the wrong way.
- Lot's wife teaches us that looking back will harden our hearts.
- The arranged marriage between Isaac and Rebekah highlights God's providential care for His people.
- Rachel and Leah reveal the challenges of living with a blended family.
- Dinah, tragically, is the victim of the first recorded rape in Scripture. From her story, we find that revenge is not so sweet.
- Although Tamar's story provides the first recorded instance of prostitution, we'll see her included in the line of the Messiah.

- Potiphar's wife initiates the first instance of sexual harassment against the godly young man Joseph. We learn that bad things happen to good people, but God can transform any situation.

May you live relationally,
Lenya Heitzig and Penny Rose

How to Get the Most Out of This Study

Did you know that abundant life doesn't just add years to your life, but it also adds life to your years? The secret to truly living rather than merely languishing is found in God's Word. We know that God reveals Himself through His Word. That's why doing a Bible study like this is so vital—because God's Word has the power to do His work in our lives. It is the catalyst that revives our hearts, renews our minds, and restores our souls. That helps to make life worth living!

This particular Bible study focuses on the women of Genesis. Although women in ancient times were often out of sight, they were never out of God's plan. To develop a complete picture of these remarkable women, we must examine the complexity of their relationships. We'll watch them struggle with imposing parents, imperfect spouses, and impulsive children. In their lives we'll see our own more clearly. You'll find yourself cheering for some while weeping with others. They will all teach us to *Live Relationally.* If you're ready, then let's get started …

Each week of the study is divided into five days for your personal time with God. There are five elements to each day's lesson. They are designed to help you fully "live" as you apply the truths you learn to your life:

1. Lift up … Here we ask you to "Lift up" prayers to God, asking Him to give you spiritual insight for the day.

2. Look at … This portion of the study asks you to "Look at" the Scripture text using inductive questions. These questions help you discover *What are the facts?* You'll learn the basic who-what-when-where-how aspects of the passage as well as some of the important background material.

3. Learn about … The "Learn about" sidebars correlate to specific questions in order to help you understand *What does this text mean?* These sidebar elements offer cultural insight, linguistic definitions, and biblical commentary.

4. Live out … These questions and exercises are designed to help you investigate *How should this change my life?* Here you are challenged to personally apply the lessons you have learned as you "Live out" God's principles in a practical way. We encourage you to write out all of the answers to the questions in this study. You may want to write the answers to the personal application questions in a journal to ensure privacy. By writing your insights from God day by day, you'll have a record of your relationship with Him that you can look back on when you need a faith boost.

5. Listen to … We finish with inspiring quotes from authors, speakers, and writers. You'll be able to "Listen to" the wisdom they've gleaned in their lives and relate it to your own.

Live Relationally is ideal for discussion in a small-group setting as well as for individual study. The following suggestions will help you and your group get the most out of your study time:

PERSONAL CHECKLIST

- Be determined. Examine your daily schedule; then set aside a consistent time for this study.

- Be prepared. Gather the materials you'll need: a Bible, this workbook, a journal in which to write your thoughts, and a pen.

- Be inspired. Begin each day with prayer, asking the Holy Spirit to be your teacher and to illuminate your mind.

- Be complete. Read the suggested Bible passage, and finish the homework each day.

- Be persistent. Answer each question as fully as possible. If you're unable to answer a question, move forward to the next question or read the explanation in the "Learn about …" section, which may offer further insight.

- Be consistent. Don't get discouraged. If you miss a day, use the weekend to catch up.

- Be honest. When answering the "Live out …" questions, allow the Lord to search your heart and transform your life. Take time to reflect honestly about your feelings, experiences, sins, goals, and responses to God.

- Be blessed. Enjoy your daily study time as God speaks to you through His Word.

SMALL-GROUP CHECKLIST

- Be prayerful. Pray before you begin your time together.

- Be biblical. Keep all answers in line with God's Word; avoid personal opinion.

- Be confidential. Keep all sharing within your small group confidential.

- Be respectful. Listen without interrupting. Keep comments on track and to the point so that all can share.

- Be discreet. In some cases, you need not share more than absolutely necessary. Some things are between you and the Lord.

- Be kind. Reply to the comments of others lovingly and courteously.

- Be mindful. Remember your group members in prayer throughout the week.

SMALL-GROUP LEADER CHECKLIST

- Be prayerful. Pray that the Holy Spirit will "guide you into truth" so that your leadership will guide others.

- Be faithful. Prepare by reading the Bible passage and studying the lesson ahead of time, highlighting truths and applying them personally.

- Be prompt. Begin and end the study on time.

- Be thorough. For optimum benefit, allot one hour for small-group discussion. This should allow plenty of time to cover all of the questions and exercises for each lesson.

- Be selective. If you have less than an hour, you should carefully choose which questions you will address and summarize the edited information for your group. In this way, you can focus on the more thought-provoking questions. Be sure to grant enough time to address pertinent "Live out …" exercises, as this is where you and the other women will clearly see God at work in your lives.

- Be sensitive. Some of the "Live out …" exercises are very personal and may not be appropriate to discuss in a small group. If you sense this is the case, feel free to move to another question.

- Be flexible. If the questions in the study seem unclear, reword them for your group. Feel free to add your own questions to bring out the meaning of a verse.

- Be inclusive. Encourage each member to participate in the discussion. You may have to draw some out or tone some down so that all have the opportunity to participate.

- Be honest. Don't be afraid to admit that you don't have all the answers! When in doubt, encourage group members to take difficult questions to their church leadership for clarification.

- Be focused. Keep the discussion on tempo and on target. Learn to pace your small group so that you complete a lesson on time. When participants get sidetracked, redirect the discussion to the passage at hand.

- Be patient. Realize that not all people are at the same place spiritually or socially. Wait for the members of your group to answer the questions rather than jumping in and answering them yourself.

Eve — Trouble in Paradise

Genesis 2:18 — 3:24

The first trouble in Paradise was man's aloneness. For six consecutive days—as God created light, the cosmos, the land and sea, the stars and planets, the creatures in the sea and sky, and every living thing that moves, including the ultimate creation of man—God declared, "It is good." But there was one thing that wasn't good: Man did not have a companion. So God created the perfect mate for Adam. She would be the counterpart for him physically, spiritually, intellectually, and socially. She was intended to complete him. She was more than a mate—she was a soul mate.

We know this woman as Eve. Although the Bible does not describe her, there is no doubt that she was the most beautiful woman who ever lived. Why? She was God's masterpiece. The Divine dipped His paintbrush into the palette of dust and clay and breathed life from His wellspring of inspiration to form a portrait of perfection. Just imagine a woman with a face more beautiful than Helen of Troy, a body more statuesque than the Venus de Milo, a personality more captivating than Cleopatra, and a smile more mysterious than the *Mona Lisa*. She ate a perfect diet, so her figure was probably flawless. Because of an untainted gene pool, she was undoubtedly without physical defect. Owing to the antediluvian atmosphere, her complexion was age-defying perfection. She was never a child, daughter, or sister. She was the first wife, the first mother, and the first woman to encounter evil incarnate. That's when real trouble in Paradise began.

Day 1: Genesis 2:18–25   **PARADISE FOUND**

Day 2: Genesis 3:1–6   **INNOCENCE LOST**

Day 3: Genesis 3:7–13   **HIDING OUT**

Day 4: Genesis 3:14–19 **JUDGMENT PRONOUNCED**

Day 5: Genesis 3:20–24 **EAST OF EDEN**

DAY 1
Paradise Found

LIFT UP ...

Thank You, Lord, that I am fearfully and wonderfully made. You have created me in Your image to glorify Your name. May I fulfill Your will in my heart and home. Amen.

LOOK AT ...

We begin our study when God made man and woman. Though God created both humans and animals, this does not mean that they are on equal footing. People are made in God's image, setting us apart from animals in a profound way. We possess a soul. The soul refers to a person's inner life. It is the center of our emotions and personality. The word *soul* is first used in Genesis: "The LORD God formed man of the dust of the ground, and breathed into his nostrils the breath of life; and man became a living being [soul]" (Gen. 2:7). In other words, humans possess intellect, emotion, and will.

For instance, dogs aren't bright enough to realize they'll never catch their own tails; cows don't weep over the beauty of a sunset; and a female praying mantis can't keep herself from chewing her spouse's head off. People, on the other hand, have the ability to acquire knowledge and experience deep feelings. They also have the capacity for self-control. While animals act instinctively, we as humans should behave transcendently. We are God's special creation endowed with the gift of "soul power."

READ GENESIS 2:18–25.

And the LORD God said, "It is not good that man should be alone; I will make him a helper comparable to him." Out of the ground the LORD God formed every beast of the field and every bird of the air, and brought them to Adam to see what he would call them. And whatever Adam called each living creature, that was its name. So Adam gave names to all cattle, to the birds of the air, and to every beast of the field. But for Adam there was not found a helper comparable to

LEARN ABOUT ...

1 One More

God verbalized a need evident in creation—the need of a companion for the man. Therefore, He decided to make another being like the man to complete him. God made woman *for* man. She, too, was created in God's image. Warren Wiersbe said, "[She was] his wife, companion, and helper."[1]

4 One Rib

During the sixth day, probably after man named the animals, God acted on man's need for a counterpart and made woman *from* man. He placed Adam into a supernatural sleep and took a piece of Adam's body to form woman. Matthew Henry said, "The man was dust refined, but the woman was dust double-refined."[2]

6 One Flesh

God created woman from man for a divine purpose: to be "a helper comparable to him" (Gen. 2:18). Only woman can fulfill the needs of man's body, soul, and spirit. This relationship is intended to take place within the context of marriage. Here we see God define marriage as a union between a husband and wife in a committed relationship for a lifetime.

him. And the LORD God caused a deep sleep to fall on Adam, and he slept; and He took one of his ribs, and closed up the flesh in its place. Then the rib which the LORD God had taken from man He made into a woman, and He brought her to the man. And Adam said: "This is now bone of my bones and flesh of my flesh; she shall be called Woman, because she was taken out of Man." Therefore a man shall leave his father and mother and be joined to his wife, and they shall become one flesh. And they were both naked, the man and his wife, and were not ashamed. Genesis 2:18–25

1. Explain the problem and solution God first spoke about in this passage.

2. Describe in detail the task God assigned to Adam.

3. Compare and contrast Adam to the rest of the living beings.

4. In your own words, describe how God created woman.

5. a. When Adam met his mate, he made a proclamation. What do you think "bone of my bones and flesh of my flesh" signified for Adam?

   b. What did he call his mate and why?

6. Here we find the first mention of marriage in Scripture. Explain God's intent for marriage.

7. a. What else do you learn about the man and wife in this passage?

   b. Why do you think this is relevant?

LIVE OUT ...

8. a. God declared that man needs companionship. Read Ecclesiastes 4:9–12, and explain some of the reasons why it is better to have a mate to come alongside you.

    b. Read the sidebar concerning "Threefold Strength," and talk about how you have experienced God's supernatural strength in your life and/or marriage.

9. Many women today struggle with the way they look, think, and feel. But when God made Eve from Adam's rib, this was not His intent. When He made *you*, He made *you* to be the person you are too. With this in mind, journal Psalm 139:13–14 into a personal psalm praising God for making you just as you are.

    > For You formed my inward parts;
    > You covered me in my mother's womb.
    > I will praise You, for I am fearfully and wonderfully made;
    > Marvelous are Your works. Psalm 139:13–14

10. Before the fall, Adam and Eve were naked and unashamed. It's probably difficult to imagine being unashamed about our looks, actions, or thoughts. But Jesus came to free us from condemnation (Rom. 8:1). Read the following Scriptures, and talk about how we can stand either ashamed or unashamed before God.

    Psalm 119:5–6

    Isaiah 41:11

    Isaiah 49:23

    Jeremiah 8:9

LEARN ABOUT ...

8 Threefold Strength

Solomon stated that "a threefold cord is not quickly broken" (Eccl. 4:12). Practically, this refers to a rope with additional strings added for strength. When God is at the center of a marriage, the marriage is fortified. This could also allude to the Trinity or to the Holy Spirit coming to indwell our hearts at salvation.

9 True Satisfaction

Woman was taken from man's rib rather than from the dust. In a sense we are unlike any other creature. Realizing this could help you feel truly satisfied about yourself. Remember that God created you as His bride to love Him and live with Him forever: "Behold, you are fair, my love! Behold, you are fair!" (Song 1:15).

○ ○ ● ○ ○

It's safe to say that none of us is perfectly content with our frame. We all wish we were better, thinner, richer, healthier, smarter, or younger. We may think that if we were different in some way, people would accept us, respect us, or love us more. Maybe we'd even love and respect ourselves more. Like Eve, we would walk in this world unashamed.

A recent University of Waterloo study determined that people's self-esteem is linked to such traits as physical appearance, social skills, and popularity. Research associate Danu Anthony noted that acceptance from others is strongly tied to appearances. Furthermore, the study found that self-esteem is connected to traits that earn acceptance from other people. "People state emphatically that it is 'what's inside' that counts and encourage their children not to judge others based on appearances, yet they revere attractive people to an astonishing degree," Anthony says. "They say they value communal qualities such as kindness and understanding more than any other traits, but seem to be exceptionally interested in achieving good looks and popularity." The bottom line is that people's looks and behavior are intimately linked to being accepted by others.[3]

As women of faith, we know that acceptance from others is not nearly as important as our acceptance *of* one Man—the God-man Jesus Christ, the second Adam. Only by accepting Jesus Christ's sacrificial death will you be made whole: "You are complete in Him" (Col. 2:10).

LISTEN TO...

The woman was formed out of man—not out of his head to rule over him; not out of his feet to be trampled upon by him; but out of his side to be his equal, from beneath his arm to be protected, and from near his heart to be loved.

—*Matthew Henry*

DAY 2

Innocence Lost

What images does the word *paradise* bring to mind? You may visualize a tropical island with sparkling blue water, swaying palm trees, and a sandy beach. Your favorite people most likely inhabit it. And since every necessity exists in abundance, you need never work. No wonder humans possess an innate desire to return to the garden and live harmoniously ever after. Environmentalists long to re-create it. Hindus hope to reincarnate it. And through meditation Buddhists attempt to replicate it. However, returning to Eden requires more than a relocation; it demands a transformation—because once you place people in paradise, innocence is lost.

When Adam and Eve arrived in Paradise, they enjoyed fresh innocence. You could describe them as naive. They'd never witnessed a crime, felt fear, or experienced regret. When Eve first encountered the Serpent, there was no reason to be suspicious. Perhaps all snakes could speak. And since no one had ever deceived her, she was especially susceptible to Satan's semantics. However, after one taste of forbidden fruit, her innocence (along with that of the human race) was lost forever. She could no longer assume that her surroundings were nonthreatening. From that point on she had to be on her guard. She would learn that what God says is much more important than why He says it.

Much like our ancestors, at birth we view the world in wonder, humans as harmless, and the future with boundless faith. But inevitably everyone experiences a loss of innocence. Whether through divorce, deceit, or disappointment, all of us eventually discover prowlers in paradise. Only God can cover our sins and lead us back to the garden.

LIFT UP ...

Father, like Eve I am susceptible to Satan's deception. Help me to be watchful and alert to the Enemy's devices. Help me to hide your Word in my heart that I might not sin against You. Amen.

LEARN ABOUT …

1 Speaking Serpent

Satan entered Eden masquerading as a serpent, one of God's creatures that He had previously declared good. As a master manipulator, he inhabits shapes and sentiments in order to deceive God's people. Scripture reveals his many disguises, from a roaring lion (I Peter 5:8) to an angel of light (2 Cor. 11:14).

LOOK AT …

Yesterday we learned that God had a solution to man's aloneness. He provided a helper who would complete Adam. Scripture reveals three different names for this companion. First, she was known as "woman," a generic term that means "man-ness." It describes her as member of man-kind, differing from other living beings. Second, she was called "Adam," depicting the union and oneness of flesh the first couple enjoyed: "Male and female created he them; and blessed them, and called their name Adam" (Gen. 5:2 KJV). Finally, Adam gave his wife the name Eve, since she would become the mother of all living things. It's interesting to note that Adam gave his wife this endearing name *after* the fall. He could have called her "Temptress" or "She-devil." Instead he prophesied concerning her future rather than pronouncing judgment on her past.

Now we turn to one of history's darkest days. Here we witness Eve succumb to temptation, thrusting all of humanity into the consequences of "the curse." You might say that your battle with sin began right here. From this point on, people are born *in* sin (with a tainted bloodline) and born *to* sin (possessing a wicked nature). Before being too harsh with Eve, try walking in her bare feet. She didn't have a Bible, a pastor, a mother, or a friend to instruct her. God had not warned her to avoid talking snakes. For Satan, it was like taking candy from a baby. Eve was dazzled by his antics.

READ GENESIS 3:1–6.

Now the serpent was more cunning than any beast of the field which the LORD God had made. And he said to the woman, "Has God indeed said, 'You shall not eat of every tree of the garden'?" And the woman said to the serpent, "We may eat the fruit of the trees of the garden; but of the fruit of the tree which is in the midst of the garden, God has said, 'You shall not eat it, nor shall you touch it, lest you die.'" Then the serpent said to the woman,

"You will not surely die. For God knows that in the day you eat of it your eyes will be opened, and you will be like God, knowing good and evil." So when the woman saw that the tree was good for food, that it was pleasant to the eyes, and a tree desirable to make one wise, she took of its fruit and ate. She also gave to her husband with her, and he ate. Genesis 3:1–6

1. Describe the Serpent in your own words.

2. Explain who initiated the conversation, and recount what was said.

3. Compare the woman's response with God's original command given in Genesis 2:16–17.

   a. To whom was that command given?

   b. What phrase did Eve omit?

   c. What phrase did Eve insert?

   d. What does this tell you about Eve's view of God?

4. List the four things the Serpent promised would happen if Eve ate of the fruit.

5. What three things motivated Eve to partake of the forbidden fruit?

6. a. What final action did Eve make?

   b. Why do you think she did it?

LEARN ABOUT …

3 Scriptural Semantics

Satan would rather that you discuss God's commands than do them. The battle is for your mind. Don't add to or subtract anything from God's Word. Instead cast "down arguments and every high thing that exalts itself against the knowledge of God, bringing every thought into captivity to the obedience of Christ" (2 Cor. 10:5).

---

5 Seems Sensible

Temptations often come in beautiful packaging; otherwise they would not be tempting. Eve's sin came through visual attraction. She decided to walk by sight and not by faith. We must never base our judgments on mere externals: "You are looking only on the surface of things. If anyone is confident that he belongs to Christ, he should consider again that we belong to Christ just as much as he" (2 Cor. 10:7 NIV).

LEARN ABOUT ...

7 Satan's Strategy

Satan attacked Eve's mind. His question raised doubts about God. Eve may have wondered some of these things: (1) Is God's word true? (2) Is God's will good? (3) Is God's way best? "I fear that somehow your pure and undivided devotion to Christ will be corrupted, just as Eve was deceived by the cunning ways of the serpent" (2 Cor. 11:3 NLT).

---

9 Spreading Sin

Eve's greatest sin was to offer the forbidden fruit to Adam. She not only ate, she also sought to propagate temptation: "What sorrow awaits the world, because it tempts people to sin. Temptations are inevitable, but what sorrow awaits the person who does the tempting" (Matt. 18:7 NLT).

LIVE OUT ...

7. There is a difference between asking God questions and questioning God. In the appropriate columns list some of the times you've asked God sincere questions as well as the times you've questioned God's sovereignty.

ASKED GOD	QUESTIONED GOD

8. Because our battle with the Enemy begins in the mind, God has given us many safeguards. Fill in the following chart to discover how to fortify your thought life. Explain what you think each instruction means.

SCRIPTURE	MENTAL SAFEGUARDS
Romans 12:2	
Ephesians 4:23	
Philippians 4:6–7	
Colossians 3:2	
1 Peter 1:13	

9. a. We learned that Eve spread her sin to Adam. Read 1 Timothy 2:11–14. Why do you think Paul cited the order of creation here?

   b. Explain who was deceived and how this led to the fall. Who do you think bears the greater burden for the fall and why?

○ ○ ● ○ ○

Certainly the Serpent took advantage of Eve's naïveté. He twisted the truth incrementally, skewing what God had commanded to question God's loving character. "Sure, He forbade the fruit, but why did He deny you something so desirable?" the snake suggested. And Eve began to reconsider God's motives. Perhaps she thought, "What if He's holding out on us? Maybe He placed enlightenment just out of reach. Is He threatened by equals?" Quickly deceit turned into doubt, and doubt tumbled into disobedience. The sin that Eve ultimately committed was covetousness—she wanted what she couldn't have.

Covetousness is the driving desire to have more, longing for what one does not possess. Sometimes it is called greed. Its underlying motivation lies in discontent with what one already has. The Bible warns, "Let your conduct be without covetousness; be content with such things as you have. For He Himself has said, 'I will never leave you nor forsake you.' So we may boldly say: 'The LORD is my helper; I will not fear'" (Heb. 13:5–6).

Abraham Lincoln once made a simple yet impactful statement on covetousness. He was walking down the street with two small boys who were both crying loudly. A passerby asked, "Why all the fuss, Abe?" Lincoln responded, "The trouble with these lads is what's wrong with the world; one has a nut and the other wants it!"

Are we any different from Eve? There are times we want the very thing we can't have. The only solution for covetousness is contentment. Just as deception began when Satan played mind games with Eve, contentment comes when you tell the Enemy to mind his own business.

LISTEN TO...

The snake pulled back the curtain to the throne room and invited Eve to take a seat. Put on the crown. Pick up the scepter. Put on the cape. See how it feels to have power. See how it feels to have a name. See how it feels to be in control! Eve swallowed the hook. The temptation to be like God eclipsed her view of God.

—*Max L. Lucado*

DAY 3

Hiding Out

"Where's Penny?" my mother demanded. Cynthia shrugged her shoulders, handed me the phone, and said, "You are so busted." I took the receiver and sheepishly said, "Hello?" My mom said, "Stop whatever you're doing and come home right now."

It all started when I heard that Jackson Browne was coming to town for a concert. I knew I had to get tickets. He was my *favorite* musician. When I mentioned it to my folks, they forbade me from going. They didn't want me out partying when I should be home cracking the books. But I ignored their warnings, went to the concert, partied like a rock star, and hid out at my friend's house afterward. I figured they'd never find out. Although I can't prove it, I think my mother is omniscient. I could never hide anything from her. Despite the fact that I got in trouble often, she continued to love me through my prodigal years.

"Adam, where are you?" could be one of the most haunting phrases ever spoken. The fact that the Creator of the universe searched through a garden for the crown of His creation—the person who had willingly disobeyed Him—is heartbreaking. No doubt God felt betrayed and disappointed. Yet He initiated reconciliation with the wayward couple. Just like me, they had been caught in the act. But they would learn never to hide from the One who loved them.

LIFT UP ...

Lord, it's so easy for me to shift the blame when I sin. But I know that my sin leaves me naked and ashamed before You. Please help me not to run and hide from You when I sin. Amen.

LOOK AT ...

Despite God's warning, we've seen Eve take a bite of the fruit of the Tree of Knowledge of Good and Evil, then share the fruit with her husband. Satan demonstrated that the art of deception is to make a lie sound like the truth. He promised that if Eve ate the fruit she would "be *like God*, knowing good and evil" (Gen. 3:5). At this point, the first couple knew only good, not evil. But after one bite, they became intimately acquainted with evil. If Satan had said, "For God knows that when you eat of it … you will be *like me,* knowing good and evil," he would have been telling the whole truth. Too late they became aware that God's word was good and that the Serpent's word was evil; they saw the goodness of God's image deformed by the wickedness of sin; and they felt the closeness of God's presence replaced with a fearful sense of dread. Sadly, there are some things that once done can never be undone. Thankfully, God still pursues people by name, calling out, "Where are you?"

LEARN ABOUT …

1 Eyes and Ears

The opening of the couple's eyes refers to the development of a conscience. Previously they had known only light, but now darkness cast a shadow. They were thrust into an inner war: "For the flesh lusts against the Spirit, and the Spirit against the flesh; and these are contrary to one another" (Gal. 5:17).

READ GENESIS 3:7–13.

Then the eyes of both of them were opened, and they knew that they were naked; and they sewed fig leaves together and made themselves coverings. And they heard the sound of the LORD *God walking in the garden in the cool of the day, and Adam and his wife hid themselves from the presence of the* LORD *God among the trees of the garden. Then the* LORD *God called to Adam and said to him, "Where are you?" So he said, "I heard Your voice in the garden, and I was afraid because I was naked; and I hid myself." And He said, "Who told you that you were naked? Have you eaten from the tree of which I commanded you that you should not eat?" Then the man said, "The woman whom You gave to be with me, she gave me of the tree, and I ate." And the* LORD *God said to the woman, "What is this you have done?" The woman said, "The serpent deceived me, and I ate." Genesis 3:7–13*

1. a. Based on their actions, what type of insight did Adam and Eve develop?

   b. How do you think this experience differed from Satan's promise in verse 5?

2. What did Adam and Eve hear, and how did they respond to the source of this sound?

LEARN ABOUT ...

3 Hide and Seek

Why did Adam and Eve hide from God? Most commentators agree that sin develops guilt, and guilt leads to fear. For the first time in their lives they were afraid of God. In a futile attempt they sought to hide from an all-knowing God. Fellowship was broken. Communion was replaced with confusion.

---

5 Naked and Ashamed

The word *naked* expresses not only the concept of going without clothing, but also the ideas of poverty, desolation, and moral bankruptcy. Earlier, Adam and Eve were unashamed of their nakedness (Gen. 2:25). After eating the fruit, they began to feel shame in every sense of the word.

---

8 Flesh and Spirit

In the strongest sense, the flesh is the earthly part of man represented by lusts and desires. The flesh is contrary to the Spirit. Those who are in the flesh cannot please God (see Rom. 8:8). Christ alone is our salvation, since by the works of the law "no flesh shall be justified" (see Gal. 2:16).[4]

3. How did God respond to Adam's absence? What does this teach you about His character?

4. a. Describe Adam's emotional state.

   b. Why do you think he felt this way?

5. Underline the word *naked,* which is repeated three times in this text. Define what you think it means in this story.

6. a. Who did Adam blame, and who did Eve blame?

   b. Explain their reasons for blaming someone else.

7. What do you think motivates us as humans to become blame shifters? How do you think we could break this pattern?

LIVE OUT ...

8. Eve's and Adam's eyes were opened so that they developed a conscience. As Christian women, our conscience and spiritual discernment enable us to fight against the works of the flesh. Read the following passage, and describe which fruit(s) of the Spirit can conquer which works of the flesh. (Example: Love conquers hatred.)

Now the works of the flesh are evident, which are: adultery, fornication, uncleanness, lewdness, idolatry, sorcery, hatred, contentions, jealousies, outbursts of wrath, selfish ambitions, dissensions, heresies, envy, murders, drunkenness, revelries.… But the fruit of the Spirit is love, joy, peace, longsuffering, kindness, goodness, faithfulness, gentleness, self-control. Against such there is no law. Galatians 5:19–23

9. We've seen the downward spiral Adam's and Eve's sin caused: They were afraid, they became ashamed, and they hid themselves. Use these three sentences to describe a time you fell into the same downward cycle.

I felt afraid when ...

I was ashamed when ...

I tried to hide by ...

10. a. We know that the first couple tried to shift the blame for their sin. Adam accused Eve, and Eve blamed the Serpent. Psalm 51 records David's confession of sin with Bathsheba after being rebuked by the prophet Nathan. Read the psalm, and describe the view of God that David expresses.

b. What does David request?

c. Ultimately who had he sinned against?

d. What does God require of the sinner?

e. If there's something you've been trying to hide or shift the blame about, confess it to God right now and experience the relief felt by King David and others through the ages.

○ ○ ● ○ ○

LEARN ABOUT ...

10 Sin and Repentance

Sin carries the notion of a law and a lawgiver. The lawgiver is God. Sin exposes everything in the character and conduct of God's creatures contrary to the expressed will of God. The sinfulness of sin lies in the fact that it is against God, even when the wrong we do is also to others or ourselves.[5]

The Internet is full of stories about a car in California that was stolen in 1981. The Web sites report that police staged an intense search for the thief, placing announcements on local radio stations and in newspapers to contact him. The owner had left a box of crackers laced with poison on the front seat of the stolen car. They were meant to be rat bait. The police and owner of the Volkswagen Beetle were desperately trying to save his life. Sadly, the thief hid from those who were trying to help him.

Both the car thief and the first couple were motivated by fear. However, their pursuers sought them to save them. So how do we know that God was not angry when He entered the garden? He was walking, not running. He arrived during the cool of the day, not in the dark of the night when fears seem to multiply. He beckoned gently rather than shouting loudly. God's presence didn't terrify the perpetrators—they were scared because they had sinned.

What about you? Do you try to hide from the One who wants to save you? It's senseless for at least three reasons. (1) You can't. "Where can I flee from Your presence?" (Ps. 139:7). (2) It hurts. "No one is good—except God alone" (Luke 18:19 NIV). (3) He cares. "[He] has come to seek and to save that which was lost" (Luke 19:10).

LISTEN TO...

Silence, O sinner, stop! Accuse not Eve and Adam.
Without that incident, it's you who would have done it.

—Angelus Silesius

DAY 4

Judgment Pronounced

On the same level as Al Capone and John Dillinger, Ma Barker was considered the mastermind of the notorious Barker-Karpis gang: robbers, kidnappers, and murderers. Although she grew up in a Christian home, Ma Barker was no angel. J. Edgar Hoover said she was "an animal mother of the she-wolf type … a veritable beast of prey." Influenced by the exploits of outlaw Jesse James, she swooned over him in person and was devastated by his death. Some say she killed her lover, billboard painter Arthur Dunlop, for ratting out her gang to the cops. She died with a tommy gun in her hands in a shoot-out with the FBI. George Barker, who left her because she wore the pants in the family, said, "She never would let me do with them [the boys] what I wanted to."[6] Some have said that Ma was an extreme example of a fallen daughter of Eve.

One of the consequences of Eve's sin was that childbirth and child rearing would be painful for all women. As Christians, we're exhorted to "train up a child in the way he should go, and when he is old he will not depart from it" (Prov. 22:6). Unfortunately, some wander off that path; and like the father in the parable of the prodigal son, we ache to see them stumble and fall. Another consequence of Eve's sin was that her relationship with Adam was compromised. God warned her, "Your desire shall be for your husband, And he shall rule over you" (Gen. 3:16). And as with Ma Barker who took the reins of leadership in her home, Eve got into trouble with not only her earthly husband, but also her heavenly Father.

LIFT UP …

Lord, You are merciful enough to find us when we sin and just enough to pronounce a penalty upon that sin. I'm so grateful that You sent Your Son to pay the ultimate penalty for my sin so that I can enjoy Your amazing grace. Amen.

LOOK AT ...

We've seen that Adam and Eve could try to run, but they could not hide themselves or their sin from God. Though they initially tried to shift the blame to someone else, we'll see how God finally forced them to face the consequences of their sin. Though God is a God of mercy, He is also a God of justice. In mercy He would allow them to live long lives, but ultimately they would receive the death sentence and return to the ashes just as He had promised.

You might say that when God sought the disobedient couple in the garden, He was prepared to hold a trial. Because God is omniscient, He was completely aware that there was something wrong in the garden of Eden. First, He pursued them as an officer of the court to bring them to justice. Next, He questioned them about their behavior as a prosecuting attorney would do. Now we'll see Him address them and Satan, their codefendant, as the divine Judge, pronouncing His sentence on them. As the One who created all three of the defendants, God had every right to judge them.

READ GENESIS 3:14–19.

So the LORD God said to the serpent: "Because you have done this, you are cursed more than all cattle, and more than every beast of the field; on your belly you shall go, and you shall eat dust all the days of your life. And I will put enmity between you and the woman, and between your seed and her Seed; He shall bruise your head, and you shall bruise His heel." To the woman He said: "I will greatly multiply your sorrow and your conception; in pain you shall bring forth children; your desire shall be for your husband, and he shall rule over you." Then to Adam He said, "Because you have heeded the voice of your wife, and have eaten from the tree of which I commanded you, saying, 'You shall not eat of it': "Cursed is the ground for your sake; in toil you shall eat of it all the days of your life. Both thorns and thistles it shall bring forth for you, and you shall eat the herb of the field. In the sweat of your face you shall eat bread till you return to the ground, for out of it you were taken; for dust you are, and to dust you shall return." Genesis 3:14–19

1. Describe how God cursed the Serpent physically.

2. a. How did He curse the Serpent spiritually?

 b. How do you think this speaks prophetically of Satan's battle with Jesus?

3. Next God pronounced His judgment on the woman.

 a. How did He punish her concerning childbirth?

 b. What did He pronounce concerning her marriage?

4. God next turned His attention to Adam.

 a. Explain why He pronounced a judgment on Adam.

 b. How did God judge Adam concerning his work?

 c. What would the ultimate punishment be for eating from the tree?

5. a. What key phrase did God use to remind Adam of his status as a created being?

 b. How would this make you feel if God talked to you in this manner?

6. God put enmity between the seed of woman (Christ) and Satan.

 a. Read Galatians 3:16. What is one interpretation of who the seed represents?

 b. Based on what you know of history and Scripture, how did Satan "bruise" the heel of the seed of the woman?

c. Paul says, "Remember that Jesus Christ, of the seed of David, was raised from the dead" (2 Tim. 2:8). How do you think this fulfills the prophecy of the seed of woman (Eve) bruising or crushing Satan's head?

LIVE OUT ...

7. God's punishment for Eve's disobedience was that there would be pain in childbearing and implied pain in child rearing. Yet Scripture considers motherhood a high calling.

a. Read the following passages and draw a line to connect them with how mothers are to be treated.

Exodus 20:12	Help your mother in her old age
Exodus 21:15–17	Make your mother proud
Proverbs 1:8	Follow your mother's instructions
Proverbs 23:22	Do not physically or verbally abuse her
Proverbs 23:25	Honor your mother

b. Talk about how you've either experienced some of the pain involved in being a mom, or how you have treated your mom.

○ ○ ● ○ ○

These verses about men ruling over women in the home have provoked controversy, especially among feminists, throughout the years. But it's good to remember that they only refer to home life. In that context, submission can be viewed as a practical rather than a punitive matter. Warren Wiersbe said, "This submission isn't identified as part of a curse or as a mandate for husbands to have sovereign power over their wives. The New Testament makes it clear that husbands and wives who love each other and are filled with the Spirit will be mutually submissive (Eph. 5:18ff; 1 Cor. 7:1–7)."[9]

It would be natural to have a desire to exalt ourselves above one another—even our husbands. After all, isn't that what Lucifer did when he rebelled against God? Isaiah records this fall from grace:

> How you are fallen from heaven,
> O Lucifer, son of the morning!
> How you are cut down to the ground,
> You who weakened the nations!
> For you have said in your heart:
> "I will ascend into heaven,
> I will exalt my throne above the stars of God." Isaiah 14:12–13

Satan's pride slithered into Eden and poisoned the hearts of men and women, bringing heartbreak. At creation God established order. The Devil disrupted that order by offering Eve forbidden fruit. God reestablished relational order not to put women down but to promote harmony in the home. Don't be deceived when the world tells you submission is slavery— you are showing the world a picture of salvation through Christ: "Just as the church is subject to Christ, so let the wives be to their own husbands in everything" (Eph. 5:24).

LISTEN TO...

The model of woman in tribal patriarchalism is the brood mare; in hedonistic naturalism, she is the bunny or plaything; in feminist ideology, she is the self-sufficient career woman; in romanticism, she is the fairy princess or maiden in distress waiting to be rescued; in biblical faith, she is the partner in ministry.

—*Donald G. Bloesch*

DAY 5

East of Eden

Have you ever been kicked out of paradise? I (Lenya) have. When I was twenty years old, I was banished from Disneyland by an armed escort who insisted that I leave the premises. Since my grandpa was a member of the Anaheim Chamber of Commerce during the 1960s, our family received free passes to make annual pilgrimages to the Magic Kingdom. We shook hands with Mickey, made our entrance on the Monorail, and had enough E tickets to ride all the main attractions twice. It was the stuff dreams were made of. But in the summer of 1977, it became my worst nightmare. My dad sent me to chaperone my brother and his best friend for a day of Disney adventure. Unknown to me, they had smuggled marijuana into "the happiest place on earth." Dangling from a gondola over Fantasyland they lit up a joint. By the time we disembarked in Tomorrowland, the Park Police were waiting to apprehend us. After some fast-talking on my part and a phone call to my mother in Michigan, the boys were released into my custody. However, we were escorted out of paradise in complete humiliation.

As traumatic as my incident was, it cannot compare to the disgrace the first couple must have experienced as they were driven from Eden. No more would they enjoy uninterrupted fellowship with their Creator. Their life of leisure would be exchanged for one of hard labor. They would be denied access to Eden's bounty forever. Partaking of forbidden fruit not only changes us, it also leads to a change of location. Prodigals inevitably find themselves leaving paradise behind.

LIFT UP ...

Lord, sin separates me from You even though I long to be close to You. Please draw me closer to the cross of Calvary, the true Tree of Life, where Jesus bought my redemption. Amen.

LOOK AT ...

Yesterday we discovered the devastating consequence of the fall. Now we come to realize that clothing is part of the curse. Matthew Henry writes, "We should have had no occasion for them, either for defense or decency, if sin had not made us naked, to our shame."[10] Had Adam and Eve refused to eat of the Tree of Knowledge of Good and Evil, they would have remained unrobed and unembarrassed. But once their eyes were opened, they saw themselves differently—what once appeared normal was now perceived as naughty. As a result, Eve became the first seamstress and sewed garments of green leaves, hoping to cover up their guilt. Apparently it didn't work. When God entered the garden, they went farther and hid behind the trees. Honestly, none of us has any reason to be proud of our wardrobe even if it's full of designer labels. Instead, our clothing can serve as a reminder of sin and a warning to avoid disobeying God's commands.

READ GENESIS 3:20–24.

And Adam called his wife's name Eve, because she was the mother of all living. Also for Adam and his wife the LORD God made tunics of skin, and clothed them. Then the LORD God said, "Behold, the man has become like one of Us, to know good and evil. And now, lest he put out his hand and take also of the tree of life, and eat, and live forever"—therefore the LORD God sent him out of the garden of Eden to till the ground from which he was taken. So He drove out the man; and He placed cherubim at the east of the garden of Eden, and a flaming sword which turned every way, to guard the way to the tree of life. Genesis 3:20–24

1. What do you learn about the first couple's relationship based on the name Adam gave his wife?

2. What clothing did God provide for the couple, and how does this compare to the clothing they chose?

3. God used the pronoun "Us" to refer to Himself. What does this tell you about His character?

LEARN ABOUT …

2 Tunics of Skin

The tunics of skin held great significance. It's likely that the animals were slaughtered before the couple's eyes. This graphically taught them what death really was and that they, too, were mortal and must one day die. It also prophesied Christ's eventual sacrifice: "Without the shedding of blood there is no forgiveness" (Heb. 9:22 NIV).

3 Trinity Is Seen

"Like one of Us" is language that points to the Trinity. Although Judaism is monotheistic, the doctrine of the Trinity is implied in the Old Testament. First, it is seen in the plural form of God's name, Elohim. Second, there are several passages where Deity is seen conversing with Himself.

4. Which aspect of the curse did God repeat and why?

5. How did God ensure that the first couple would never be able to eat from the Tree of Life?

6. Why do you think God prevented the first couple from partaking of the Tree of Life?

LIVE OUT ...

7. We've seen that Adam's wife was known by three different names, the last of which was Eve. List some of the names or nicknames that you have been given. Who gave them to you and what do they mean?

8. The couple literally clothed themselves in fig leaves, while God dressed them in tunics of skin, offering the first blood sacrifice. Paul uses the analogy of "putting on" clothing to show that we can wear spiritual attributes much as we would wear beautiful garments. Below, list some of your favorite attire and how it makes you feel physically; then read Colossians 3:12, and list the characteristics you'd like to wear spiritually.

FROM MY CLOSET
Example: coat makes me warm

FROM GOD'S WORD
kindness offers warmth to others

9. God sent Adam and Eve out of the garden of Eden, and an angel prevented them from ever returning. Journal about a time you had to leave someplace. How did it make you feel? Where did you go?

○ ○ ● ○ ○

Who would want to make a sheep taste like a toad? Biochemists at the University of Wyoming did, in the hope of reducing coyote attacks on the 18.5 million sheep grazing throughout the United States at the time. The task took on top priority after a ban on the use of predator poisons on public lands was passed. Which brings us to the toads. Toads are inedible for almost every animal, especially coyotes. A certain chemical in the skin makes them revolting to your average coyote. Other exotic concoctions were also tested: Tabasco, skunk spray, and cougar urine. The hope was that a coyote snacking on a sheep would experience a repulsive, sickening taste, encouraging the predator to drop sheep from its menu. Ideally, scientists hoped to create a "New Generation" of coyotes that would shudder at the sight of sheep.[12]

Don't you wonder why God didn't come up with a plan like that in the garden of Eden? He could have made the fruit on the Tree of Knowledge of Good and Evil stinky or ugly or out of reach. Really, if an electric shock fence surrounded it or security alarms were attached to it, perhaps Adam and Eve would have stayed away. You have to ask yourself, "Why did God plant the tree in the first place?" If He had not, there wouldn't have been anything to tempt them. But if He had protected the first couple from temptation, they wouldn't have had free will. If there had been no choice between good and evil, right and wrong, they would have been no better than robots. Adam and Eve needed to be challenged with choice. Would they obey God or not? Would they submit to His rules or make their own? You face the same moral dilemma. Oh, that sin would stink and temptation would taste like toads!

LISTEN TO...

The stars shine on brightly while Adam and Eve pursue their way into the far wilderness. There is a sound through the silence, as of the falling tears of an angel.

—*Elizabeth Barrett Browning*

Noah's Wife—Behind Every Great Man

Genesis 6:1–7:7

"Behind every great man is a great woman" continues to ring true, though no one knows who said it first. The phrase asserts that men owe their success to women who play a role behind the scenes in the lives of their men. Lord Thomas Dewar confirmed this, noting, "The road to success is filled with women pushing their husbands along."[1]

Looking at America's long legacy of first ladies, we discover women who embodied this saying. Dolly Madison supported orphanages; Nancy Reagan taught our youth to "Just say no." When running for reelection, George W. Bush said that the best reason to vote for him was to keep Laura in the White House. The Smithsonian Institution acknowledges that although "unelected and unpaid, [first ladies] occupy a position of power defined as much by their own personalities and interests as by public perceptions and social expectations. Americans expect the first lady to be a symbol of home, family, and womanhood— although the meaning of those ideals changes with every generation. She is also a political partner, from the campaign trail to White House receptions. While some first ladies support the presidency behind the scenes … others use their title to effect change in their own right."[2]

Mrs. Noah is certainly one of the first ladies of the faith. Although unnamed, she is mentioned five times in Genesis as Noah's wife. Likely she was a righteous woman; otherwise she would not have entered the ark. Since her sons and their wives also made the journey, we can safely assume that she was a godly mother and mentor. It's important to remember that unnamed does not mean unimportant. She was no doubt a great source of comfort and encouragement to her husband and children.

Day 1: Genesis 6:1–4   **GIRLS BEHAVING BADLY**

Day 2: Genesis 6:5–10   **FAMILY VALUES**

Day 3: Genesis 6:11–16   **HOUSEBOAT**

Day 4: Genesis 6:17–22   **ALL IN THE FAMILY**

Day 5: Genesis 7:1–7   **HOME AWAY FROM HOME**

DAY 1

Girls Behaving Badly

LIFT UP ...

Lord, You have given me great influence in the lives of the men in my family. By Your guidance may I model Your character to them and give them a godly heritage. Amen.

LOOK AT ...

So far we've studied Eve, the first woman who fell from God's grace because of her willfulness. We now move forward to a time when the curse culminated in coarse living. Girls were behaving badly as they crossbred with men of suspicious backgrounds. As humanity spiraled out of control, God was compelled to intervene. Thankfully, there was one family that stood out in the crowd. While the rest of society was raunchy, they were righteous. Rich with a family history in godliness and grace, Noah was the honored recipient of a call from God.

Imagine how difficult it must have been for Mr. and Mrs. Noah to raise their children in a society bent on sin. Their home must have been a haven from the influences on the street. How did they instill family values in their children? Perhaps they retold the story of the fall as well as the sin of Cain, warning of the consequences of disobedience. Maybe they encouraged their children to be like Enoch, their great-grandfather, who walked with God and was raptured. We can learn much from their example as we teach our children to be in this world but not of it.

READ GENESIS 6:1–4.

Now it came to pass, when men began to multiply on the face of the earth, and daughters were born to them, that the sons of God saw the daughters of men, that they were beautiful; and they took wives for themselves of all whom they chose. And the LORD said, "My Spirit shall not strive with man forever, for he is indeed flesh; yet his days shall be one hundred and twenty years."

LEARN ABOUT …

2 Sons of God

Commentators dispute the identity of these "sons of God." The phrase could refer to nonhumans (i.e., fallen angels). It could also refer to men from the line of Cain joining with godly women.[3] The third possibility is unequally yoked marriage between godly men and ungodly women.

3 Strive with God

To *strive* means to quarrel or contend. It often involves a case between unequal parties. But one day striving must end and judgment begin. Here God proclaimed a 120-year limit. Most agree that this was the amount of time given to Noah to build the ark and sinners to repent before the flood.

5 Scared of Giants

"Giants" in both Genesis 6 and Numbers 13 comes from the Hebrew word *nephilim*, which literally means "fallen ones," referring to the antediluvian rebellion. Some scholars believe the *nephilim* descended from famous rulers and mighty warriors. Those whom humans saw as "men of renown," God viewed as "fallen ones."

There were giants on the earth in those days, and also afterward, when the sons of God came in to the daughters of men and they bore children to them. Those were the mighty men who were of old, men of renown. Genesis 6:1–4

1. The word *now* places us at a point in time. Read Genesis 5:30–32, and describe when this story takes place.

2. a. What does the text say about "the sons of God"?

   b. What is your reaction to this account of "the sons of God" and "the daughters of men"?

3. What did the Lord decree and why?

4. Describe the giants—what they were like and how they came into being.

5. Read Numbers 13:32–33, and describe the inhabitants of the land of Canaan many centuries later.

6. What does the presence of these "giants" tell you about the world in which Noah and his wife lived?

LIVE OUT …

7. a. We've looked back as far as Noah's father and sons. Let's climb a little higher in his family tree. Read Genesis 5:21–29. What repeated phrase describes Enoch's (Noah's great-grandfather) unusual departure?

   b. What record does Methuselah (Noah's grandfather) hold, and how old was Methuselah when he died?

c. Why did Lamech (Noah's father) give Noah his name?

8. God's Spirit strove with the population in Noah's day, hoping they would repent and be saved from the coming judgment. Isaiah said, "Woe to him who strives with his Maker!" (Isa. 45:9).

a. Describe a situation in which you argued with God.

b. How did the argument end?

c. What did you learn?

9. Today we've seen various theories regarding the giants. The fact is that all of us face giants of one sort or another. Journal a prayer asking God to help you conquer any "giant" that you face.

LEARN ABOUT …

7 Sent of God

Methuselah's name is significant. It literally means "dart," but prophetically it means "when he dies it will come."[4] Bestowing this name on Methuselah would make Enoch, his father, a prophet. The year that Methuselah died, the flood occurred. His long life attests to God's incredible grace and patience before judgment.

---

8 Sovereignty of God

God's sovereignty expresses His supreme rulership. Sovereignty is not an attribute of God but a prerogative based upon the perfections of His divinity. All forms of existence are within the scope of His dominion. God created humans with the power to choose between good and evil. However, He rules in wisdom and grace.[5]

○ ○ ● ○ ○

Jesus warned that "as it was in the days of Noah, so it will be also in the days of the Son of Man: They ate, they drank, they married wives, they were given in marriage, until the day that Noah entered the ark, and the flood came and destroyed them all" (Luke 17:26–27). Each generation hopes that it is the one that will see Christ's return. And ours is no different from the days of Noah. In this new millennium we eat, drink, marry … and girls have gone wild.

For college coeds, spring break means breaking loose. One poll tells us that 30 percent of the women interviewed believe sun and alcohol are an "essential part of life," 74 percent said that spring break meant increased sexual activity, 40 percent said that they passed out, and 13 percent reported having sex with more than one partner. The American Medical Association opined that women on spring break "use alcohol as *an excuse* to engage in outrageous behavior." The implication is that if women would drink as much at home as they do on vacation, they'd be engaging in more public sexual activity. Columnist Ana Marie Cox notes, "The truth is we all do stupid things when we're drunk—but we all want to do stupid things."[6] What a sad commentary that our seemingly educated young women *want* to do stupid things! Isn't it time to wise up?

What's the lesson for those of us living in the twenty-first century? God did indeed judge the people of Noah's time. He also judged the inhabitants of Sodom and Gomorrah. As you observe our society, it's logical to assume that God will not strive with us much longer. We will all face a day of reckoning. The Bible has thrown you a lifeline—take hold of it before it's too late.

LISTEN TO...

If God doesn't judge America for its immorality, then He owes Sodom and Gomorrah an apology.

—*Billy Graham*

DAY 2
Family Values

"Family values" is a term first used by conservatives to support Judeo-Christian ideology. These supporters contend that the nuclear family is the core of society. They oppose abortion, pornography, premarital sex, homosexuality, some aspects of feminism, cohabitation, and depictions of sexuality in the media.

In contrast to the view of family values held by conservatives, liberals have sought to co-opt the term to support unbiblical lifestyles. Their ideology promotes such practices as sex education that excludes abstinence, abortion on demand, teen access to contraception, same-sex marriages, and gay parenting.

Vice President Dan Quayle introduced "family values" as a political term during a speech in 1992 that attributed the Los Angeles riots to a breakdown of family values. Quayle specifically cited the decay of moral values and family structure in American society as the cause of these riots. He used as an example the television program *Murphy Brown*. He believed that Candice Bergen's character, the single and pregnant Murphy Brown, mocked the importance of fathers and redefined the nuclear family as a "lifestyle choice." One source reports that "Quayle drew a firestorm of criticism from feminist and liberal organizations, and was widely ridiculed by late-night talk show hosts for saying this.… Ironically, the show's star, Candice Bergen, herself said in an interview after the show was canceled that she agreed with him."[7]

Noah's family also faced an attack on traditional family values. They were surrounded by every kind of wickedness. Not only were family values decaying, but godly values were also nonexistent—except in the case of Noah.

LIFT UP ...

Thank You, Lord, for teaching us the values that are right in Your eyes. Help me to show my family Your righteousness. Amen.

LEARN ABOUT ...

I The Mind

"Intent of the thoughts" can be translated "imagination." The Hebrew word implies "to fashion from pottery." John Phillips writes, "Man fashioned wicked philosophies, they formed obscene artifacts, they eagerly espoused filthy causes, they made fashionable vile sins, they poured society into their mold."[8] Paul warned, "Don't copy the behavior and customs of this world" (Rom. 12:2 NLT).

LOOK AT ...

Yesterday introduced us to giants, who were the offspring of mixed marriages. The Israelites would encounter these giants again when they crossed into the Promised Land and once more in the times of the kings.

After the fall, humanity experienced an enormous population boom but continued on a rapid moral decline. The depravity reached such depths that God regretted creating humans. Twice in today's text the word *sorry* is used to describe God's emotions. *Sorry* is translated "repent" in some Bible versions. It seems contradictory to think that a perfect God would repent of anything. However, the true meaning of *repent* helps us to understand God's frame of mind. In one sense, the word *repent* means to sigh, to breathe strongly, or to be sorry. In another sense, it means to pity, console, or ease oneself. How tragic that God's crowning creation became His greatest regret. That we could be a disappointment to God is sobering, for God intended humans to be His greatest joy: "You created all things, and they exist because you created what you pleased" (Rev. 4:11 NLT). May we live our lives in such a way that God is satisfied instead of sorry.

READ GENESIS 6:5–10.

Then the LORD saw that the wickedness of man was great in the earth, and that every intent of the thoughts of his heart was only evil continually. And the LORD was sorry that He had made man on the earth, and He was grieved in His heart. So the LORD said, "I will destroy man whom I have created from the face of the earth, both man and beast, creeping thing and birds of the air, for I am sorry that I have made them." But Noah found grace in the eyes of the LORD. This is the genealogy of Noah. Noah was a just man, perfect in his generations. Noah walked with God. And Noah begot three sons: Shem, Ham, and Japheth. Genesis 6:5–10

1. Describe what the Lord saw.

2. How did the Lord feel about this?

3. What did He decide to do about this and why?

4. Who caught the Lord's attention and why?

5. a. What four phrases describe Noah's character?

   b. Which of these phrases would you most like to describe you? Why?

6. List Noah's sons. If you know the story of Noah and the flood, explain why they become important later.

LIVE OUT ...

7. God's description of humanity's depravity is devastating. Read 1 Timothy 1:8–10 to discover some of the sins the antediluvians (people living before the flood) were engaged in. Using the word EVIL as an acronym, list some of the ways you see people sinning today.

   E

   V

   I

   L

8. We've discovered that our sin caused God to grieve. Use Ephesians 4:29–31 as a template to write a personal prayer

LEARN ABOUT ...

2 The Heart

Genesis 6 is a stark contrast to Genesis 1. In the beginning God saw that everything was good, but by the time of Noah all things human were evil. This caused God great grief. *Grief* comes from a primitive root that means to carve or pain. In other words, our sins cut God to the heart.

5 The Man

The description of Noah could reveal the plan of salvation. Finding grace represents forgiveness. Being "just" implies that he was justified before a holy God. That Noah was declared "perfect" reveals that he was without blemish, having been washed from his sins. That he walked with God portrays the saint's ongoing process of sanctification.

7 The Flesh

There are two types of evil: physical and moral. Moral evil is sin, disorder in the moral world. The greatest evil is the failure of rational human beings to conform in character and conduct to the will of God.[9] "The face of the LORD is against those who do evil, to cut off the remembrance of them from the earth" (Ps. 34:16).

asking God to forgive you for the ways you may have brought Him sorrow.

> Let no corrupt word proceed out of your mouth, but what is good for necessary edification, that it may impart grace to the hearers. And do not grieve the Holy Spirit of God, by whom you were sealed for the day of redemption. Let all bitterness, wrath, anger, clamor, and evil speaking be put away from you, with all malice.
> Ephesians 4:29–31

9. Noah's qualities foreshadowed the steps to salvation. In the space provided, talk about a time when you've walked in Noah's footsteps to faith:

I found grace in God's eyes when … (see Eph. 2:8)

I knew I was justified when … (see Rom. 5:1)

I knew God saw me as perfect when … (see James 1:4)

I walk with God when … (see Eph. 4:1–3)

∘ ∘ ● ∘ ∘

Nineteenth-century Scottish preacher Andrew Kennedy Hutchison Boyd is best remembered for what some called "chirping" articles in *Fraser's Magazine*. One editorial contrasted the influence of good and evil: "I do not know why it is that by the constitution of the universe, evil has so much more power than good to produce its effect and to propagate its nature. One drop of foul will pollute a whole cup of fair water; but one drop of fair water has no power to appreciably improve a cup of foul.

Sharp pain, present in a tooth or a toe, will make the whole man miserable, though all the rest of his body be easy; but if all the rest of the body be suffering, an easy tooth or toe will cause no perceptible alleviation."[10]

It can be the same in a home, workplace, or classroom. One person's negativity can influence the atmosphere. Everyone knows that at home "If Mama ain't happy, ain't nobody happy." Down on the farm the saying goes "One bad apple spoils the whole barrel." At school you've been warned "Bad company corrupts good morals." The message within each of these sayings is that sin is highly contagious.

During the time of Noah, evil was pervasive and growing exponentially. One small family faced a tidal wave of wickedness. Lest the last bastion of goodness be overwhelmed, God developed a plan. He would rescue them just in the nick of time and begin the human race all over again with Noah's descendants.

LISTEN TO...

Evil is the real problem in the hearts and minds of men. It is not a problem of physics but of ethics. It is easier to denature plutonium than to denature the evil spirit of man.

—Albert Einstein

DAY 3

Houseboat

Jackie Gleason's immortal words—"This house is my castle!"—still resonate today. I suppose that Noah could have told his wife, "A houseboat is a man's refuge, honey." In truth, a home should be a haven from the world around us. It's the place where we feel safe from pressures clamoring on the outside. Inside its four walls we find acceptance from the people whose opinions truly matter. When our hearts are overwhelmed, like Dorothy, we may also lament, "There's no place like home."

Noah lived in a world that was crashing in around him. And God had a solution: "It's time to move." Have you ever felt like that? Has God ever interrupted your plans by uprooting you from your cozy nest only to drop you into uncharted waters? Let's face it, no woman looks forward to the day her husband comes home and says, "The boss says it's time to move." But that's exactly what Noah would have to do. And they weren't moving up in this world. They would likely be leaving a two-camel tent to live in a floating zoo. But the old saying is true: "Home is where the heart is." Whether you live in a single story, a duplex, or a trilevel ark, it's not the house that makes a home. It's the people who dwell in it. You have to admire Mrs. Noah for going along for the ride.

LIFT UP ...

Father, just as You had a saving plan for Noah and his family by way of the ark, You also have a saving plan for me and my family by way of the cross of Christ Jesus. Thank You for Your provision. Amen.

LOOK AT ...

Yesterday we learned that the inhabitants of the earth had become increasingly wicked. Their sin stood in stark contrast to Noah's steadfast heart. While God sorrowed over humanity's rebellion, He found comfort in His righteous friend.

Today we continue to see this contrast widen as God enlisted Noah for a rescue operation. He gave this faithful man a gigantic task: Build an ark. We'll discover that the ark would be shaped in a way that was perfectly suited for floating rather than sailing. This is a beautiful illustration of God's sovereignty. He would take the helm to steer the boat through tumultuous water. He would guide it to its predetermined destination. Imagine the kind of trust that Noah and his family must have had as they climbed aboard and realized that there was no navigational system. But isn't that similar to our journey of faith? God wants us to sit back and allow Him to route our course. Have you relinquished control of your future to the hand of the One who can ensure safe passage to the distant shore?

LEARN ABOUT ...

1 Violent

The Hebrew term behind the word *violence* refers to physical and ethical injustice. It means to do wrong or be malicious, cruel, unjust, or oppressive in dealing with others. From the time of Adam and Eve until the days of Noah, violence continued to expand until it covered the face of the earth.

---

3 Vile

Corrupt literally means decayed. The earth itself had not grown corrupt, but the people living on the earth had. They had given in to fleshly lusts, including violence, bringing judgment upon themselves. In essence God said to them, "I will dig your grave, for you are vile" (Nah. 1:14).

READ GENESIS 6:11–16.

The earth also was corrupt before God, and the earth was filled with violence. So God looked upon the earth, and indeed it was corrupt; for all flesh had corrupted their way on the earth. And God said to Noah, "The end of all flesh has come before Me, for the earth is filled with violence through them; and behold, I will destroy them with the earth. Make yourself an ark of gopherwood; make rooms in the ark, and cover it inside and outside with pitch. And this is how you shall make it: The length of the ark shall be three hundred cubits, its width fifty cubits, and its height thirty cubits. You shall make a window for the ark, and you shall finish it to a cubit from above; and set the door of the ark in its side. You shall make it with lower, second, and third decks." Genesis 6:11–16

1. Underline the word *earth* in today's text, and describe the earth's condition in Noah's time.

2. Circle all the references to God in the text. How did God respond to the earth's condition?

3. Reread the text, and explain how the earth had become corrupted.

LEARN ABOUT …

5 Vessel

The word *ark* means chest. It was made of gopherwood (probably cypress), making it light and durable. The pitch made it watertight. The ark consisted of a number of "nests," or small rooms, arranged in three tiers. It was built in the form of a chest, with flat bottom and roof, and was intended to float rather than sail.[11]

7 Vassal

The earth refers to the planet, to the soil on the ground that God cursed after the fall, and to the people who populate the planet. God is sovereign over the earth. All its living creatures, including mankind, are subject to His rule.[12] "The earth is the LORD's, and all its fullness, the world and those who dwell therein" (Ps. 24:1).

9 Vexed

Noah brought his family to a wooden ark so they could be rescued from God's wrath. As Christians we can lead our families to the wooden cross to save them from sin and death: "Believe on the LORD Jesus Christ, and you will be saved, you and your household" (Acts 16:31).

4. Who did God include in His plans? Look back to yesterday's lesson, and explain why he was included.

5. Describe the means of deliverance from the coming destruction and who was intended to use it.

6. Highlight the word *make* in the text; then describe the details of the vessel's construction.

LIVE OUT …

7. What do you learn about God from Genesis 6:11–16, and why is this important for us know?"

8. The people in Noah's day were violent and corrupt. List some ways people today behave in the same ways.

9. According to Hebrews 11:7, Noah had a plan of salvation for his household. With this in mind, write about some ways you can lead your family to the Lord.

∘ ∘ ● ∘ ∘

Whoever said that humans are basically good was basically wrong. Even we Americans who claim to love truth and justice don't live up to that claim. The book *The Day America Told the Truth* offers some astonishing statistics: Ninety-one percent of Americans lie routinely; 31 percent of those married admit to having had an extramarital affair lasting over a year; 86 percent of youth regularly lie to their parents; and 75 percent lie regularly to their best friends. Wrongdoing doesn't end with failure to tell the truth, either. One in five young people loses his or her virginity before the age of thirteen. Sadly, two-thirds of those asked about religion said it plays no role in shaping their opinions about sex.[13]

It's easy to look at Noah's day and judge humanity for its corruption and violence. We can detach ourselves and shake our heads, thinking, "Whew, they got what was coming to 'em." But it just takes a brief look at the world around us to recognize that we're not that different. All you have to do is surf the Internet, surf through your cable or satellite networks, or read the newspaper to realize that the same corruption and violence are woven into the fabric of our society.

Rather than being women who point a finger at the corruption, let's offer the only solution to the problem. We can point the way to the cross. Just as Noah was known as a "preacher of righteousness" (2 Peter 2:5), be known as one who spends her time loving the unlovely, sharing the gospel, and "redeeming the time, because the days are evil" (Eph. 5:16).

LISTEN TO...

We have a real problem in this country when it comes to values. We have become the kind of society that civilized countries used to send missionaries to.

—*William Bennett*

DAY 4

All in the Family

From eye or hair color to favorite foods and mental acumen, you and your kids have more in common than you realize. Did you know that a brand-new study revealed that snoring trends are all in the family? Researchers at Cincinnati Children's Hospital Medical Center evaluated 681 infants (average age 12.6 months) and found that babies who snored regularly were three times more likely to have parents who also sawed logs nightly.[14] Sadly, another study out of the University of Washington demonstrates that the emotional well-being of children is strongly linked to their parents' mental health. In turn, parents' mental health is linked to their offspring's emotions and behavior. Troubled children are likely to have troubled parents, and vice versa.[15] Some professionals argue whether behavior is the result of nurture or nature. The answer appears to be both. Some characteristics are inherited, while others are ingrained. The old saying rings true: "The acorn doesn't fall far from the tree."

The sons of Noah were no exception to this rule. They would be a key part of their father's workforce. In fact, they could have named their family business "Noah & Sons Shipbuilders." These men were nurtured in a family that feared the Lord. That they entered the ark indicates that they, too, were considered righteous. God ratified this idea by including them in His covenant, ensuring that their families would be rescued from the coming flood. We don't know whether their eyes were brown or blue. We do know that their hearts beat as one with their father's.

LIFT UP ...

Lord, help me to listen to Your instructions and to follow each detail that You share. Please help me to pass on those lessons to my loved ones so we can live righteously. Amen.

LOOK AT ...

It's been sobering to read about the complete depravity of humankind during Noah's days. Their corruption permeated all realms of society as seen in phrases like "all flesh" and "the earth is filled" describing the chaos.

Now we see God's rescue operation begin to unfold. That God saves some while submerging others demonstrates His ability to balance judgment with mercy. Although most were lost in the darkness of those days, there were a scarce few who radiated God's light. God knew how to separate the two. Noah, therefore, foreshadowed another judgment that will come upon the whole earth. This reckoning will be introduced at the return of Jesus Christ. At that time He will rescue believers from a planet that is once again utterly corrupt. However, instead of water, fire will consume the ungodly. Peter wrote, "The world that then existed perished, being flooded with water. But the heavens and the earth which are now preserved by the same word, are reserved for fire until the day of judgment and perdition of ungodly men" (2 Peter 3:6–7). At the time of this future reckoning, where will your family be? May you be wise like Noah and warn them of the wrath to come.

LEARN ABOUT ...

2 Covenant

In the biblical sense a covenant implies much more than a contract or simple agreement. A contract always has an end date, while a covenant is a permanent arrangement. Another difference is that a contract generally involves only one part of a person, such as a skill, while a covenant covers a person's total being.[16]

READ GENESIS 6:17–22.

"And behold, I Myself am bringing floodwaters on the earth, to destroy from under heaven all flesh in which is the breath of life; everything that is on the earth shall die. But I will establish My covenant with you; and you shall go into the ark—you, your sons, your wife, and your sons' wives with you. And of every living thing of all flesh you shall bring two of every sort into the ark, to keep them alive with you; they shall be male and female. Of the birds after their kind, of animals after their kind, and of every creeping thing of the earth after its kind, two of every kind will come to you to keep them alive. And you shall take for yourself of all food that is eaten, and you shall gather it to yourself; and it shall be food for you and for them." Thus Noah did; according to all that God commanded him, so he did. Genesis 6:17–22

1. Explain how God would judge the earth. Circle the words that describe the full extent of this destruction.

2. By contrast, what were God's plans for Noah? Who else was included?

3. Underline the word *kind* in the passage, and then list the kinds of creatures that would also inhabit the ark.

4. a. How would Noah gather the animals?

   b. What was his responsibility to them?

5. Besides building the ark, what further task was Noah assigned to ensure survival?

6. If you were God, what kind of report card would you give Noah regarding his assignment and why?

LIVE OUT ...

7. God made a covenant with Noah and his sons. He has also made a covenant with those who believe in His Son. Read Hebrews 9:13–28.

   a. Contrast the blood of goats and calves with the precious blood of Christ (vv. 13–14 and vv. 19–28).

   b. Who are included in the new covenant and by what means (v. 15)?

   c. Describe what must occur for a testament to be "in force" (vv. 16–18).

8. God caused the animals to cooperate with Noah as they gathered to the ark. Has God ever helped you do the impossible? Journal about a task He gave you to do and how He assisted in its fulfillment.

9. We discovered that one of Noah's defining traits was complete obedience. Using the word OBEY as an acrostic, list some of the ways God is asking you to obey Him.

O

B

E

Y

∘ ∘ ● ∘ ∘

The late Roland Q. Leavell said in his book, *Evangelism: Christ's Imperative Commission*, that of all the reported church members:

5 per cent do not exist,

10 per cent cannot be found,

20 per cent never pray,

25 per cent never read the Bible,

30 per cent never attend church services,

40 per cent never give any money to the church,

50 per cent never go to Sunday School,

60 per cent never go to church Sunday night,

70 per cent never give to missions,

80 per cent never go to prayer meeting,

90 per cent never have family worship, and

95 per cent never win a soul to Christ.[17]

If these statistics are correct, it means that only 5 percent of Christians are being obedient to the Great Commission. Jesus told His followers, "Go into all the world and preach the gospel to every creature. He who believes and is baptized will be saved; but he who does not believe will be condemned" (Mark 16:15–16). Just as Noah was a preacher of righteousness to his generation, we must evangelize the people of our time. Of course this is done through the way we live as well as the words we say. When was the last time you gave your testimony or shared the gospel with others? It's very likely that the only thing that comforted Noah as he witnessed his friends and neighbors drowning was the assurance that he had done everything he could to rescue them.

Listen to...

Faith and obedience are bound up in the same bundle. He that obeys God, trusts God; and he that trusts God, obeys God.

—*Charles Haddon Spurgeon*

DAY 5

Home Away from Home

I'll never forget the summer I (Penny) was ten years old. For family vacations, my parents bought a big blue RV that we quickly nicknamed the Blue Goose. We packed our gear and headed to Colorado for two weeks. My parents, two brothers, our toy poodle, Pokey, and I piled in and headed north for summer in the beautiful outdoors. Unfortunately, we didn't realize that Colorado in June is sometimes like a winter wonderland. My cute little shorts sets offered no defense against the freezing cold. We ended up stuck in the Blue Goose for days on end. Our outdoor family fun turned into cooped-up family feuds. My brothers decided to gang up on me in endless games of Monopoly and Clue. Pokey escaped the confinement and ran into a lake to chase some birds. It took hours to warm his shivering little body after my dad rescued him from nearly drowning. The walls of our home away from home began to close in on us. One day we cried out, "Can't we just go back to Albuquerque?" My folks agreed, and we turned the blue monstrosity south and headed home. That week my dad put the RV up for sale.

Can you imagine climbing onto a big boat filled with every type of animal, knowing you were headed into a storm? Now add in-laws to the equation. Not only that, you would have absolutely no control over your destination or the timing of your landing. It's amazing that Noah's family came through the storm in their home away from home completely intact, ready to begin life anew.

LIFT UP ...

Though I may not understand why some trials flood my life, Lord, I know You are always there for me. Thank You for continually keeping me protected. Amen.

LOOK AT ...

When God entered into a covenant relationship with Noah, his wife, their sons, and their wives, He promised to give the family protection from the coming flood. Thus, we see God's character in providing a godly remnant of committed followers. Throughout history

LEARN ABOUT ...

1 Come In

Perhaps the most welcome words we can hear are "Come in." After 120 years of construction, God told Noah that it was time for his family to enter the ark. Only those who were considered righteous could cross the threshold: "The righteous is delivered from trouble" (Prov. 11:8).

2 Clean and Unclean

Most of us know the story of Noah taking the animals into the ark two by two. But there were some species where more animals were needed. The clean animals would be used for sacrificial purposes, so they would require more than two animals to keep the species alive.

God has always protected a few faithful people from judgment or calamity. In this case, God rescued Noah and his family, using them to populate the earth anew. In addition, He would also save the animals. In a sense, He would create a fresh start for the earth and the human race.

God is more than willing to give each of us a new beginning. Don't wait for a flood of judgment or a vast calamity in order to cry out for God's help. Simply cry out for God's protection through the blood of His Son. The Bible is clear: "If anyone is in Christ, he is a new creation; old things have passed away; behold, all things have become new" (2 Cor. 5:17).

READ GENESIS 7:1–7.

Then the LORD said to Noah, "Come into the ark, you and all your household, because I have seen that you are righteous before Me in this genera-tion. You shall take with you seven each of every clean animal, a male and his female; two each of animals that are unclean, a male and his female; also seven each of birds of the air, male and female, to keep the species alive on the face of all the earth. For after seven more days I will cause it to rain on the earth forty days and forty nights, and I will destroy from the face of the earth all living things that I have made." And Noah did according to all that the LORD commanded him. Noah was six hundred years old when the floodwaters were on the earth. So Noah, with his sons, his wife, and his sons' wives, went into the ark because of the waters of the flood. Genesis 7:1–7

1. What instruction did God give to Noah and his household and why?

2. What was Noah told to do with the animals and why?

3. a. After how many days would the rain begin?

   b. Why do you think God chose to wait?

4. Describe what would happen as a result of the floodwaters.

5. What do you learn about Noah in this passage?

6. What do you learn about Noah's wife in this passage?

LIVE OUT ...

7. Noah and his family were invited to come into the ark for safety. Read the following verses, and describe some of the blessings of answering the invitation to "come." Talk about whether you have personally experienced these blessings.

   Matthew 11:28

   Matthew 16:24

   Matthew 25:34–36

   Revelation 22:17

8. We know God instructed Noah to bring clean animals on the ark, looking toward the time he would make sacrificial offerings. We can make an offering of prayer. With this in mind, rewrite Psalm 51:10–11 into a personal prayer asking God to cleanse you of sin.

   > Create in me a clean heart, O God,
   > And renew a steadfast spirit within me.
   > Do not cast me away from Your presence,
   > And do not take Your Holy Spirit from me. Psalm 51:10–11

9. a. There is no record of Mrs. Noah's response to Noah's encounters with God or the journey to new life on the ark. Try to put

LEARN ABOUT ...

6 Closed In

Scripture implies that God was in the ark with Noah and his family. Noah waited seven days for the flood to begin. Then "the LORD shut him in" (Gen. 7:16). Adam Clarke said, "God took him under his especial protection, and as he shut him [Noah] in, so he shut the others out."[18]

7 Come to Christ

Only seven people followed Noah into the ark to be protected and repopulate the planet. Jesus beckoned: "Come, follow me" (see Luke 18:22). As with Noah, only a faithful few followed Him. Ultimately, His crucifixion conquered sin and death. Following His resurrection and ascension, His disciples spread the message of eternal hope to the world.

8 Cleansed

After the flood, Noah built an altar and offered sacrifices for ritual purity and cleansing: "Noah built an altar to the LORD, and took of every clean animal and of every clean bird, and offered burnt offerings on the altar" (Gen. 8:20). After that, God sent a rainbow, promising never to flood the earth again.

yourself in her place. How do you think she might have felt as her husband spent 120 years building a boat based on instructions from God?

b. How do you suppose the world treated her family during this time?

c. What do you think she might have thought, felt, or done as she sat on the boat with her family seven extra days, waiting for the rain to come?

d. What feelings might she have endured as she watched the floods devastate the world she knew?

e. How do you relate to Mrs. Noah? (Perhaps you've followed a husband who was called by God, been mocked by the world for your faith, waited for a promise that was late in coming, or watched as others faced the consequences for sin.)

○ ○ ● ○ ○

Modern society is often run on a first-name basis. Some people in authority even allow their subordinates to address them by their given name. When Dwight D. Eisenhower ran for office, he didn't ask people to address him as "General." His slogan was "I like Ike." As a people, we even call famous and powerful people by their first names. We know the flamboyant singer/actress Cher. We've seen Madonna try to transform herself before our eyes from a "material girl" pop singer to a jet-setting superstar, mother, children's book author, and kabbalah devotee. Because we know their names, we think we know the person.

That's why it might feel a bit disconcerting to study over one hundred years in the life of a woman who has remained unnamed. We call her only Mrs. Noah or Noah's wife. Though we don't know her name, we do know the person. She was a woman of faith who was saved from judgment. She steadfastly continued the work God gave her. She probably was kind. After all, her sons and daughters-in-law consented to being cooped up in the ark with her. She must have been a hard worker. Think about caring for all of those animals! And she must have been humble. She didn't say, "Make sure you spell my name right when you put this in the Bible." Though we don't know her name, Jesus may have had Noah's wife in mind when He said, "Blessed are the meek, for they shall inherit the earth" (Matt. 5:5).

LISTEN TO...

Meek endurance and meek obedience, the accepting of his dealings, of whatever complexion they are and however they may tear and desolate our hearts, without murmuring, without sulking, without rebellion or resistance, is the deepest conception of the meekness which Christ pronounced blessed.

—Alexander Maclaren

Sarah—Stand by Your Man

Genesis 12 & 20

Tammy Wynette's "Stand by Your Man" is one of the most covered songs in country music history. Sadly, as the feminist movement gained popularity during the 1970s, many women denounced the song as well as its singer. However, Wynette defended the song. On a talk show with Jay Leno, she insisted that the song was not a call for women to give in to the old double standard but was instead pointing out that they should be willing to forgive. She also said that a husband should be willing to stand by his wife as well.[1] Tammy's song truly elevated the sanctity of marriage, while feminists sought to tear it apart.

Marriage is more than a union; it's a right of passage. As women we graduate from one relationship to another. We transition from being a daughter to becoming a wife. With this transition, our alliances also shift from father to husband. "Daddy's little girl" is transformed into her spouse's "better half." While one bond breaks, another forms into the tie that binds. Jesus said, "'For this reason a man shall leave his father and mother and be joined to his wife, and the two shall become one flesh[.]' So then, they are no longer two but one flesh. Therefore what God has joined together, let not man separate" (Matt. 19:5–6). In other words, you must stand by your man through thick and thin.

One shining example of this stick-to-itiveness was Sarah, the bride of Abraham. We'll watch her leave her parents, people, and place of birth to cleave to her husband during some of the most difficult circumstances imaginable—famine, flight, fatigue, and falsity.

Day 1: Genesis 12:1–9   LEAVING AND CLEAVING

Day 2: Genesis 12:10–20   TRUSTING AND OBEYING

Day 3: Genesis 20:1–7   SLEEPING AND DREAMING

Day 4: Genesis 20:8–13   WATCHING AND WAITING

Day 5: Genesis 20:14–18   GIVING AND TAKING

DAY 1

Leaving and Cleaving

LIFT UP ...

God, thank You for creating us with the capacity for deep and satisfying relationships. May I be a woman who is stable and trustworthy for my family and friends. Amen.

LOOK AT ...

In the previous lesson, we gained insight into Mrs. Noah, one of the Bible's nameless women. We learned through her life that anonymous does not mean inconsequential. Like many unsung heroines, she happily served behind the scenes as her husband and sons became renowned.

Now we meet one of the Bible's top ten women of valor. Sarah, Abraham's wife, is truly the matriarch of the faith. We'll see a complex woman who would at one moment exhibit a meek and quiet spirit and the next stand up to her husband when there was conflict in the home. As she walked through her life, she came to understand that the hand of God is more powerful than the wishes of man. Peter wrote, "Sarah obeyed her husband, Abraham, and called him her master. You are her daughters when you do what is right without fear of what your husbands might do" (1 Peter 3:6 NLT).[2] When your husband asks you to do something that doesn't make sense, how do you respond? If you cooperate rather than complain, you'll see God intervene in ways that you never imagined.

READ GENESIS 12:1–9.

Now the LORD had said to Abram: "Get out of your country, from your family and from your father's house, to a land that I will show you. I will make you a great nation; I will bless you and make your name great; and you shall be a blessing. I will bless those who bless you, and I will curse him who curses you; and in you all the families of the earth shall be blessed." So Abram departed as the LORD had spoken to him, and Lot went with him. And Abram was seventy-five years old when

LEARN ABOUT ...

I Motherland

The ancient city of Haran still exists today in northern Mesopotamia. Originally located in Paddan Aram, it was on the busy caravan road connecting Nineveh with Babylon and Damascus with Tyre. A natural stopping place for Abraham and his father, Terah, on their trek to Palestine, Haran was a center for the moon god cult.[3]

3 Fatherland

God promised to make "a great nation" out of Abraham. He became the father of a new race of people (the Jews) and was the founding father of three religions: Judaism, Islam, and Christianity. God promised to judge nations with either a blessing or a curse, depending upon how they treat Abraham and Isaac's descendants: "Abraham was, humanly speaking, the founder of our Jewish nation" (Rom. 4:1 NLT).

5 No-Man's-Land

Abraham was stuck in no-man's-land, meaning that God took him to a place that was not yet his. God promised that Canaan would be given to Abraham's descendants, but Abraham wasn't powerful enough to expel the Canaanites. In addition, their sins had not reached the point where God would bring judgment.

he departed from Haran. Then Abram took Sarai his wife and Lot his brother's son, and all their possessions that they had gathered, and the people whom they had acquired in Haran, and they departed to go to the land of Canaan. So they came to the land of Canaan. Abram passed through the land to the place of Shechem, as far as the terebinth tree of Moreh. And the Canaanites were then in the land. Then the LORD appeared to Abram and said, "To your descendants I will give this land." And there he built an altar to the LORD, who had appeared to him. And he moved from there to the mountain east of Bethel, and he pitched his tent with Bethel on the west and Ai on the east; there he built an altar to the LORD and called on the name of the LORD. So Abram journeyed, going on still toward the South. Genesis 12:1–9

1. a. List all that Abraham was asked to leave behind.

   b. How might that have made him feel?

   c. What do you imagine Sarah felt about this?

2. What phrase in God's instructions indicates that Abraham did not know exactly where he was going?

3. a. List the blessing that would follow Abraham's leap of faith.

   b. How might this promise have influenced him?

   c. What might Sarah's reactions have been?

4. List those who accompanied Abraham on this journey and what kind of supplies they might need.

5. What places were included in their journey, and where did they finally set up camp?

6. Abraham did something twice. Underline the activity. Why do you think he did this?

LIVE OUT ...

LEARN ABOUT ...

8 Promised Land

Many assume that entering the Promised Land is a picture of the believer passing from earth to heaven. In fact, it represents the believer inheriting the promises of God on earth. To possess our inheritance we must endure trials and temptations, combat and conquests. "Imitate those who through faith and patience inherit the promises" (Heb. 6:12).

9 Holy Land

Noah built the first altar after the flood. The next several altars mentioned are connected to Abraham and his wanderings. The first was at Shechem to symbolize his eventual possession of the land. Near Bethel and at Hebron he built altars to sacrifice animals and call upon the name of the Lord.[4]

7. Abraham and Sarah were asked to leave all that was familiar to them. Jesus asks the same of His followers. Rewrite the following passage into a personal prayer relinquishing all that you possess into God's hands.

> "If anyone desires to come after Me, let him deny himself, and take up his cross, and follow Me. For whoever desires to save his life will lose it, but whoever loses his life for My sake will find it. For what profit is it to a man if he gains the whole world, and loses his own soul?" Matthew 16:24–26

8. Abraham would empty his arms only to be filled with the promises of God. So too, as we deny all to follow the Lord, He fills our lives with great and precious promises. Read Galatians 3:26–29.

   a. Who does God consider as members of His family, and how does this happen?

   b. What divisions has Christ abolished?

   c. What additional benefit does the believer experience in Christ?

9. This season in Abraham's life consisted of tents and altars. The tent was where he spent time with people, and the altar was where he communed with God. In the columns below, list the places you

have lived and places you have worshipped. Then write about one memorable encounter you had in each of these places.

Ex. worshipped at a retreat   Ex. lived in a college dorm

○ ○ ● ○ ○

In marriage, God established the principle of leaving and cleaving. This is an essential part of becoming one flesh. Drs. Greg and Michael Smalley say, "There are many ways to cleave to one another—physically, emotionally, relationally, and spiritually."

1. Physically:

Putting geographical distance between the couple and extended family offers these benefits:

Relying on each other for daily support.
Not relying on parents for moral support.
Establishing new roles and lifestyles.

2. Emotionally:

Sharing your inmost desires with your spouse rather than others allows you to:

Keep personal issues between you and your spouse.
Prevent excessive external demands from stressing the marriage.
Place your spouse first in decision making.

3. Relationally:

Placing your spouse as the primary relationship helps make a break with the past. Your spouse will know that—after God—he or she holds first place in your heart. Break from the past by:

Getting rid of old letters, pictures, and possessions.

Being sensitive when talking about past relationships.

If necessary, attending counseling together.

4. Spiritually:

Together, talk through spiritual issues like biblical interpretations, church attendance, and prayer habits. Here's a list of ways to cleave spiritually:

Pray for and with each other.

Attend church together.

Serve in some type of church or mission service together.

Read the Bible and memorize Scripture together.[5]

Abraham might have been a baseball player who knew that you can't get to second base if you keep your foot on first. He willingly left his home and went where God told him. His beautiful wife Sarah left everything to go with him. There were some hits and misses on the journey, but God considered their pilgrimage a home run.

LISTEN TO...

Let your home be your parish, your little brood your congregation, your living room a sanctuary, and your knee a sacred altar.

—*Billy Graham*

DAY 2

Trusting and Obeying

Before entering Egypt, Abraham convinced his wife to tell a little white lie. But is there really such a thing? If your spouse asks, "Does this make me look fat?" replying, "It makes you look like an elephant," isn't helpful. However, lies are not acceptable, especially with loved ones. Robert Butterworth, a Los Angeles psychologist, says, "If you can't get honesty from your spouse, who can you get it from?" Although the truth hurts, it doesn't have to be brutal. Butterworth cautions, "You don't have to be cruel when you tell the truth." He recommends prefacing hard truths with "I know this might upset you" to express sensitivity.

Mark Meadows, a sociology professor at San Diego's Union Institute, says couples can spot falsehoods by watching for these signs:

Body language. Crossed arms, sweaty brows, or a fidgety demeanor can signify discomfort.

Eye contact. If you're not making eye contact, it's unlikely you're getting the whole truth.

Hesitation. Stuttering, stalling, and changing the subject are clear signals that something's not right.

Inconsistencies. If your partner says your friends are great but is never available to meet them, something fishy may be going on.

If honesty hasn't been the best policy in your relationship so far, how do you start over? Trust can be rebuilt, but it takes time and tenderness. The first step toward forgiveness is to understand why we tell lies. Meadows says, "People lie for two reasons: to protect themselves or to protect others." If your mate lied instead of telling you what his mother *really* thinks about you, go easy on him.[6] Abraham was afraid, but that didn't excuse his moral failure. It made it harder for Sarah to trust and obey him in the future.

LIFT UP …

Lord, I know that You "hate every false way." Please search my heart and reveal any crooked places that don't please You. Then forgive me and make me love righteousness and truth. Amen.

LOOK AT ...

We've seen that Abraham and Sarah were partners in their pilgrimage as well as in the promises of God. For the Lord to fulfill His covenant with Abraham to make him a great nation and bless his seed, Sarah had to be included in the deal. As the saying goes, it takes two to tango. Therefore, if Abraham was to become the father of Israel, Sarah had to be its mother.

After a stellar start, today we'll see the couple facing a roadblock. Famine forced them to flee from Canaan. Heading in an unexpected direction caused Abraham to fear—and we know that fear is the opposite of faith. His lapse in faith put Sarah in a compromising situation. Sarah even agreed to a lie. Scripture is silent concerning how Sarah felt about the lie, but we know that God protected her while she was staying with Pharaoh.

We all land in situations that put our faith to the test. Sometimes we are asked to follow our husbands into unknown territory. Sometimes those in authority over us fail—and we are forced to suffer the consequences alongside them. But God can turn failures into bright futures. Remember, "God causes everything to work together for the good of those who love God and are called according to his purpose for them" (Rom. 8:28 NLT). He did it for Sarah; He can do it for *you!*

READ GENESIS 12:10–20.

Now there was a famine in the land, and Abram went down to Egypt to dwell there, for the famine was severe in the land. And it came to pass, when he was close to entering Egypt, that he said to Sarai his wife, "Indeed I know that you are a woman of beautiful countenance. Therefore it will happen, when the Egyptians see you, that they will say, 'This is his wife'; and they will kill me, but they will let you live. Please say you are my sister, that it may be well with me for your sake, and that I may live because of you." So it was, when Abram came into Egypt, that the Egyptians saw the woman, that she was very beautiful. The princes of Pharaoh also saw her and commended her to Pharaoh. And the woman was taken to Pharaoh's house. He treated Abram well for her sake. He had sheep, oxen, male donkeys, male and female servants, female donkeys, and camels. But the LORD plagued Pharaoh and his house with great plagues because of Sarai, Abram's wife. And Pharaoh called Abram and said, "What is this you

Learn About ...

I Famine

God often uses circumstances to test His people. Perhaps Abraham expected milk and honey only to discover dust and drought. The fruitful land turning barren accomplished two things: (I) The ungodly Canaanites were punished, and (2) the patriarch was tested. Warren Wiersbe writes, "Tests often follow triumphs."[7]

2 Fear

Egypt scared Abraham to death. He worried that the Egyptians would kill him to kidnap his wife. Hebrew folklore perpetuates the mystery of Sarah's remarkable beauty that only seemed to increase with age. The ancients believed that caravan traveling greatly diminished youth and beauty. Yet after a long trip, Abraham feared that Sarah was prettier than ever.

3 Faith

Faith is a confident belief in God involving a commitment to His will. *Fausset's Bible Dictionary* elaborates on Hebrews II:I—"Faith is the substance of things hoped for (i.e., it substantiates God's promises ... it makes them present realities), the evidence (... 'convincing proof' or 'demonstration') of things not seen.... Where sight is, there faith ceases."[8]

have done to me? Why did you not tell me that she was your wife? Why did you say, 'She is my sister'? I might have taken her as my wife. Now therefore, here is your wife; take her and go your way." So Pharaoh commanded his men concerning him; and they sent him away, with his wife and all that he had. Genesis 12:10–20

1. Describe what happened "now."

2. a. Explain what Abraham feared and how he handled it.

   b. What does this teach you about him?

3. a. Recount what happened to Sarah.

   b. How might this have made her feel?

4. Contrast the lives of Abraham and Pharaoh during this season.

5. a. Who rectified this situation?

   b. What lesson can you learn for your life?

6. Put yourself in Sarah's place, and describe how you think this final outcome might have made her feel.

Live Out ...

7. True faith begins where human resources end. When food ran out, so did Abraham's faith. Journal about a time when one of your necessities dried up and how it affected your faith. What did God teach you, and how did you grow from the experience?

8. Fear and faith cannot coexist. One ultimately consumes the other. "Fear not" is a repetitive scriptural command. Place a check in the appropriate box to indicate the things that make you afraid.

☐ Loneliness: "Fear not, for I am with you; be not dismayed" (Isa. 41:10).

☐ Weakness: "Fear not … I will help you" (Isa. 41:14).

☐ Insignificance: "Fear not … I have called you by your name" (Isa. 43:1).

☐ Enemies: "Be strong … do not fear nor be afraid of them" (Deut. 31:6).

☐ Embarrassment: "Fear not; for thou shalt not be ashamed" (Isa. 54:4 KJV).

• Death: "Fear not them which kill the body, but are not able to kill the soul" (Matt. 10:28 KJV).

Journal a prayer asking God to give you faith to overcome your fear. Tell Him that you will walk in faith despite your feelings.

9. a. We reaffirmed that "faith is being sure of what we hope for and certain of what we do not see" (Heb. 11:1 NIV). List some of the ways you are choosing to walk by faith and not by sight.

b. What scriptural promises are you holding on to, waiting to see their fulfillment?

○ ○ ● ○ ○

It's hard to believe that shortly after arriving in the Promised Land, Abraham made an exodus to Egypt. Egypt often symbolizes the world system and its bondage, while the land of Israel is a portrait of our future inheritance and God's blessings. Too late Abraham learned that it's

LEARN ABOUT …

8 Faithful

We can trust God because He keeps His promises. Our faith is based upon His faithfulness. Although Abraham and Sarah had a lapse in faith, God did not. He rectified the situation, and everyone, including Pharaoh, saw God's faithfulness. Paul reminded Timothy, "If we are faithless, He remains faithful; He cannot deny Himself" (2 Tim. 2:13).

9 Future

Faith is for the here and now. But it's also for the future. It would have been better for the couple to remain in the Promised Land during a famine than to enjoy feasting in Pharaoh's entourage: "Better a handful with quietness than both hands full, together with toil and grasping for the wind" (Eccl. 4:6).

impossible to run from your problems, because oftentimes *you* turn out to be the problem. In Canaan he was afraid of famine. In Egypt he feared foul play. One bad choice led to another—fleeing opened the way to fibbing.

Was asking Sarah to assert that she was Abraham's sister and not his wife a bold-faced lie? Not exactly. Sarah and Abraham did have blood ties. She was his half sister—we discover in Genesis 20 that they had the same father but different mothers. Some would say that Abraham was just stretching the truth. In reality, a half-truth is a whole lie. You can lie just as easily by withholding information as you can by disseminating misinformation. An Arabian proverb says, "To tell a lie might help you to have lunch, but not to have supper." Somehow Pharaoh became aware of Abraham's deception. That's when their free lunch ended.

Let's ask ourselves whether we are much different from the parsing patriarch. In the United States we live with a "credibility gap." We fudge on our income tax returns, thereby pilfering millions of dollars per year from the government. Doctors fake reports to make a profit from Medicare patients. Prize athletes use steroids to beef up their statistics. In the words of a *Time* magazine essay, ours is "a huckstering, show-bizzy world, jangling with hype, hullabaloo, and hooey, bull, baloney, and bamboozlement."[9]

LISTEN TO...

The beginning of anxiety is the end of faith; and the beginning of true faith is the end of anxiety.

—George Müller

DAY 3

Sleeping and Dreaming

The philosopher George Santayana said, "Those who cannot learn from history are doomed to repeat it." Now some propose that there is a scientific reason why people fail to learn from their mistakes. Dr. Jacqueline Beals writes, "A genetic polymorphism that reduces dopamine receptor density has been linked to a decreased ability to learn from errors. The German study, published in the December 7 issue of *Science*, shows that carriers of the dopamine receptor D2 (*DRD2*) *Taq 1A* allele are less able to learn from negative conse-quences."[10] The scientists believe decreased dopamine levels might mean certain people can't learn to do right after they've done wrong.

As believers, we know why people make the same mistakes again and again: sin. The sin nature was genetically imputed to us at the fall. Regardless of how we try to overcome this character defect, it is human nature to sin. Yet God in His goodness comes alongside us—and since the New Testament age, He has come to dwell inside us—to help us change our ways and do what is right in His sight.

We know that Abraham and Sarah fudged the truth when they were in Egypt by telling Pharaoh that Sarah was Abraham's sister. Thankfully, God protected Sarah's virtue and their marriage. Now we'll see how the couple foolishly repeated their error with another powerful ruler after God visited them with the assurance of a son to be the heir of promise. They should have known better. They should have learned from their mistake.

LIFT UP ...

Father God, please help me to learn from my mistakes rather than repeat them. I want to be a person who is able to change my ways for good. Help me to be the person You want me to be in the power of Your Holy Spirit. Amen.

LOOK AT ...

We move ahead approximately twenty-two years, from around 1918 BC to around 1896 BC.[11] Chapters 18—19 found Abraham at Mamre under the terebinth tree, meeting with

LEARN ABOUT ...

2 Going South

Gerar was a Philistine city in southern Palestine. A wealthy city on a caravan route, Gerar was also known as an agricultural community. The destruction of Sodom and Gomorrah could have caused another famine and led Abraham, Sarah, and their household to journey south. Isaac also went to Gerar during a time of famine (see Gen. 26:1).

---

3 God's Sovereignty

God supernaturally prevented Sarah from having a sexual relationship with anyone but Abraham. He had promised that through Sarah Abraham would bring forth a child who would birth the race of chosen people. Through this genealogical line the Messiah would come to deliver His people: "The Deliverer will come out of Zion" (Rom. 11:26).

God, who had appeared in human form (a theophany) with two of His angels. Abraham asked God to spare Sodom and Gomorrah if even ten righteous people could be found there. God promised to do so (see Gen. 18:16–33). Unfortunately, ten were not found, and the towns were destroyed with fire from heaven.

We pick up our story in Genesis 20, when Abraham and Sarah moved to a new place and faced a crisis similar to the one in Genesis 12. Unfortunately, they changed locations but failed to change a sinful pattern. Let's learn from this couple that you can run but you can't hide from God. He wants to change us. Sometimes He'll even use unbelievers to show us the error of our ways.

READ GENESIS 20:1–7.

And Abraham journeyed from there to the South, and dwelt between Kadesh and Shur, and stayed in Gerar. Now Abraham said of Sarah his wife, "She is my sister." And Abimelech king of Gerar sent and took Sarah. But God came to Abimelech in a dream by night, and said to him, "Indeed you are a dead man because of the woman whom you have taken, for she is a man's wife." But Abimelech had not come near her; and he said, "Lord, will You slay a righteous nation also? Did he not say to me, 'She is my sister'? And she, even she herself said, 'He is my brother.' In the integrity of my heart and innocence of my hands I have done this." And God said to him in a dream, "Yes, I know that you did this in the integrity of your heart. For I also withheld you from sinning against Me; therefore I did not let you touch her. Now therefore, restore the man's wife; for he is a prophet, and he will pray for you and you shall live. But if you do not restore her, know that you shall surely die, you and all who are yours." Genesis 20:1–7

1. Look back to Genesis 17:1, 17:17, and 18:1, and recount Abraham's and Sarah's ages and place where they lived at this time.

2. In today's text we see the transitional word *And* to bring us here.

Describe where Abraham journeyed. How do you think the phrase "to the South" might be interpreted in Scripture?

3. a. What happened to Sarah?

   b. How were Sarah and Abraham complicit in allowing this to happen?

   c. Describe how God intervened to protect Sarah.

4. How did Abimelech explain himself to God?

5. Explain why God wanted Abimelech to restore Sarah to Abraham.

6. What would the consequences be for Abimelech and his people if he did not send Sarah back to Abraham?

LIVE OUT ...

7. God spoke to Abimelech in a dream. In the columns below list some of the ways God speaks to you. Beside each column, describe how you know it is God and not an imposter speaking to you.

HOW GOD COMMUNICATES   **HOW I KNOW IT IS HIM**

8. Sarah again conspired with Abraham to lie about their relationship as husband and wife. You might call lying Sarah's "besetting sin." Examine your heart for a pattern of sin that keeps repeating itself in your life. Then confess it to God, and ask Him to help cleanse you of it once and for all.

LEARN ABOUT ...

5 God's Spokesman

In Abimelech's dream God described Abraham as a prophet. A prophet was a person who spoke for God and communicated God's message. Unfortunately, in this case Abraham's actions did not live up to his words. Nevertheless, God did not take Abraham's spiritual gifts away.

7 Good Sleep

In the Bible, dreams were sometimes prophetic or ways to make known God's will. God spoke to Jacob in a dream to renew the covenant and reassure Jacob of His protection. Two dream cycles required interpretation: The first related to Joseph (Gen. 37:5–10); the second involved Daniel (Dan. 2:14–45). Both dreams pertained to future events.[12]

8 Give Up Sin

Abraham and Sarah agreed from the start to lie about their relationship. However, when it got them into trouble with Pharaoh, they could have decided to speak the truth. Instead, they continued to lie. This placed them and the people they encountered at risk and ultimately led to their poor witness for the God they served.

9. In the book of Esther, King Ahasuerus asked Queen Vashti to do something against her conscience.

   a. Read Esther 1:10–19, and recount what happened to this queen because of her refusal to obey her husband.

   b. Though Queen Vashti was not a believer, she is a good example of following her conscience rather than the dictates of an ungodly husband. Read Acts 5:26–32, and talk about how one might respond to authority when asked to do something that goes against God's principles. Do you think this extends to the marriage relationship? Why or why not?

∘ ∘ ● ∘ ∘

When I (Penny) was in college, I had fallen away from walking with the Lord. But He was chasing after me in some surprising ways. Members of Campus Crusade for Christ stopped by my dorm room and invited me to meetings; my grandmother often called to tell me she was praying for me; and I had recurring dreams about Jesus. I knew that God was trying to get my attention. In a few years, I returned to a real relationship with Christ.

Paul Johnson wrote,

> We take less notice of dreams than the ancients, because we are more sophisticated. One reason why Judaism, and Christianity which sprang from it, were so much an advance on pagan religions is that they attached comparatively little importance to dreams. True, there are 116 references to dreams in the Old Testament, but most are clustered in two sections: 52 in Genesis in the early patriarchal period and 29 in the book of Daniel. Only 14 dreams are specifically recorded. In each case, moreover, God is the initiator for particular purposes and his meaning is plain—no need for the interpretative dream-books of paganism. As Daniel told Nebuchadnezzar, only God discloses the secrets of dreams…. The message of the Bible is that God regards dreaming as a secondary mode of communication.[13]

God's written Word is the primary means by which He imparts His wisdom to humans. He also speaks through people, the Holy Spirit, our circumstances, and sometimes even our dreams. Is God trying to get a message to you as He did to me? Listen to His voice and turn to Him quickly.

LISTEN TO ...

Our heart oft-times wakes when we sleep; and God can speak to that, either by words, by Proverbs, by Signs and Similitudes, as well as if one was awake.

—*John Bunyan*

DAY 4

Watching and Waiting

Should you journey to Germany to explore its many art galleries, you would come across one studio that houses an unusual painting called *Cloud Lane*. Displayed at the end of lengthy dim corridor, from a distance the picture appears full of gloomy clouds that evoke an unsettling feeling. As you slowly approach, the chaos on the canvas begins to coalesce into a beautiful scene. Instead of hanging clouds, you see hovering angels triumphantly descending en masse.

Too often we view our trials in much the same way. Instinctively we want to run from approaching shadows. But if we would look more closely through the eyes of faith, we'd see a host of angels coming with deliverance and hope.[14] It's really true that with God every cloud has its silver lining.

Based on Abraham's encounter with Pharaoh, you'd think he would have learned that looks are deceiving. A drought had caused him to doubt God's provision. He went off to Egypt without affording God the opportunity to "supply all [his] need according to His riches in glory" (Phil. 4:19). Some of us never see God's miraculous provision, because we're too busy trying to fulfill our needs through the arm of the flesh. The encounter with Abimelech provided Abraham a second chance at weathering the storms of life. When tempests gather, have you considered that perhaps they are God's harbingers? The psalmist wrote, "Sing praises to God and to his name! Sing loud praises to him who rides the clouds. His name is the LORD—rejoice in his presence!" (Ps. 68:4 NLT).

LIFT UP …

I know that You, Lord, work all situations out for my good and Your ultimate glory. But I must give You the chance. Help me not to run from trials, but to trust You in the midst of them. Amen.

LOOK AT ...

Did you know that the first time the term *prophet* is used in Scripture is when Abraham was in a season of moral failure? The truth that God uses men with feet of clay is both uplifting and downright confusing. Our expectations for ministers are higher than our expectations for ourselves. In reality, there is no such thing as sinless perfection for leaders or laypersons. As Christians we aim to sin less and less. But when we fail, we can still find forgiveness. John reminds believers that Christ cleanses from sins both past and present: "If we say that we have no sin, we deceive ourselves.… If we confess our sins, He is faithful and just to forgive us our sins and to cleanse us from all unrighteousness" (1 John 1:8–9). The truth is we should be looking for sin in our own hearts before doing exploratory surgery on others.

Now our text shows us that Abimelech's divine dream turned into Abraham's worst nightmare—public humiliation. The patriarch was exposed as a liar and a coward. He discovered that there was no excuse for his shenanigans. Situations like this perfectly illustrate the saying "Your sins will find you out." Paul explained it like this: "Do not be deceived, God is not mocked; for whatever a man sows, that he will also reap. For he who sows to his flesh will of the flesh reap corruption, but he who sows to the Spirit will of the Spirit reap everlasting life" (Gal. 6:7–8).

READ GENESIS 20:8–13.

So Abimelech rose early in the morning, called all his servants, and told all these things in their hearing; and the men were very much afraid. And Abimelech called Abraham and said to him, "What have you done to us? How have I offended you, that you have brought on me and on my kingdom a great sin? You have done deeds to me that ought not to be done." Then Abimelech said to Abraham, "What did you have in view, that you have done this thing?" And Abraham said, "Because I thought, surely the fear of God is not in this place; and they will kill me on account of my wife. But indeed she is truly my sister. She is the daughter of my father, but not the daughter of my mother; and she became my wife. And it came to pass, when God caused me to wander from my father's house, that I said to her, 'This is your kindness that you should do for me: in every place, wherever we go, say of me, "He is my brother."'" Genesis 20:8–13

LEARN ABOUT ...

1 Afraid

John Phillips wrote, "The fear of God was so overwhelming that Abimelech, even though furious, could scarcely keep himself from trembling with fright even as he sat on his throne. And all around him his courtiers were in an equal panic."[15] Solomon said, "By the fear of the LORD one departs from evil" (Prov. 16:6).

---

3 Appalled

Abimelech believed that Abraham's deceit had extensive consequences. Not only would it impact the ruler, it would taint his entire realm. It's true; the sins of a king corrupt his kingdom. Look at Jeroboam. "He did evil in the sight of the LORD ... and in his sin by which he had made Israel sin" (1 Kings 15:26).

---

6 Appealed

Abraham appealed to Sarah's affection by asking her to lie in order to save his life. She cooperated with her husband, risking her reputation along with his. She could have influenced him to fear God rather than man. They rationalized their deception with a flimsy partial truth.

1. a. What did Abimelech do next?

    b. How did others respond?

2. How do you know that Abraham's deception was far reaching?

3. a. Rephrase Abimelech's final question to Abraham.

    b. Describe how this might have made Abraham feel.

4. What two excuses did Abraham give for his ploy?

5. How did he rationalize his deception?

6. a. Rephrase Abraham's instructions to Sarah.

    b. How would a request like this make you feel?

LIVE OUT ...

7. The fear of the Lord affected a king and his kingdom as Abimelech sought to right the wrong he had committed. Fill in the following chart to discover the benefits of fearing God.

SCRIPTURE	BENEFITS OF FEARING THE LORD
Psalm 111:10	
Proverbs 10:27	
Proverbs 14:26–27	
Proverbs 22:4	

8. Abimelech was aware that his actions as ruler of the nation would impact his nation. Explain whether you believe that this principle

is true. Use examples from history or current events to make your point.

9.   Sarah was put in a difficult situation concerning whether to obey God or her husband. First Peter 3:1–6 sheds insight into her decision making. Read the text; then answer the following questions.

   a. How are women encouraged to handle disobedient husbands (vv. 1–2)?

   b. Compare and contrast inner and outer beauty (vv. 3–4).

   c. How did "holy women" reveal that they trusted God (v. 5)?

   d. What things did Sarah do and not do to make herself a godly woman (v. 6)?

· · ● · ·

LEARN ABOUT …

7 Awed

The term "the fear of the Lord" carries the idea of reverence and awe. It is based upon a loving relationship with God whereby those who love Him desire to obey Him. The fear of the Lord is also closely related to living a godly life.

9 Adorned

Often we see the word *adornment* and think of outward adornments like earrings or makeup. But the embellishments that God values are inward, like attitudes or actions: "As a ring of gold in a swine's snout, so is a lovely woman who lacks discretion" (Prov. 11:22). Sarah's beauty grew with age because her devotion to God grew and matured.

Dissimilar people often view the same thing with completely different perspectives. There's an old story about three people who were visiting the Grand Canyon—an artist, a pastor, and a cowboy. As they stood on the edge of that massive abyss, each one responded with an exclamation. The artist said, "Ah, what a beautiful scene to paint!" The minister cried, "What a wonderful example of the handiwork of God!" The cowboy mused, "What a terrible place to lose a cow!"[16]

You know the old saying "Beauty is in the eye of the beholder." Well, it appears that everyone who beheld Sarah thought she was a knockout. However, with most advantages in life, our greatest strength can become our greatest weakness. In Sarah's case, her lovely countenance opened the door to compromise. She could have been the spokesmodel for the famous shampoo advertisement, "Don't hate me because I'm beautiful." Powerful potentates changed their position from coveting her to casting her out of their kingdoms.

What are you doing with the gifts God has bestowed upon you? As long as you use them for His glory, they will remain a blessing. But once you begin to rely on them for personal advantage, they can become a curse. Solomon may have learned this the hard way. What God intended to bless a nation, Solomon started to use for personal benefit. His wisdom led to wealth, and he began to seek many women. Eventually the miserable king wrote, "Remove falsehood and lies far from me; give me neither poverty nor riches—feed me with the food allotted to me; lest I be full and deny You, and say, 'Who is the LORD?' Or lest I be poor and steal, and profane the name of my God" (Prov. 30:8–9).

LISTEN TO …

The essence of lying is in deception, not in words: a lie may be told by silence, by equivocation, by the accent on a syllable, by a glance of the eye attaching a peculiar significance to a sentence.

—*John Ruskin*

DAY 5

Giving and Taking

One of the greatest gifts we can give is to help someone become a better person. Who has motivated you to improve in some area? An elementary school teacher who helped you win the spelling bee? A coach who went the extra mile? A parent who lavished love?

David B. Bohl said, "The essence of all growth starts with a willingness to change for the better.… Many times we are faced with situations that are actually growth opportunities in disguise."[17] The first time Sarah and Abraham went to a foreign land and lied about their relationship, they didn't learn from their experience. How do we know? Twenty years later they repeated their mistake. Have you ever noticed that if you continue in sin, God will force you to face it until you repent? *Now* it was time for them to learn from their mistakes.

Bohl wrote, "The second quality of growth is an unremitting willingness to shoulder whatever responsibility changing entails. The buck stops, and starts, with ourselves. It's important to realize that changing for the better sometimes will not come easy. You will sometimes have to shoulder tremendous liability to make it happen."[18] For Abraham and Sarah, perhaps the biggest blow was being reprimanded by a pagan leader.

LIFT UP …

Jesus, help me to take any rebuke to heart as a wake-up call to restore my relationship with You. Thank You for Your grace in forgiving me and renewing me into deeper fellowship with You. Amen.

LOOK AT …

We've seen Abraham and Sarah caught in a lie when they were trying to save their skins. Thankfully, God preserved Sarah's purity, thus preserving the line of the Messiah. No doubt Abimelech questioned their character. At worst he could have viewed them as a traveling con artist team and thrown them into prison. At best they were naive in thinking they could get away with lying again. Scripture is clear that you can "be sure your sin will find you out" (Num. 32:23). The pagan Abimelech was more gracious to Abraham and Sarah than they

LEARN ABOUT …

2 Restored

To *restore* means to return to the starting point or convert. In the King James Version it has been translated "fetch home again." Here it carries the idea of restitution, where what was taken away was given back and additional value added: "He shall make restitution for his trespass in full, plus one-fifth of it" (Num. 5:7).

3 Rebuked

Sometimes the greatest rebuke comes in the form of kindness. Abimelech lavished Abraham with worldly goods and prime real estate. In addition, he treated Sarah graciously by sending her back unharmed. God also treats people kindly to bring them back: "God's kindness leads you toward repentance" (Rom. 2:4 NIV).

4 Request

Prayer is simply communicating with God. One aspect of prayer is making requests known to God to fulfill our needs and the needs of others. Here, Abraham interceded for healing on behalf of Abimelech and the women who had been afflicted. Perhaps during this prayer Abraham prayed for forgiveness as well.

were to him, because he let them go away with dignity. How tragic that an unbeliever was forced to rebuke believers—it must have stung badly. Even more remarkable is God's grace in forgiving the couple. He continued to refer to Abraham as a prophet. He did not go back on His covenant promise. And He never brought up this incident in the New Testament by pointing out Abraham's failure. How wonderful to serve a God who forgives and chooses to forget.

READ GENESIS 20:14–18.

Then Abimelech took sheep, oxen, and male and female servants, and gave them to Abraham; and he restored Sarah his wife to him. And Abimelech said, "See, my land is before you; dwell where it pleases you." Then to Sarah he said, "Behold, I have given your brother a thousand pieces of silver; indeed this vindicates you before all who are with you and before everybody." Thus she was rebuked. So Abraham prayed to God; and God healed Abimelech, his wife, and his female servants. Then they bore children; for the LORD had closed up all the wombs of the house of Abimelech because of Sarah, Abraham's wife. Genesis 20:14–18

1. In what ways did Abimelech compensate Abraham for taking Sarah?

2. What was the silver intended to provide for Sarah?

3. How did she feel instead? How would you have felt in her shoes?

4. How did Abraham respond, and what was the result?

5. Why had God closed the women's wombs?

LIVE OUT ...

6. a. We've seen how Sarah was restored to Abraham and even given more. Fill in the following chart to discover what God restores to His people.

SCRIPTURE	WHAT GOD RESTORES
Psalm 51:12	
Isaiah 57:15–18	
Joel 2:25–26	
Matthew 17:11	

b. What divine restoration project does God have you involved in?

c. Which Scripture offers you the most comfort and why?

7. a. Sarah was rebuked by Abimelech's actions. Read Proverbs 9:8–9. What do you learn about being rebuked?

b. How do you usually respond when you are rebuked?

8. We saw Abraham pray for Abimelech and his family to be restored to health. One good acronym for structured prayer is CATS. Use this acronym to pray on behalf of someone who needs restoration.

Confession:

Adoration:

Thanksgiving:

Supplication:

LEARN ABOUT ...

6 Recompense

Abimelech gave gifts to recompense Abraham. The idea comes from *shalom* or making peace. Jesus said, "Blessed are the peacemakers, for they shall be called sons of God" (Matt. 5:9). It's unclear whether Abimelech became a believer, but we know he feared God and acted accordingly. We're told, "As much as depends on you, live peaceably with all men" (Rom. 12:18).

8 Reverence

Talking to God in prayer is the ultimate display of reverence. "Draw near to God and He will draw near to you" (James 4:8). God wants to hear and respond to our prayers. He urges us to "call upon Me and go and pray to Me, and I will listen to you" (Jer. 29:12).

○ ○ ● ○ ○

The cosmetic industry tries to tell women that they can restore their youthful skin by purchasing products to add a glow or take away wrinkles. Most of us have tried a variety of products to stop the aging process. Sadly, it seems that the only thing that gets renewed is the manufacturer's bank account. Let's face it, we're all getting older, and no amount of restorative cream can change that.

In the 1980s the Sistine Chapel began a large restoration project. Michelangelo's frescoes and important artwork by Botticelli, Perugino, Rosselli, and others had been ravaged by time. Accumulated dirt, smoke from candles, and layers of varnish had caused the masterpieces to lose their luster. A team of experts spent over a decade cleaning and restoring the Sistine ceiling. The cleaning revealed unexpectedly brilliant colors that had not been seen for centuries.

Whether it is human skin or a piece of artwork, humans desire restoration after something has begun to decay. In Sarah and Abraham's case, they had lost their reputation as followers of God. So Abimelech made an offering of animals, servants, slaves, and silver in an effort to restore the couple to their previous condition. However, let's not get confused about who Abimelech sought to appease. Though Sarah and Abraham were the beneficiaries, Abimelech made his offering to God.

Have you lost your luster? Do you feel that you are living your life in black and white rather than in Technicolor? Maybe it is time to turn back to God and ask Him to peel away the layers of grime or the wrinkles that have kept you away from Him. He is only a prayer away. He truly is the God of restoration: "Restore us, O God of our salvation, and cause Your anger toward us to cease" (Ps. 85:4).

LISTEN TO ...

It may well be that a faith that has made experience of falling and restoration has learned a depth of self-distrust, a firmness of confidence in Christ, a warmth of grateful love which it would never otherwise have experienced.

—*Alexander Maclaren*

Hagar—Where Do I Fit In?

Genesis 16 & 21:8–21

Indian culture divides itself into a caste system. Ancient Hindu writings reveal that there are four "varnas" or rankings of people within society—Brahman, the highest caste; Kshatriya; Vaishya; and Sudra, the lowest caste. Brahmans serve as teachers, scholars, and priests. The Dalits, unclean members of the Sudra, are also known as "untouchables" and work in unhealthy and unpleasant jobs. Those who come in contact with Dalits are excluded from temple worship and required to undergo ceremonial cleansing to purge themselves from impurity.

However, Indians are not the only society that embraces cultural segregation. The British also operate within a class system. Formed during the Victorian era, this system was probably influenced by the colonization of India. The British created an "intricate hierarchy of people which contrasted the new and old rich, the skilled and unskilled, the rural and urban and many more."[1]

During the patriarchal era there were defined classes of people too. Abraham was viewed as a chieftain or sheikh by his contemporaries. He was the leader of a large tribe that included a military contingent, family members, and slaves. Where did Hagar fit in? She was in the lowest class for many reasons. She was a woman. A slave. A foreigner. And unmarried.

Although humanity likes to classify and elevate one person above another, the advent of Christ leveled the playing field. Paul wrote, "There is neither Jew nor Greek, there is neither slave nor free, there is neither male nor female; for you are all one in Christ Jesus" (Gal. 3:28).

Day 1: Genesis 16:1–4   **WHAT WERE YOU THINKING?**

Day 2: Genesis 16:5–9   **WHY SHOULD I?**

Day 3: Genesis 16:10–16   **WHO ARE YOU?**

Day 4: Genesis 21:8–15   **WHY ME?**

Day 5: Genesis 21:16–21   **WHAT NOW?**

DAY 1
What Were You Thinking?

LIFT UP ...

Father, let me embrace whatever You send my way as good and perfect. Please help me to influence those around me to take the right step and to do the right thing. Amen.

LOOK AT ...

As we begin Genesis 16, we remain involved in the lives of Abraham and Sarah. We know that God had made a covenant with them to send them a son—the heir of promise. However, the couple had waited ten years and grown old without receiving the promise. At this time their faith began to waver. They began to look for other solutions. But they would learn the hard way that God's delays are not denials. What about you? Are you waiting for the fulfillment of a promise made long ago? Don't give up hope. Don't give in to doubt. The Lord's timing is always just right.

Unfortunately, Sarah became desperate and devised a hasty scheme. Sending her husband into the arms of another woman, she thought she'd hurry God along. Let's not fall into the same trap. *God* things come to those who wait: "Those who wait on the LORD shall renew their strength; they shall mount up with wings like eagles, they shall run and not be weary, they shall walk and not faint" (Isa. 40:31).

READ GENESIS 16:1–4.

Now Sarai, Abram's wife, had borne him no children. And she had an Egyptian maid-servant whose name was Hagar. So Sarai said to Abram, "See now, the LORD has restrained me from bearing children. Please, go in to my maid; perhaps I shall obtain children by her." And Abram heeded the voice of Sarai. Then Sarai, Abram's wife, took Hagar her maid, the Egyptian, and gave her to her husband Abram to be his wife, after Abram had dwelt ten years

LEARN ABOUT ...

2 Servant

An Egyptian name, *Hagar* resembles the Arabic word for flight. Legend holds that Hagar was an Egyptian princess, perhaps the daughter of Pharaoh. Although some commentators believe that she was one of the female slaves presented to Abraham by Pharaoh during his visit to Egypt, she properly belonged to Sarah.[2]

---

4 Surrogate

Ten years earlier Abraham and Sarah received the promise of an heir. Determined to become a mother, Sarah sought a child by a means now known as surrogacy. It was widely popular in the East and recorded by the Code of Hammurabi, one of the earliest and best-preserved law codes from ancient Babylon.

---

6 Spiteful

Although culturally acceptable, surrogacy was not part of God's plan. He had promised a literal heir; anything less would be of the flesh. Once Hagar conceived, a rift developed within Abraham's household. The handmaiden became an affront to the mistress. Her haughty attitude would one day bring heartbreak. Abraham listened to his wife instead of God.

in the land of Canaan. So he went in to Hagar, and she conceived. And when she saw that she had conceived, her mistress became despised in her eyes. Genesis 16:1–4

1. "Now" what was happening in the lives of Abraham and Sarah?

2. Describe the new character introduced in our study.

3. Who did Sarah blame for her infertility? Do you think she was justified? Share a Scripture to support your theory.

4. What do you learn about Sarah from the solution she offered?

5. a. How did Abraham respond to this plan?

   b. What insight into him does this give you?

6. Recount the outcome of this plan and how it affected Hagar.

LIVE OUT ...

7. Hagar had no choice in becoming a maidservant. As believers, Christ asks us to become servants by choice. Jesus said, "If anyone desires to be first, he shall be last of all and servant of all" (Mark 9:35).

   a. List some areas where you come in first and some in which you are last.

   b. Now rewrite Mark 9:35 into a personal prayer of humility.

8. Sarah wanted the right thing but went about it the wrong way.

Make a list of things you've done or witnessed that were done with good intentions but produced bad results.

RIGHT THING	WRONG WAY
Ex. Desire a husband	Marry an unbeliever

9.   When Hagar got what Sarah wanted, she felt she had the upper hand. Later this got Hagar into a lot of trouble. It's easy to put people down when things are going our way. Journal about a time this was true of you.

○ ○ ● ○ ○

Hagar had a choice. She could have treated Sarah with respect or even compassion because of her infertility. In ancient Eastern cultures barrenness was seen as a curse or punishment from God. If Hagar had stayed in her place as a humble servant instead of responding in pride and petulance, things could have turned out differently. Sadly, she chose to despise her mistress.

Ernest Gordon, an American POW in the Kwai prison camp during WWII, observed how wounded Japanese prisoners were treated by their own people as they were returned to Bangkok. His book *Through the Valley of the Kwai* tells the tale of how he and his fellow captives treated their captors with dignity:

They [the Japanese] were in a shocking state. I have never seen men filthier. Uniforms were encrusted with mud, blood, and excrement. Their wounds, sorely inflamed and full of pus, crawled with maggots. The maggots, however, in eating the putrefying flesh, probably prevented gangrene.

It was apparent why the Japanese were so cruel to their prisoners. If they didn't care for their own, why should they care for us? ...

Without a word most of the officers in my section unbuckled their packs, took out part of their ration and a rag or two, and, with water canteens in their hands, went over to the Japanese train.

Our guards tried to prevent us, bawling, "No goodka! No goodka!" But we ignored them and knelt down by the enemy to give water and food, to clean and bind up their wounds. Grateful cries of "Aragatto!" ("Thank you") followed us when we left.[3]

LISTEN TO ...

Before you can cure the diseases of the body, you must cure the diseases of the soul—greed, ignorance, prejudice, and intolerance.

—*Paul Ehrlich*

DAY 2

Why Should I?

While two heads may be better than one, having two wives is never a good idea. *Polygamy* comes from the Greek and means "many marriages." It defines any form of marriage in which either person has more than one mate at a time. Social biology broadens the term to include multiple matings of any form. In contrast, monogamy describes a relationship where each person has only one spouse.

When studying Abraham, we encounter a complex relationship between the patriarch, his wife, and a legal concubine. Bear in mind that at this time there was no written Law or Ten Commandments denouncing polygamy. There was, however, God's Word spoken directly to individuals. For instance, Adam was told that a man must "leave and cleave" to establish a nuclear family. The question is, over the centuries, had Abraham received this oral instruction? Coming from Ur of the Chaldees, Abraham was raised in a society that accepted multiple wives and concubines as common practice. Now Abraham would learn that two women was one too many.

When God gave Moses the Law, He forbade adultery. Adultery is defined as any sexual relationship outside of marriage. God further affirmed the sanctity of marriage when He said, "The king must not take many wives for himself" (Deut. 17:17 NLT). Although in the Old Testament polygamy and divorce were tolerated, in the New Testament Jesus explained that this was not God's divine ideal: "Moses, because of the hardness of your hearts, permitted you to divorce your wives, but from the beginning it was not so. And I say to you, whoever divorces his wife, except for sexual immorality, and marries another, commits adultery" (Matt. 19:8–9).

LIFT UP …

Lord, too often I ask, "Why should I stay where I'm not comfortable?" Help me to learn contentment whether I am abased or I abound. Amen.

Look at ...

Yesterday we saw how the parents of the promise had lost heart because of a ten-year delay in the fulfillment of God's covenant. Infertility led to instability in Sarah's heart. Instead of recalling God's prior faithfulness in delivering her from the hands of powerful men, she fixated on her empty womb. In desperation she recruited Hagar as a surrogate.

When the pregnancy plan came to fruition, the women responded poorly. Hagar responded boastfully and Sarah spitefully. Trials have a way of bringing out either the best or the worst in us. That's because they have the uncanny ability to expose our hearts. If you jostle a jar of perfume, sweetness pours forth. If you jam into a vessel of lemon juice, sourness spills out. Jesus reminds us, "Out of the abundance of the heart the mouth speaks. A good man out of the good treasure of his heart brings forth good things, and an evil man out of the evil treasure brings forth evil things" (Matt. 12:34–35). What springs out of your mouth when things don't go your way?

READ GENESIS 16:5–9.

Then Sarai said to Abram, "My wrong be upon you! I gave my maid into your embrace; and when she saw that she had conceived, I became despised in her eyes. The LORD judge between you and me." So Abram said to Sarai, "Indeed your maid is in your hand; do to her as you please." And when Sarai dealt harshly with her, she fled from her presence. Now the Angel of the LORD found her by a spring of water in the wilderness, by the spring on the way to Shur. And He said, "Hagar, Sarai's maid, where have you come from, and where are you going?" She said, "I am fleeing from the presence of my mistress Sarai." The Angel of the LORD said to her, "Return to your mistress, and submit yourself under her hand." Genesis 16:5–9

1. Compare Sarah's response to unexpected consequences with those of Adam and Eve.

2. a. How did Sarah bring God into the equation?

   b. Have you ever done the same thing? If so, when?

3. Explain how Abraham responded to the conflict.

4. What was the outcome of Abraham's approach?

5. a. Who did Hagar encounter as she "fled"?

   b. Recount their conversation.

6. Describe the internal conflict that Hagar may have felt in response to the Lord's command.

LIVE OUT ...

7. Sin caused Sarah to behave irrationally, from an untamed tongue to an uncontrolled temper. Place a check in the boxes below to note the ways you have behaved irrationally. Then ask God to check your heart and cleanse you from these sins.

   ❏ Gossip and backbiting
   ❏ Outburst of anger
   ❏ Manipulating others
   ❏ Cold shoulder
   ❏ Physical violence
   ❏ Overeating
   ❏ Overspending
   ❏ Other _____

8. Hagar bore the brunt of Sarah's wrath. Have you ever come out on the short end of the stick? If so, journal about a situation where you were blamed for something you did not do. How did it make you feel, and what did you do about it?

LEARN ABOUT ...

2 Irrational

Sarah now began to reap what she had sown. Instead of taking responsibility as mastermind of this scheme, she blamed her husband. Next she vented her anger on Hagar, who had simply followed orders. Finally, she tried to rationalize her actions by invoking God as judge, hyperspiritualizing the situation.

4 Irresponsible

In a patriarchal society the man was truly king of his castle. Abraham could have quashed the whole surrogate scheme from the start. And when the women spiraled out of control, he should have served as mediator. Instead he allowed the squabble to ferment. Sadly, Abraham abdicated his rightful role, and Hagar fell victim.

5 Irresistible

"The Angel of the Lord is a mysterious messenger of God, sometimes described as the Lord Himself, but at other times as one sent by God. The Lord used this messenger to appear to human beings who otherwise would not be able to see Him and live."[4] His presence and pronouncement were an irresistible inducement for Hagar.

8 Responsibility

Blame shifting goes all the way back to the garden. The first step toward repentance is to take responsibility for our own sins and let the blame fall in the right place. "Suppose you sin by violating one of the LORD's commands. Even if you are unaware of what you have done, you are guilty and will be punished for your sin" (Lev. 5:17 NLT).

9 Resolution

Sometimes God asks us to remain in a painful situation. Many trials are ongoing. If we resolve to obey, we will be rewarded: "Blessed is the man who endures temptation; for when he has been approved, he will receive the crown of life which the Lord has promised to those who love Him" (James 1:12).

9. Hagar received a difficult request—return to a scornful woman and submit. Do you know somebody in a painful place? Rewrite the following verse into a prayer of comfort on that person's behalf.

> Praise be to the God and Father of our Lord Jesus Christ, the Father of compassion and the God of all comfort, who comforts us in all our troubles, so that we can comfort those in any trouble with the comfort we ourselves have received from God. For just as the sufferings of Christ flow over into our lives, so also through Christ our comfort overflows. 2 Corinthians 1:3–5 NIV

○ ○ ● ○ ○

Many people are forced to learn how to live with chronic pain—the kind that lasts longer than the injury that caused it. According to the Society for Neuroscience, it afflicts nearly 100 million people in the United States. The toll of the suffering is hard to measure, and the methods used to diagnose it are inexact. But chronic pain is a $100-billion-a-year burden on American society.

In the United States alone, according to the latest surveys and estimates:

Chronic headaches, including migraines, affect about 45 million people. The costs—including lost productivity, medical expenses, and the estimated 157 million missed workdays—add up to $50 billion annually.

Arthritis affects more than 40 million people, and as the population ages over the next two decades, that number is expected to reach 60 million.

Low back pain strikes two-thirds of adults. Problems usually go away on their own, but chronic

pain lingers in about 15 percent of cases, leaving 7 million people partially
or completely disabled.

At least 16,000 people die each year from gastrointestinal problems
caused by nonsteroidal anti-inflammatory drugs (NSAIDs), widely used
pain relievers such as ibuprofen and aspirin.[5]

Not all pain is physical. Countless people live with chronic emotional pain. In Hagar's case,
her hurt came at the hands of her boss. She would be chided and chastised as long as she
remained under Sarah's employ. And there were no pills to relieve her emotional ills. But an
encounter with God would bring untold comfort and joy. Prayer still serves as one of the
best painkillers in the world!

LISTEN TO...

You don't have to be alone in your hurt! Comfort is yours. Joy is an option. And it's all
been made possible by your Savior. He went without comfort so that you might have it. He
postponed joy so that you might share in it. He willingly chose isolation so that you might
never be alone in your hurt and sorrow.

—Joni Eareckson Tada

DAY 3

Who Are You?

"Who are you?" is not an easy question to answer. We are complex creatures. No single adjective can serve to define us. We are a compilation of our roles, relationships, realities, and aspirations. Another reason the answer eludes us is that we are always evolving. No one is static. Circumstances and life's cycles change us. You are not the same person that you once were. Like Bill Gates, you may have felt like a nobody in high school, while in adulthood you may have become an entrepreneur. Or like Oprah, your life could have begun impoverished only to end empowered. But most importantly, the real you is the one God created you to be.

It's fascinating to see how God views people. He doesn't merely see what we are but who we can become. He doesn't see just your abilities but also your possibilities. Take Simon, the disciple who buckled under pressure by denying Christ three times. Jesus renamed him Peter (literally "a rock"), upon whose strong confession Christ would build His church. Remember Gideon? When God found him hiding in a winepress sifting wheat, He declared him a "mighty man of valor." At that moment Gideon was gutless, but after a touch from God he became full of gusto! Hagar had a similar experience. She ran away from Sarah as a godless foreigner and returned as a believing matriarch. Isn't it wonderful that Jesus sees you for what you can be and not as a has-been? Listen carefully, and you'll hear Him saying, "Follow me, and I will make you more than you ever dreamed you could be!"

LIFT UP ...

God, You have been faithful to find me wherever I have roamed. You know my tears and collect them in a bottle. Thank You for Your presence both now and forever. Amen.

LOOK AT ...

Yesterday, the Angel of the Lord was introduced for the first time in Scripture. Amazingly, this apparition came to a Gentile woman rather than Abraham and Sarah, the couple of promise. Though they had spurned Hagar, God stretched out His arms.

Today we will discover that the Angel promised Hagar something that only God could perform. Also, when Hagar called this being God, He accepted the acknowledgment. However, when the apostle John mistakenly worshipped an angel, he was rebuked: "And I fell at his feet to worship him. But he said to me, 'See that you do not do that! I am your fellow servant, and of your brethren who have the testimony of Jesus. Worship God!'" (Rev. 19:10). Therefore, we can conclude that when Hagar met the Angel of the Lord, she was, indeed, meeting the Lord. Commentators call such a divine encounter a *theophany*, which indicates a pre-incarnate manifestation of Jesus Christ to meet special needs or accomplish special tasks. Warren Wiersbe writes, "The fact that the Son of God took on a temporary body, left heaven, and came down to help a rejected servant-girl surely reveals His grace and love."[6]

Where were you when you encountered Christ? Like Hagar, you were probably a sinner not a saint, hiding from and not hunting for God, a modest worker not a majestic woman. Isn't His grace amazing?

READ GENESIS 16:10–16.

Then the Angel of the LORD said to her, "I will multiply your descendants exceedingly, so that they shall not be counted for multitude." And the Angel of the LORD said to her: "Behold, you are with child, and you shall bear a son. You shall call his name Ishmael, because the LORD has heard your affliction. He shall be a wild man; his hand shall be against every man, and every man's hand against him. And he shall dwell in the presence of all his brethren." Then she called the name of the LORD who spoke to her, You-Are-the-God-Who-Sees; for she said, "Have I also here seen Him who sees me?" Therefore the well was called Beer Lahai Roi; observe, it is between Kadesh and Bered. So Hagar bore Abram a son; and Abram named his son, whom Hagar bore, Ishmael. Abram was eighty-six years old when Hagar bore Ishmael to Abram.
Genesis 16:10–16

LEARN ABOUT ...

1 A Nation

Just as He had promised Abraham and Sarah, the Lord promised Hagar that she would bear a son. He would also bring from this heir a great nation. Ishmael is the progenitor of the Arabs. His name means "God will hear." He married an Egyptian wife and had twelve sons and one daughter. His daughter, Mahalath, married Esau.

---

2 A Nuisance

New Unger's Bible Dictionary says that Ishmael was a wild and wayward child. Likely the freedom of desert life and his role as heir-almost-apparent made him impatient and overbearing. Ill-tempered, he treated Sarah harshly. Earning a scant living by sword and bow might have wounded his proud spirit, making him what the Angel had predicted.[7]

---

3 A Name

Hagar called God *El Roi*—the God who sees. The well where the encounter took place is similarly named "The well of the Living One who sees me." Isn't it comforting to know that God doesn't expect us to go it alone? Not only does He see our plight, He does something about it.

1. List the blessings that the Angel of the Lord promised to Hagar. How would this make her feel?

2. Describe the personality traits Hagar's son would possess.

3. a. What name of God is introduced?

   b. Why was it given?

4. Where did this conversation take place?

5. Upon her return, what event occurred?

6. Who named Hagar's son, and what time reference was given?

LIVE OUT ...

7. a. Blessings follow obedience. After Hagar humbly returned to her master, she bore a child. In Deuteronomy 28:1–25 the Lord contrasts the blessings of obedience with the curses of disobedience. Read that passage, and note all forms of the words *bless* and *curse*. In the columns below, list areas of life that would be blessed for obedience or cursed for disobedience.

   BLESSED   **CURSED**

   b. What conclusions do you draw from this exercise?

8. Ishmael would become the father of the Arab ethnic group. Tradition holds that the genealogy of the prophet Muhammad reaches all the way back to Hagar. Looking at history and current events, describe how the Angel's prophecy regarding Ishmael has been fulfilled.

9. Hagar encountered El Roi—the God who sees. More remarkable than God seeing her is that she saw *Him*. Using the word SEES as an acrostic, describe ways you've seen God.

S

E

E

S

○ ○ ● ○ ○

Conflict in the Middle East flows from generation to generation like a river of tears and bad blood. This bitterness dates back to 1910 BC with Abraham's two sons, Ishmael and Isaac. The patriarch's estranged children initiated an unending current of personal rejection, revenge, and mutual loss. Sadly, the Jewish and Arab conflict affects all of us. It's a drain on our national resources as our military tries to provide stability to the region. It endangers the lives of our children who are part of the peacekeeping forces throughout the Middle East. It robs the world of security as terrorist tentacles reach across oceans and into countries too numerous to name. And it costs us at the gas pump. If only Abraham and Sarah could have had a do-over for the fateful decision to enlist a surrogate.

LEARN ABOUT ...

7 A Note

To *obey* is to carry out the will of another, especially God. Biblically, obedience is related to hearing. Therefore, obedience is a positive, active response to what a person hears. In the Old Testament covenant between God and man, obedience was the basis for knowing God's blessing. Man's failure to obey God resulted in judgment.

9 A Knowledge

The term "the eyes of the Lord" is used twenty times in Scripture. Of course we know that God is spirit, not inhabiting a physical body. Therefore He does not have eyes in the human sense. But He does see. In fact, nothing escapes His view: "The eyes of the LORD run to and fro throughout the whole earth" (2 Chron. 16:9).

God made Hagar promises about her son too. But the child brought with him a painful prophecy: "His hand shall be against every man, and every man's hand against him." This principle was especially true during the rebirth of Israel in 1948. Many Middle Eastern states acted quickly as aggressors against the nascent nation and used both military measures and terrorist action. Israel has almost always retaliated with force. The prophetic fistfight continues today. A second prophecy—"he shall dwell in the presence of all his brethren"— has also been realized. A more literal translation is "he shall dwell over against his brother." The expression is a Hebrew idiom meaning to dwell in a state of hostility.[8] In other words, Ishmael's descendants would live side by side with their brothers, but in a state of hostility. It perfectly describes the situation today.

LISTEN TO...

If God sees the sparrow fall, paints the lily short and tall, gives the sky its azure hue, surely then he cares for you.

—Unknown

DAY 4

Why Me?

When was the last time you said it? It might have been when the guy you thought was Mr. Right turned out to be Mr. Wrong. Or maybe the job didn't fit anymore and you were forced to move on. A disobedient child, a careless driver, or a bad diagnosis can cause you to throw your hands up in indignation and say, "*Why me?* Why does everything have to go wrong for me?"

When the "Why me?" blues begin to dominate our lives, we can turn bitter. It's so much better to look for the good in a situation. We can be thankful we found out about Mr. Wrong before it was too late. Or rejoice that moving from an old job provided new prospects. Or pray for the prodigal. The best thing to do when we start crying, "Why me?" is to look up. God promises, "I will instruct you and teach you in the way you should go; I will guide you with My eye" (Ps. 32:8).

Hagar and Ishmael had reached a turning point. Ishmael was a young man, probably about fifteen years old. Though he was Abraham's firstborn son, his mother was only a slave. He would not be Abraham's successor after all—his half brother, Isaac, would inherit everything. The boy who had been groomed to take Abraham's place must have been gravely disappointed. Hagar might have wondered why she had been allowed to give birth to a son only to see his inheritance ripped away by Isaac's birth. It would have been easy for Hagar to ask, "Why me?"

LIFT UP ...

Father, sometimes the things required of us are difficult. Please help me to obey You without grumbling or complaining. Help me trust You to work all things out for good. Amen.

LOOK AT ...

We last saw Hagar with her baby son, Ishmael. Now we move forward five chapters and approximately fifteen years. Following the Angel of the Lord's instructions, Hagar and Ishmael remained under Abraham's protection. Then Isaac, the son of promise, was born to Sarah and Abraham. God supernaturally enabled the aged couple to produce their own child. Their son, Isaac, would one day father Jacob, and their descendants would multiply to

LEARN ABOUT ...

I Mock Another

At Isaac's feast, his older brother, Ishmael, scoffed at him. The word means to mock, laugh in derision, or treat with contempt. The writer may have been making a play on words, since Isaac's name means laughter. But Ishmael's scornful chuckles would bring grief: "Fools mock at sin, but among the upright there is favor" (Prov. 14:9).

4 Make a Nation

The Angel of the Lord first came to Hagar and promised to multiply her descendants. Now He promised Abraham He would make a "nation" from his son Ishmael. The Hebrew word translated as "nation" comes from the word *goy*, which refers to a group of individuals who are considered as a unit with respect to origin, language, land, jurisprudence, and government.

become the Hebrew people. God's promise to Abraham to "make [him] a great nation" (Gen. 12:2) would be fulfilled. Isaac, not Ishmael, would be the son to receive the inheritance.

Although Isaac was the son of promise, God also made a promise to Hagar that her son Ishmael would father multitudes. However, it would be impossible for the sons to live together. One of the two boys would have to leave and make his way in the world. Ishmael too must have asked, "Why me?"

READ GENESIS 21:8–15.

And Abraham made a great feast on the same day that Isaac was weaned. And Sarah saw the son of Hagar the Egyptian, whom she had borne to Abraham, scoffing. Therefore she said to Abraham, "Cast out this bondwoman and her son; for the son of this bondwoman shall not be heir with my son, namely with Isaac." And the matter was very displeasing in Abraham's sight because of his son. But God said to Abraham, "Do not let it be displeasing in your sight because of the lad or because of your bondwoman. Whatever Sarah has said to you, listen to her voice; for in Isaac your seed shall be called. Yet I will also make a nation of the son of the bondwoman, because he is your seed." So Abraham rose early in the morning, and took bread and a skin of water; and putting it on her shoulder, he gave it and the boy to Hagar, and sent her away. Then she departed and wandered in the Wilderness of Beersheba. And the water in the skin was used up, and she placed the boy under one of the shrubs. Genesis 21:8–15

1. a. What did Sarah observe at the feast?

   b. Why do you think Ishmael might have been acting this way?

2. What did Sarah request and why?

3. Describe how Abraham felt and why he felt this way.

4. How did God comfort Abraham regarding his sons' futures?

5. What action did Abraham take?

6. Describe where Ishmael and Hagar wound up.

LIVE OUT ...

7. Ishmael scoffed at Isaac, setting up a chain reaction of events that led to his expulsion from his father's home. Fill in the following table to learn more about the scoffer (or mocker).

SCRIPTURE	LESSONS ABOUT THE SCOFFER/MOCKER
Proverbs 9:7–8	
Proverbs 15:12	
Proverbs 21:24	
Proverbs 22:10	

8. Sarah pointed out Ishmael's behavior and asked Abraham to send Ishmael away. Doing this was "very displeasing" for Abraham. Describe a circumstance in your life when you have had to be separated from one you love very dearly. How did it affect you, and how were you comforted?

9. Hagar seemed to give up when she ran out of supplies. She didn't remember God's promise to provide for her. Perhaps you are in a situation like Hagar, wandering in a wilderness seemingly without relief. Take the following steps of faith to renew your spiritual vigor:

    Step 1. Remember what God has promised you in the past. (Ex. God has promised to supply your needs.)

LEARN ABOUT ...

6 Moving Along

Ishmael and Hagar set out and wandered in the wilderness. The wilderness of Beersheba was midway between the Mediterranean Sea and the southern end of the Dead Sea. Beersheba was considered the southern extremity of the Promised Land. At Beersheba God appeared to Hagar (Gen. 21:17), Isaac (Gen. 26:23–33), and Jacob (Gen. 46:1–5).[9]

8 Mourning Another

Abraham had clearly bonded with his son Ishmael as he had grown into young adulthood. Now he was forced to give the inheritance to Isaac, releasing Ishmael to make it in the world. The word *displeased* in our text means "broken to pieces." Abraham would have a broken family and a broken heart.

9 Memory Altered

Keeping God's promises in the forefront of our minds helps when times get rough. God's Word is powerful enough to transform any situation. If you're walking in the wilderness of despair, look to the Scriptures to pull you out of the depths: "Revive me, O LORD, according to Your word" (Ps. 119:107).

Step 2. Rely on God's character. (Ex. God is trustworthy.)

Step 3. Request God's help. (Ex. Call on God in your time of need.)

∘ ∘ ● ∘ ∘

When I (Penny) was twelve years old, I learned one of our family secrets. My grandmother told me how her father had taken her brother and moved to California. She never saw her father again. She only remembered him saying, "Good-bye, my happy home." I later found out that there were rumors he had walked in and found his wife with another man. My grandmother was devastated. She cried herself to sleep every night for a year over losing her brother and father. That's when she turned to Christ and He became the source of her strength.

It's heartbreaking to hear of the disintegration of a family. To read about Hagar and Ishmael packing their things and heading to the desert is gut wrenching. We know this separation was permanent. We don't know if Abraham saw his older son again. The boy he raised to be his heir was sent into the desert to forge a new destiny.

Commentators remind us that we are looking at this through the lens of Western society. Isaac's birth really had changed everything. In ancient Eastern society, a son fathered by a slave would not share in the inheritance of legitimate sons. Furthermore, according to the Code of Hammurabi 171, children born of a slave and a freeman would be given their freedom after the father's death. If this code held sway or there was similar thinking in Abraham's household, Ishmael would have been released when Abraham died.[10] Eventually, Ishmael and Hagar would have left Abraham's camp. But they did not leave God's watchful eye.

LISTEN TO...

The Lord my pasture shall prepare, and feed me with a shepherd's care; His presence shall my wants supply, and guard me with a watchful eye.

—*Joseph Addison*

DAY 5
What Now?

As He had promised Sarah, God promised Hagar that her son would develop into a great nation. Her offspring, the Arab peoples, form a strong arm in Abraham's family tree. As Isaac was delivered from death on Mount Moriah, Ishmael was divinely delivered from death in the wilderness. They both took wives, fathered children, and subdued territory. Today there are twenty-one Arab states with a combined population of 175 million. The Arab states contain 5.3 million square miles of oil-rich land.

Abraham stands as the father of monotheism. *Time* calls him an "interfaith superstar.... He changed history by espousing just one God, and thus became sacred to Muslims, Jews and Christians."[11] Isaac's descendants developed the Jewish religion while Ishmael's later produced Islam. Christianity, the third major monotheistic religion, also claims Abraham as its "father of faith."

However, the patriarch sprang from a long line of idol worshippers. *Time* continues, "Abraham was born, according to tradition, into a family that sold idols—a way of emphasizing the polytheism that reigned in the Middle East before his enlightenment."[12] Ur, Abraham's hometown, served pagan gods, the foremost being the god of the sword and the moon god. Interestingly, Islam adopted the moon and the sword as the symbols of its faith. Equally interesting, the name *Allah* is derived from the Babylonian name for the moon god, pronounced "Il-yah."

You might say that the three monotheistic religions struggle with sibling rivalry. Centuries after Abraham's death, they are still contesting his will. Who *are* the true heirs of God's promises to Abraham? Paul wrote, "Therefore know that only those who are of faith are sons of Abraham. And the Scripture, foreseeing that God would justify the Gentiles by faith, preached the gospel to Abraham beforehand, saying, 'In you all the nations shall be blessed.' So then those who are of faith are blessed with believing Abraham" (Gal. 3:7–9).

LIFT UP ...

Lord, thank You for bringing me into the family of faith. Please help me to be ever watchful for You wherever I may roam. Amen.

LOOK AT ...

2 He Hears

The word *voice* has several connotations. Here it most likely means "to lift up one's voice and weep." It signifies many things, including crying out for help, mourning for present or anticipated tragedy, and the "sound" of disaster. "Lord, hear my voice! Let Your ears be attentive to the voice of my supplications" (Ps. 130:2).

3 He Answers

Isn't it comforting to know that God's ear is attuned to the cry of your voice? Not only does He hear, He responds with words of comfort and practical help. "I sought the LORD, and He heard me, and delivered me from all my fears" (Ps. 34:4).

Yesterday we saw Hagar and Ishmael expelled from Abraham's camp, wandering in the wilderness of Beersheba. Bereft of supplies, Ishmael was left alone under a shrub. Today we see that though they may have been abandoned from a human standpoint, God would keep His promises to Hagar concerning her son.

In Galatians 4:21–31, Paul wrote of Sarah, Hagar, Isaac, and Ishmael in a symbolic fashion. He used the women to illustrate the difference between the law (Hagar) and grace (Sarah), works (Hagar) and faith (Sarah). Paul used Isaac to illustrate the new nature and Ishmael to depict the old nature. He concluded by urging believers to "'cast out the bondwoman and her son, for the son of the bondwoman shall not be heir with the son of the freewoman.' So then, brethren, we are not children of the bondwoman but of the free" (Gal. 4:30). True freedom is found when we cast off our old nature that has been corrupted by sin and put on the new nature that comes from new birth and new life in Christ: "If the Son makes you free, you shall be free indeed" (John 8:36).

READ GENESIS 21:16–21.

Then she went and sat down across from him at a distance of about a bowshot; for she said to herself, "Let me not see the death of the boy." So she sat opposite him, and lifted her voice and wept. And God heard the voice of the lad. Then the angel of God called to Hagar out of heaven, and said to her, "What ails you, Hagar? Fear not, for God has heard the voice of the lad where he is. Arise, lift up the lad and hold him with your hand, for I will make him a great nation." Then God opened her eyes, and she saw a well of water. And she went and filled the skin with water, and gave the lad a drink. So God was with the lad; and he grew and dwelt in the wilderness, and became an archer. He dwelt in the Wilderness of Paran; and his mother took a wife for him from the land of Egypt. Genesis 21:16–21

1. "Then" what did Hagar do and why?

2. a. Circle the word *voice* that is repeated in this text. To whom does this word refer?

   b. What do you observe about the voices?

3. Now underline each use of "God" as well as the verb that follows. What do you learn about Him?

4. Describe the gamut of emotions you believe Hagar might have experienced.

5. Recount the many provisions God made for this mother and child.

6. Where do we leave Hagar and Ishmael? What alliance was formed?

LIVE OUT ...

7. a. The angel of God instructed Hagar to get up and get going to get out of her present situation. Sometimes serving others is the best way out to get out of a bad situation. List some practical ways to serve others when you are feeling down.

   b. Have you ever done this? Has it helped you to feel better?

8. God opened Hagar's eyes to the well of water standing nearby. God has put many things right in front of our eyes too.

   a. Match the following Scripture passages with the things God has provided right before our eyes.

LEARN ABOUT ...

5 He Provides

Hagar named God El Roi, the God Who Sees. Another of His names is Jehovah Jireh, the God Who Provides. Whether you are in a wilderness needing water or in a workplace needing wisdom, God can provide you exactly what you need. "My God shall supply all your need according to His riches in glory by Christ Jesus" (Phil. 4:19).

7 He Compels

When Hagar and Ishmael cried out, the Lord answered them. He asked Hagar to "arise, lift up the lad and hold him with your hand." In other words, they would need to take an active step of faith rather than wallow in self-pity. Faith and works go hand in hand. James said, "Faith without works is dead" (James 2:20).

8 He Knows

God is able to answer your prayer even before you pray it. This doesn't mean that He doesn't want to hear your prayer—He does! But even before you utter your prayer, God knows what you need: "Before they call, I will answer; and while they are still speaking, I will hear" (Isa. 65:24).

Psalm 26:3	God's help
Psalm 101:6	God's law
Psalm 119:18	God's loving-kindness
Psalm 121:1–2	God's people

b. From which of these have you turned your eyes away? How would keeping your eyes on them help strengthen your faith?

9. Despite God's comfort and provision, Hagar eventually went back to her native country of Egypt to seek a wife for her son. We know that Egypt symbolizes the world. Describe some ways you've noticed that the world lures believers to come "home." How do you fight those temptations?

o o ● o o

There's always a choice between following the way of the world and following God's way. We'll never know what might have happened had Hagar decided not to get her son a wife from Egypt. What if she had asked Abraham to provide Ishmael a wife from among the people of God? What if she had gone to Abraham's homeland, Ur, as Eliezer would do for Isaac, to seek a spouse for her son Ishmael? Perhaps if she had chosen a wife who believed in the one true God, things would have turned out differently. But we cannot rewrite history. We can only learn its lessons. The result of Hagar's decision has been heartbreak. Ishmael founded a "nation" or people group and fulfilled the prophecy, becoming "a wild man." The Bible says, "His descendants settled in the area from Havilah to Shur, near the border of Egypt, as you go toward Asshur. And they lived in hostility toward all their brothers" (Gen. 25:18 NIV). Sadly, the hostility between the Arabs and the Jews continues today.

It's been said that we must make good choices or our choices will make us. The story of Ruth and Orpah illustrates this principle. Both women had a choice of which path to take. They had been living in the pagan land of Moab and married Jewish husbands who died. Their mother-in-law, Naomi, decided to go back to her home in Bethlehem, where God was providing bread for His people. Ruth the Moabitess chose to go with her mother-in-law. Orpah chose to stay behind in the pagan land and disappeared from the biblical record. In a step of faith, Ruth and Naomi went to the Promised Land. There, Ruth met Boaz, a prosperous Bethlehemite who took her under his wing and married her. Ruth, like Sarah and Abraham, became a part of the lineage of Jesus Christ. It was the right choice.

LISTEN TO...

Be entirely tolerant or not at all; follow the good path or the evil one. To stand at the crossroads requires more strength than you possess.

—Heinrich Heine

Lot's Wife—Living in the Past

Genesis 19:1–29

Have you ever met someone who lives in the past? They use phrases like "used to," "back then," or "when I was younger." In these people's minds, the past was better than the present or the future. They seem to dwell in the land of long ago.

The problem with living in the past is that it holds no hope for the future. But that's not really the case—many people have found new beginnings with new promises for the future. But in order to move forward we must let go of the past. One writer advised,

> Take a moment to write down every defining moment in your life;
> it might have been a time that your teacher praised you for your work
> that you put a lot of effort on, it might have [been] the time your parents
> divorced, [or] a rejection you felt from a friend. Once you have written
> down all those moments ask yourself what have you learn[ed] from that
> experience and how has it shaped the person you are today. It is only when
> we learn from our past that we can then let that go from our lives. If we
> spend our whole waking lives being dictated by our past we don't have an
> opportunity to look forward to shape our future.[1]

This week we'll meet Lot's wife, who simply could not let go of the past. Her defining moment became a moment of defiance as she turned to look back. She was unwilling to move forward, so she became stuck in the past.

Day 1: Genesis 19:1–7   **THE WELCOME MAT**

Day 2: Genesis 19:8–11   **KNOCKING AT THE DOOR**

Day 3: Genesis 19:12–16   **FIRE ESCAPE**

Day 4: Genesis 19:17–23   **RELOCATION PLAN**

Day 5: Genesis 19:24–29   **HOMESICK**

DAY 1
The Welcome Mat

LIFT UP ...

Lord, I know my surroundings and my friends influence who I am. Please help me to surround myself with those things that glorify You so that I can be a light in my community and in my home. Amen.

LOOK AT ...

This week we meet another unnamed Bible woman: Lot's wife. Like Noah's wife, she is associated with a time of judgment. But unlike Noah's wife, there is no evidence that she was either good or godly. Jesus told us to "remember Lot's wife" (Luke 17:32) as a warning to be ready for Christ's return, when He will judge the world.

In order to know Lot's wife, we need to know Lot. Lot accompanied his uncle Abraham from Ur of the Chaldees. Both men owned large herds of cattle. Eventually, the herdsmen began to quarrel over the pastureland, so the men decided to separate. Abraham offered Lot the first choice of land. Lot chose the fertile, well-watered land in the Jordan River valley. He "pitched his tent even as far as Sodom" (Gen. 13:12). When a coalition of kings raided Sodom and took Lot captive, Abraham rode to Lot's rescue. The king of Sodom went to meet with Abraham in order to thank him. Lot moved in a downward spiral: from Abraham's company, to dwelling near Sodom, to dwelling in Sodom. Most likely, his wife was a woman from Sodom. Today we'll see that God was good enough to send angels into Sodom to warn Lot of the destruction to come. God is also sending us a message that one day He will judge the world. Will we be living in Sodom, or the kingdom of God?

READ GENESIS

Now the two angels came to Sodom in the evening, and Lot was sitting in the gate of Sodom. When Lot saw them, he rose to meet them, and bowed himself with his face toward the

LEARN ABOUT ...

2 Incandescent Visitors

Angels are created spiritual beings with superhuman power and knowledge. They are charged with caring for people and serving them in times of need. They also guide and instruct good people. Angels meet a wide variety of human needs, including relieving hunger and thirst, overcoming loneliness and dread, and delivering God's people from danger.[2]

---

6 Insistent Townspeople

In the Middle East, it was expected that visitors be treated with great hospitality and courtesy. Apparently the depravity of Sodom had reached such a high level that the men of the city were willing to assault and rape their guests rather than offer them the protection dictated by the customs of their day.

---

7 Interceding Host

It's interesting to note that Lot referred to the townspeople as "brethren." Perhaps he was trying to remind them that they should act civilly. Or perhaps he considered himself one of them. In any case, he at least recognized that their actions toward the angelic visitors were wicked.

ground. And he said, "Here now, my lords, please turn in to your servant's house and spend the night, and wash your feet; then you may rise early and go on your way." And they said, "No, but we will spend the night in the open square." But he insisted strongly; so they turned in to him and entered his house. Then he made them a feast, and baked unleavened bread, and they ate. Now before they lay down, the men of the city, the men of Sodom, both old and young, all the people from every quarter, surrounded the house. And they called to Lot and said to him, "Where are the men who came to you tonight? Bring them out to us that we may know them carnally." So Lot went out to them through the doorway, shut the door behind him, and said, "Please, my brethren, do not do so wickedly!" Genesis 19:1–7

1. Describe who came to Sodom and when they arrived.

2. Skim Genesis 18, and recount where the angels had been prior to this.

3. How did Lot react to the angels? What did he invite them to do?

4. a. How did the angels respond to this invitation?

   b. Why do you think they didn't want to go to Lot's house?

5. Why do you think Lot "insisted strongly" that the angels stay with him?

6. Describe how the townsmen acted toward the angels.

   w did Lot respond?

LIVE OUT ...

8. Two angels came to Sodom, and Lot invited them home. What does Hebrews 13:2 teach you about offering hospitality to strangers? How can you do this in a world that grows more and more dangerous?

9. a. Though Lot called the men of the city brethren, 2 Peter 2:7–10 offers more insight into Lot's character. How does Peter describe Lot? What effect did the men of Sodom have on Lot (vv. 7–8)?

   b. What does God promise the godly (v. 9)?

   c. What does He promise the unjust (v. 9)?

   d. Have you ever felt oppressed by the people or society surrounding you? How have God's promises helped lift you up?

10. Lot faced the crowd of men and stood against wickedness. The first place to fight wickedness is in our own hearts. Rewrite Psalm 139:23–24 into a personal prayer asking God to cleanse you of any wicked way.

   Search me, O God, and know my heart; try me, and know my anxieties; and see if there is any wicked way in me, and lead me in the way everlasting. Psalm 139:23–24

o o ● o o

The *Los Angeles Times* ran an article entitled "For Gays in Las Vegas, the Welcome Mat Is Out." It said, "When Andy Steele and Michael Turner

LEARN ABOUT ...

8 Inappropriate Worship

While angels are spiritual beings, they are not God. Only God is worthy of our worship. Too often, people make the mistake of worshipping what is created rather than the Creator. Some people have even worshipped angels. Paul warned, "Let no one cheat you of your reward, taking delight in false humility and worship of angels" (Col. 2:18).

9 Indescribable God

To the oppressed, God promises to lighten the load. Jesus said, "My yoke is easy and My burden is light" (Matt. 11:30). To the tempted, He offers a way out: "God is faithful, who ... with the temptation will also make the way of escape, that you may be able to bear it" (1 Cor. 10:13).

stepped off their plane in Las Vegas, the first-time visitors from Britain were anxious about how welcome they would be as an openly gay couple." The men decided to stay at the Blue Moon Resort, a hotel frequented by gay men. The taxi driver knew where the hotel was and seemed unconcerned with their choice of lodgings. Turner said, "Most of the taxi drivers know the Blue Moon is a gay resort, but they go out of their way to be friendly and helpful." Steele added, "They say that people around here are not bothered [by] whether you're gay, straight or whatever."[3] Las Vegas consistently ranks second—behind New York—as the most popular place for gay and lesbian couples to visit, according to Community Marketing Inc., a San Francisco company that researches gay and lesbian travel habits.

In Lot's day, the welcome mat would have been out for the gay community in Sodom as well. But a Do Not Enter sign should have been posted. The Lord told Abraham, "The outcry against Sodom and Gomorrah is great, and … their sin is very grave" (Gen. 18:20).

Listen to…

Wickedness never goes unpunished, and righteousness is never unrewarded.

—*W. Graham Scroggie*

DAY 2

Knocking at the Door

The knock-knock joke is probably one of the first jokes you ever learned. It stems from a time-honored "call and play" exercise demanding a response. The standard knock-knock joke has five lines:

1. The humorist says, *Knock, knock!*

2. The recipient replies, *Who's there?*

3. The humorist gives a response, sometimes involving a name to set up the pun.

4. The recipient repeats the response followed by *who?*

5. The humorist gives the punch line, which typically involves a pun or misuse of a word. Here are a few examples of some classic knock-knock jokes:

Knock, knock!
Who's there?
Doris.
Doris who?
Doris open, I'm going to come in.

Knock, knock!
Who's there?
Delores.
Delores who?
Delores my shepherd … (a play on *The Lord is my shepherd.*)

Knock-knock jokes are entrenched in American culture as well as in the cultures of the United Kingdom, Ireland, France, Australia, Canada, and South Africa. In other nations, such as Brazil and Germany, they are practically unknown. In French the jokes begin with the phrase "Toc-Toc," and in Afrikaans they begin with "Klop-klop."[4]

It was no joke when the citizens of Sodom knocked on Lot's door and asked for entrance to his home. The men of the town, young and old, were bent on having their way with the angelic visitors to Lot's home. If you wanted to make a knock-knock joke, you might say,

> Knock, knock
> *Who's there?*
> Lot.
> *Lot who?*
> Lots of trouble.

The men of Sodom would find that going to Lot's house was more trouble than it was worth.

Lift up ...

Lord, in a world where sin is accepted and often encouraged, I desire to live a pure and holy life. Teach me to do Your will Your way. Help me to stand firm against unrighteousness. Amen.

Look at ...

We've seen that two angelic visitors made their way from Hebron to Sodom and came to lodge at Lot's house. They were investigating the wicked happenings in Sodom to bring justice to the perverse place. The fact that Lot was sitting in the city gates indicates that he had been acting as an elder in the city and held the prominent position of a judge. Most commentators agree that he probably received this post as a result of his relationship with the powerful Abraham, who had rescued him and the town during the war with King Chedorlaomer and three other kings (see Gen. 14:8). Now we see that Lot acted with much less courage than his uncle Abraham when faced with danger. Rather than protecting his family members and seeking the Lord's help, he took matters into his own hands and made an offer that brought shame to his name and threatened his family with greater violence.

READ GENESIS 19:8–11.

"See now, I have two daughters who have not known a man; please, let me bring them out to you, and you may do to them as you wish; only do nothing to these men, since this is the reason they have come under the shadow of my roof." And they said, "Stand back!" Then they said, "This one came in to stay here, and he keeps acting as a judge; now we will deal worse with you than with them." So they pressed hard against the man Lot, and came near to break down the door. But the men reached out their hands and pulled Lot into the house with them, and shut the door. And they struck the men who were at the doorway of the house with blindness, both small and great, so that they became weary trying to find the door.

Genesis 19:8–11

1. What did Lot offer the men of Sodom in place of the angels and why?

2. In your own words, recount the townsmen's verbal response to Lot.

3. Describe the townspeople's physical response to Lot.

4. Imagine you were trying to protect someone of great importance. Describe how you think Lot felt at this point.

5. How was Lot saved from the men of Sodom?

6. Describe what happened to the men of Sodom.

LEARN ABOUT …

1 Virgin Daughters

Perhaps Lot thought that by offering his daughters he would bring the men to their senses. Perhaps he realized that releasing the angels to the citizenry would be an abomination in God's eyes. But Matthew Henry said, "Of two sins we must choose neither, nor ever do evil that good may come of it."[5]

3 Violent Dealings

Because Lot refused to give the men what they desired, they turned into a mob and threatened to physically harm him. Their sexual sin swelled into violence and threatened to peak in murder. Solomon warned, "He who is often rebuked, and hardens his neck, will suddenly be destroyed, and that without remedy" (Prov. 29:1).

6 Visual Disturbance

Three types of blindness are described in the Bible: sudden blindness, gradual blindness, and chronic blindness. Blindness was often viewed as punishment for evildoing. Jesus said, "For judgment I have come into this world, that those who do not see may see, and that those who see may be made blind" (John 9:39).[6]

LIVE OUT ...

7. a. Read Judges 19:22—20:8. How does this story resemble today's portion of Scripture?

    b. How is it different?

    c. How did the nation of Israel respond to the atrocity that occurred?

    d. How did you respond when you read Lot's offer about his daughters and when you read the story about the concubine in Gibeah?

8. a. Today we saw that sinful people who were able to see were made blind. According to Zephaniah 1:17, why does God pronounce this punishment?

    b. According to Zephaniah 1:18, when will this occur?

    c. Are you eagerly watching for this day, or are you turning a blind eye to the possibility that Christ will come again? Please explain.

o o ● o o

Not too long ago, my (Penny's) husband was told he was going blind because of a fast-growing cataract. Thankfully, a new type of surgery was developed only months before that could replace the lenses of his eyes. If his condition had occurred even a year earlier, they could have done nothing to help him. Today, his vision is 20/20. He sees with new eyes.

Throughout Scripture God associated physical blindness with a lack of spiritual understanding. Jesus used this metaphor as well. In fact, He told His followers that the religious rulers of the day were "blind leaders of the blind" (Matt. 15:14). There is an eye in our hearts that can "see" the things of God. Sadly, the world, the flesh, and the Devil have dimmed our vision. We need someone to open our eyes and help us see.

Throughout His earthly ministry Jesus performed many miracles. He walked on water, He raised the dead, He healed the sick, and "to many blind He gave sight" (Luke 7:21). Jesus proclaimed,

> "The Spirit of the LORD is upon Me,
> Because He has anointed Me
> To preach the gospel to the poor;
> He has sent Me to heal the brokenhearted,
> To proclaim liberty to the captives
> And recovery of sight to the blind." Luke 4:18

The Spirit of God and the Son of God can perform eye surgery so we can see with the eyes of our hearts. Won't you allow God to give you new eyes?

LISTEN TO...

Never let a man imagine that he can pursue a good end by evil means, without sinning against his own soul. The evil effect on himself is certain.

—*Robert Southey*

DAY 3

Fire Escape

Remember doing fire drills in school? The bells sounded, and rows of children diligently headed for the nearest exit, then waited outside for the all-clear bell to sound. It's a good idea to plan fire drills in our homes as well. Statistics show that roughly ten people a day die in home fires. Tens of thousands more are injured. But if we're prepared for a fire, we can get out quickly and survive. Here are a few tips on planning a fire escape:

Install smoke detectors, and make sure the batteries are charged.

Draw an escape plan.

Agree on a meeting place outside for a head count.

Consider installing a fire-sprinkler system.

Practice your escape plan at least twice a year.

Make sure everyone can unlock all doors and windows quickly, even in the dark.

When the angels sounded the alarm for Sodom, Lot ran to tell his family members about the coming fire. Sadly, the sons-in-law believed that Lot was sounding a false alarm. They failed to heed the warning and wound up enduring the fires of judgment. When God sounds the trumpet to call His people home, will you be eagerly listening for His cry, or will you stay behind because you're unprepared?

LIFT UP ...

Father, thank You for Your mercy by which I was saved. Help me to show mercy to those who have not yet experienced Your salvation. Amen.

LOOK AT ...

Through the intervention of the angels, Lot escaped from his violent neighbors. It could be that until the angels caused the supernatural blindness, Lot did not realize that the "men" who came to visit were messengers from God. Or perhaps he immediately recognized that they were angels in disguise and that he, the only righteous man in town, knew of their presence. Whatever the case, there was imminent danger: God determined to send the fires of judgment upon the wicked cities of Sodom and Gomorrah. Clearly the angels had not found ten righteous men among the residents of the city on their reconnaissance mission. The prophet Ezekiel lists God's reasons for judging the two cities: "This was the iniquity of your sister Sodom: She and her daughter had pride, fullness of food, and abundance of idleness; neither did she strengthen the hand of the poor and needy. And they were haughty and committed abomination before Me; therefore I took them away as I saw fit" (Ezek. 16:49–50). It's a startling reminder that God can do with the world as He sees fit. When we compare Sodom's sins with the things we see in our own world, we realize that things today are much the same as they were back then. How many righteous people would the angels find if they came to your town?

LEARN ABOUT …

2 Mocked

Lot didn't have the civil authority to keep the mob at bay to protect his guests, nor did he hold the moral authority to convince his family of the coming judgment. His witness was shaky at best, perhaps even nonexistent. He blended in so well that he could not stand out or stand up for truth when the time came.

READ GENESIS 19:12–16.

Then the men said to Lot, "Have you anyone else here? Son-in-law, your sons, your daughters, and whomever you have in the city—take them out of this place! For we will destroy this place, because the outcry against them has grown great before the face of the LORD, and the LORD has sent us to destroy it." So Lot went out and spoke to his sons-in-law, who had married his daughters, and said, "Get up, get out of this place; for the LORD will destroy this city!" But to his sons-in-law he seemed to be joking. When the morning dawned, the angels urged Lot to hurry, saying, "Arise, take your wife and your two daughters who are here, lest you be consumed in the punishment of the city." And while he lingered, the men took hold of his hand, his wife's hand, and the hands of his two daughters, the LORD being merciful to him, and they brought him out and set him outside the city. Genesis 19:12–16

1. What do the "men" (angels) instruct Lot to do with his family and why?

LEARN ABOUT ...

4 Morning

God waited until morning for the family to leave. Perhaps He delayed judgment one more night so Lot's family could travel by daylight. Perhaps He waited so the sons-in-law could reconsider their decision. Whatever the reason, God again showed that "the longsuffering of our Lord is salvation" (2 Peter 3:15).

---

7 Merciful

To be *merciful* means to commiserate, to pity, or to spare. In this case, God sympathized with Lot, pitying him, and showed that He was willing to save the lives of Lot and his family members from the judgment to come. God offers mercy even when someone is undeserving: "Therefore He has mercy on whom He wills" (Rom. 9:18).

---

8 Mindful

Carnal Christians can be transformed by waging a spiritual battle. The struggle between the flesh and spirit begins in the mind: "For to be carnally minded is death, but to be spiritually minded is life and peace. Because the carnal mind is enmity against God; for it is not subject to the law of God, nor indeed can be" (Rom. 8:6–7).

2. a. Who did Lot try to rescue?

   b. What method did he use?

3. a. How did they respond?

   b. How do you think Lot may have felt about this?

4. In your own words, recount what the angels said when morning dawned.

5. After the angels warned him to leave, Lot "lingered." Why do you think he reacted this way?

6. What action did the angels take and why?

7. a. What attribute of God is revealed in the angels' saving Lot and his family?

   b. When was the last time you experienced this attribute of God?

LIVE OUT ...

8. Today we learned that Lot blended in with the world around him so that no one believed him when he spoke the truth from the Lord. As Christians we call this being carnal.

   a. Read 1 Corinthians 3:1–3, and describe how a carnal Christian acts.

   b. Talk about a time when you experienced being with a carnal Christian (or were one yourself). How did it affect your outlook on God and/or His Word?

9. Lot and his family lingered even after the angels told them it was time to move. Has there ever been a time when you hesitated to obey God's voice? What were the consequences?

10. The angels showed the Lord's mercy by taking the family's hands and bringing them outside the city. Use the word HAND as an acrostic to describe how you will lend a helping hand to someone who needs to experience God's mercy this week.

H

A

N

D

LEARN ABOUT ...

9 Moving

To *linger* means to question, hesitate, or express reluctance. When the angels told Lot to retrieve his family, he instantly obeyed. But when they told him to leave Sodom, he hesitated. He and his family were narrowly saved: "Others save with fear, pulling them out of the fire, hating even the garment defiled by the flesh" (Jude v. 23).

o o ● o o

How do we balance mercy and judgment when we encounter sinful people who face the consequences for their sin? Well-known author C. S. Lewis wrote about the dilemma of hating the sin and loving the sinner:

> I remember Christian teachers telling me long ago that I must hate a bad man's actions, but not hate the bad man: or, as they would say, hate the sin but not the sinner.
>
> For a long time I used to think this a silly, straw-splitting distinction: how could you hate what a man did and not hate the man? But years later it occurred to me that there was one man to whom I had been doing this all my life—namely myself. However much I might

dislike my own cowardice or conceit or greed, I went on loving myself. There had never been the slightest difficulty about it. In fact the very reason why I hated the things was that I loved the man. Just because I loved myself, I was sorry to find that I was the sort of man who did those things.[7]

God abhors sin, yet He is able to love the sinner. He loved us enough to send His only Son to pay the price for our sins. This was indeed God's mercy at its height. His mercy extends to all who choose to accept this precious gift. When we judge ourselves first and accept this love gift from God, we can become willing messengers to those who are living in the Sodom and Gomorrah of today's world, lest they face the judgment that is sure to come.

LISTEN TO...

Mercy imitates God, and disappoints Satan.

—John Chrysostom

DAY 4

Relocation Plan

Sometimes we grow so accustomed to our surroundings that we don't realize how dangerous they are. This was true for Lot and his family. Aesop told the fable of "The Town Mouse and the Country Mouse" to make this point.

> A town mouse went to visit his cousin in the country. The country mouse made his cousin welcome. Beans and bacon were all he could offer, but he offered them freely. The town mouse turned up his nose at this country fare, and said, "I don't suppose you can expect anything better in the country. Come with me, and I will show you how to live." So the two mice set off for town and arrived late at night.
>
> "You will want some refreshment after our journey," said the town mouse, and took his country cousin into the dining room. There they found the remains of a fine feast. Soon the two mice were eating jellies and cakes and everything nice. Suddenly they heard growling and barking.
>
> "What is that?" said the country mouse.
>
> "It is only the dogs of the house," answered the other.
>
> "Only?" said the country mouse. "I do not like that music at my dinner!" At that moment the door flew open and in came two huge mastiffs. The two mice scampered down and ran off.
>
> "Good-bye, cousin," said the country mouse.
>
> "What! Going so soon?" said the other.
>
> "Yes," he replied. "Better beans and bacon in peace than cakes and jam in fear."[8]

LIFT UP ...

Lord, please enable me to accept the changes that come from You. I want to live a life that is flexible and sensitive to the movement of Your Holy Spirit. Please remove areas of my life that resist the work that You are doing and help me to follow You. Amen.

LEARN ABOUT ...

I Flee

Some commentators believe the Angel of the Lord—in other words, God Himself—was waiting outside the city to give Lot and his family instructions. Others believe that one of the angels served as the spokesman for the two. Either way, there was an urgency about the message: "Run for your life!"

LOOK AT ...

God sent angels to save Lot from the violence of the townspeople of Sodom. They also took his hand and helped his family flee from the destruction of Sodom. This insight into the ministry of angels is awe inspiring, especially as we consider that Lot was inclined to linger in his home even when faced with judgment. Lot is a picture of the carnal or worldly Christian. By wanting to have the best of both worlds, he almost lost everything. But God interceded and saved Lot from the coming destruction, albeit as if by fire.

Lot's problem was not that he lived *in* the world, but that he and his family became *of* the world. As believers, God does not call us to walk away from the world, but He does tell us, "Do not love the world or the things in the world" (1 John 2:15). Lot was walking a fine line, and it almost cost him his life. Does the world have a hold on your heart, or do you hold the things of the world lightly? Your answer makes all the difference in the world.

READ GENESIS 19:17–23.

So it came to pass, when they had brought them outside, that he said, "Escape for your life! Do not look behind you nor stay anywhere in the plain. Escape to the mountains, lest you be destroyed." Then Lot said to them, "Please, no, my lords! Indeed now, your servant has found favor in your sight, and you have increased your mercy which you have shown me by saving my life; but I cannot escape to the mountains, lest some evil overtake me and I die. See now, this city is near enough to flee to, and it is a little one; please let me escape there (is it not a little one?) and my soul shall live." And he said to him, "See, I have favored you concerning this thing also, in that I will not overthrow this city for which you have spoken. Hurry, escape there. For I cannot do anything until you arrive there." Therefore the name of the city was called Zoar. The sun had risen upon the earth when Lot entered Zoar. Genesis 19:17–23

1. a. What instructions did Lot's family receive once they were outside Sodom?

   b. Who do you think was speaking to Lot?

2. What reason did Lot give for failing to obey the angel's directions?

3. How did he cover his disobedience with politeness?

4. a. Where did Lot want to go instead and why?

   b. Do you think this was good reasoning? Please explain.

5. How did the angel respond to Lot's request?

6. a. Why did he urge Lot to hurry?

   b. How do you feel about Lot at this point in time?

7. What was the name of the city to which Lot fled, and at what time did he arrive?

Live out ...

8. The command to run to the mountains is similar to Christ's prediction concerning the great tribulation. Read Matthew 24:15–17, and see where the people should go when they see the abomination of desolation. Why do you think the mountains will provide a safe haven?

Learn About ...

4 Plea

Lot was more afraid of going to unknown territory in the mountains than of facing the judgment looming over the place he was leaving behind. Therefore, he asked for a "little" favor: that instead he be allowed to go to a small town nearby. The angel granted his request as an example of God's permissive will rather than His perfect will.

7 Wee

Zoar, which means little or small, was one of five cities that lay on the plain of the Jordan River valley. It was one of the Cities of Kikkar or Circle. Prior to this it was called Bela (see Gen. 14:2). This wee little city was the only one spared in the destruction of the cities on the plain.[9]

8 Free

Some people believe the abomination of desolation occurred during the reign of Antiochus Epiphanes. Others believe his reign foreshadowed the coming of Antichrist, who will establish a worship and economic system that brings relentless trouble to Judea. The only way to be free will be to flee.

9. a. We saw Lot plead with the angel to allow him to go to Zoar rather than the mountains. How did you feel about the angel allowing Lot to have his way in this instance? Why?

   b. What does this show you about God's character?

   c. Read Genesis 19:30. Where did Lot ultimately wind up living?

10. Although Lot was weak willed and lingered in Sodom, God showed him favor. Journal about a time God showed you favor when you were least deserving of receiving it.

○ ○ ● ○ ○

One evening a woman was driving home when she noticed a huge truck behind her that was driving uncomfortably close. She stepped on the gas to gain some distance from the truck, but when she sped up, the truck did too. The faster she drove, the faster the truck drove.

Frightened, she exited the freeway. But the truck stayed with her. The woman then turned up a main street, hoping to lose her pursuer in traffic. But the truck ran a red light and continued the chase.

Reaching the point of panic, the woman whipped her car into a service station and bolted out of her auto, screaming for help. The truck driver sprang from his truck and ran toward her car. Yanking the back door open, the driver pulled out a man hidden in the backseat. It turned out that the woman was running from the wrong person. From his high point of view, the truck driver had spotted a would-be rapist in the woman's car. The chase wasn't an effort to harm her but to save her even at the cost of his own safety.[10]

God had the vantage point of seeing that it would be better for Lot to settle in the mountains. But Lot was more comfortable in the familiar plains. So often we settle for the familiar and fear the heights. Take heart!

God knows what is best and will guide you from the danger and desolation, though the journey may seem fraught with fear.

LISTEN TO...

Measure not God's love and favour by your own feeling. The sun shines as clearly in the darkest day as it does in the brightest. The difference is not in the sun, but in some clouds.

—*Richard Sibbs*

DAY 5

Homesick

A homesick cat traveled three hundred miles to return home even though his owner gave him away. Ranulph, a black tomcat named after explorer Ranulph Fiennes, was given to new owners in the north of England. He made the journey back to Archiestown, Scotland, surprising owner Gil Bray by showing up on his doorstep. It seems that Bray's wife had given the cat to a friend because she worked long hours. When Ranulph reappeared, the Brays called their friends to confirm that Ranulph had gone missing.

"I'm totally amazed but delighted he's back," Bray told a Glasgow newspaper. "He certainly lived up to his namesake's reputation as an adventurous traveler. He is half the weight he was when he left, and the local vet reckons he has honed up his hunting skills during the trek, probably living off mice, small birds and scraps."

Fortunately, the cat arrived just a few days before the Brays were scheduled to move to Glasgow.[11] Perhaps Ranulph had a homing instinct that drove him to head for home. His journey led him back to a loving family.

Things were quite different for Mrs. Lot. She was commanded, "Do not look behind you" (Gen. 19:17). It's a spiritual principle; God asks His children to move forward with no turning back. Paul wrote, "One thing I do, forgetting those things which are behind and reaching forward to those things which are ahead, I press toward the goal for the prize of the upward call of God in Christ Jesus" (Phil. 3:13–14).

LIFT UP ...

Father, when You pronounce judgment on my past sin, help me never to look back on it with longing. I want to remember that those around me are affected by my second thoughts. I'd rather look forward to You than back on the past. Amen.

LOOK AT ...

We've seen that the angels pulled Lot's family from their home and helped them escape from Sodom to the town of Zoar. Now we'll see God keep His promise to destroy the cities because of their wickedness. Jesus compared the story of Lot with the judgment that will come suddenly at the end of days. He said,

> As it was ... in the days of Lot: They ate, they
> drank, they bought, they sold, they planted, they built;
> but on the day that Lot went out of Sodom it rained
> fire and brimstone from heaven and destroyed them all.
> Even so will it be in the day when the Son of Man is
> revealed. In that day, he who is on the housetop, and his
> goods are in the house, let him not come down to take
> them away. And likewise the one who is in the field,
> let him not turn back. Remember Lot's wife. Whoever
> seeks to save his life will lose it, and whoever loses his
> life will preserve it. Luke 17:28–33

The best thing you can do is lose your life to Christ in order to gain salvation.

LEARN ABOUT ...

I Fire and Brimstone

Brimstone is a combustible mineral found near active volcanoes. It burns with a very disagreeable odor. In Hebrew and Greek it denotes divine fire, barrenness, and devastation. Brimstone was considered an agent of God's judgment (Gen. 19:24). In the New Testament it symbolically represents the future punishment of the wicked (see Rev. 9:17–18).

READ GENESIS 19:24–29.

Then the LORD rained brimstone and fire on Sodom and Gomorrah, from the LORD out of the heavens. So He overthrew those cities, all the plain, all the inhabitants of the cities, and what grew on the ground. But his wife looked back behind him, and she became a pillar of salt. And Abraham went early in the morning to the place where he had stood before the LORD. Then he looked toward Sodom and Gomorrah, and toward all the land of the plain; and he saw, and behold, the smoke of the land which went up like the smoke of a furnace. And it came to pass, when God destroyed the cities of the plain, that God remembered Abraham, and sent Lot out of the midst of the overthrow, when He overthrew the cities in which Lot had dwelt. Genesis 19:24–29

1. What form of judgment came upon Sodom and Gomorrah?

2. What else was included in this judgment?

3. a. Describe what happened to Lot's wife.

   b. Why do you think she did this?

4. Describe Abraham's actions.

5. What do you think went through Abraham's mind at this point?

6. How do you know that Lot's salvation was linked with Abraham's prayer?

LIVE OUT ...

7. a. In today's society, not many Christians seem to give fire-and-brimstone messages for fear of offending the audience. How did this lesson on the judgment of Sodom and Gomorrah affect you personally?

   b. How will it impact the way you share your faith with others?

8. Peter wrote a thought-provoking statement when he said, "For the time has come for judgment to begin at the house of God; and if it begins with us first, what will be the end of those who do not obey the gospel of God? Now 'If the righteous one is scarcely saved, where will the ungodly and the sinner appear?'" (1 Peter 4:17–18).

   a. How do you think we should go about judging ourselves as believers?

   b. What is the end of those who do not obey the gospel?

c. In today's lesson, who was a picture of the righteous "scarcely saved"?

d. Who was a portrait of the ungodly?

9. We know Lot's wife looked back with longing. Check the boxes of some things that might tempt you to look back from following Christ.

☐ Old relationships   ☐ Current trends   ☐ Worldly treasures

☐ Old habits   ☐ Convenient surroundings   ☐ Friends and family

☐ Other

LEARN ABOUT ...

9 Long For

Longing for the things of this world leads only to dissatisfaction. Trends change, treasures rust, and people disappoint us. How much better to long for the things of God! The psalmist wrote: "My soul longs, yes, even faints for the courts of the LORD; my heart and my flesh cry out for the living God" (Ps. 84:2).

· ○ ● ○ ·

"Ladeez and Gentlemen! Welcome to the Greatest Show on Earth!" bellows the man in the red silk jacket, white riding breeches, black boots, and silk top hat. Everyone's eyes are glued to the center of the three-ring circus. They expect to be dazzled. You can smell the popcorn in the air. You can feel the expectation building. Children's eyes are wide with amazement. Parents turn back in time to the thrill of believing in the impossible. The ringmaster proudly introduces "the Flying Wallendas," the most famous tightrope walkers of all time.

The patriarch of the family, Karl Wallenda, had answered an ad for "an experienced hand balancer with courage." Born to a family of acrobats, jugglers, and clowns, Wallenda knew the job was a perfect fit. In 1922 he began his own act and married fellow performer Helen Kreis.

The Wallendas headlined the Barnum and Bailey circus in Akron, Ohio, when a wire slipped and the tightrope walkers fell to the ground.

A reporter wrote that they fell so gracefully it seemed they were flying. Thus, the Flying Wallendas were born.

In 1978 Karl was walking between the towers of the Condada Holiday Inn in San Juan, Puerto Rico, when he plunged to his death. His wife said that for the first time he was focusing on falling rather than on walking the tightrope.[13]

The same is true for us spiritually. Rather than looking selfishly inward or backward at the world, we must keep our focus upward toward God, "looking unto Jesus, the author and finisher of our faith" (Heb. 12:2).

LISTEN TO...

My dear brother, let God make of you what He will, He will end all with consolation, and shall make glory out of your suffering.

—Samuel Rutherford

Rebekah—A Fairy-Tale Romance

Genesis 24

"Once upon a time" is the perfect opening to any fairy tale. Fairy tales are fantastic fictional stories featuring characters from folklore or the imagination. These creatures vary from elves and giants to trolls and talking animals. Dating back thousands of years, most of these tales involve far-fetched plots and usually end "happily ever after." In modern times, we often speak of circumstances that have "a fairy-tale ending." Sometimes we use specific fairy tales to describe real-life situations. For instance, Princess Diana's life was called a "Cinderella story" during the early years of her romance with Prince Charles. The mischievous kid who pulls the fire alarm as a prank becomes known as "the boy who cried wolf."

While we must never mistake the true stories in Scripture for fiction or folklore, some of these accounts include plotlines with miraculous interventions and dreamlike qualities. The romance between Isaac and Rebekah serves as one of the Bible's greatest love stories. Its rich narrative includes some elements of a fairy tale: a solemn oath, an arduous journey, a chance encounter, and a golden gift. Once the beautiful heroine and the handsome heir meet, they experience love at first sight. Their future begins to unfold as a dream come true. If you are a hopeless romantic, you'll be thrilled to discover that Genesis 24 is the longest chapter in the book. Only thirty-one verses describe creation, while sixty-seven are devoted to Isaac's courtship of Rebekah. This true story depicts the divine romance at the heart of the universe—it is a picture of Jesus and His bride, the church. As you read along, you'll find yourself included in this "fairy-tale romance."

Day 1: Genesis 24:1–12 — ONCE UPON A TIME

Day 2: Genesis 24:13–28 — THE WISHING WELL

Day 3: Genesis 24:29–49 — THE BEST MAN?

Day 4: Genesis 24:50–60 — SHOWERED WITH BLESSINGS

Day 5: Genesis 24:61–67 — HAPPILY EVER AFTER

DAY 1

Once upon a Time

LIFT UP ...

Lord, thank You for always going before me. Help me to trust in Your plan and purpose for my life. As I seek to be the woman You have called me to be, give me the strength to wait patiently on You. Amen.

LOOK AT ...

So far in our study of the women in Genesis, we've seen Eve endure the fall, Noah's wife survive the flood, Sarah unite to the "father of faith," Hagar overcome the folly of Sarah's surrogacy scheme, and Lot's wife turned into salt. Through each life, we've caught a glimpse of Jesus in Genesis. Christ's sinless sacrifice was foretold as an innocent animal was sacrificed to cover the consequences of sin. Just as the wooden ark rescued Noah's family from the coming judgment, the wooden cross promises to redeem believers from the final judgment. The Savior's birth was foreseen in God's promise that through Abraham and Sarah's offspring "all the families of the earth shall be blessed" (Gen. 12:3). Hagar's water from the miraculous well in the wilderness reminds us that those who drink of Jesus, the living water, will thirst no more. Now our study turns to Rebekah. Her idyllic courtship and marriage to Isaac is a heavenly picture of God the Father sending the Spirit into the world to obtain a bride for His only begotten Son.

READ GENESIS 24:1–12.

Now Abraham was old, well advanced in age; and the LORD had blessed Abraham in all things. So Abraham said to the oldest servant of his house, who ruled over all that he had, "Please, put your hand under my thigh, and I will make you swear by the LORD, the God of heaven and the God of the earth, that you will not take a wife for my son from the daughters of the Canaanites, among whom I dwell; but you shall go to my country and to my family, and take a wife for my son Isaac."

LEARN ABOUT ...

2 Stately Servant

Previously in Genesis the name of Abraham's chief servant was revealed as Eliezer. According to tradition, if Abraham had failed to produce a physical heir, his chief servant would have become the adopted heir. "Abram said, 'Lord GOD, what will You give me, seeing I go childless, and the heir of my house is Eliezer of Damascus?'" (Gen. 15:2).

3 Solemnly Swear

Commentators offer several explanations about the significance of putting a hand under another's thigh during an oath. Some say it was a solemn way of signifying that if the oath was violated, the children, yet unborn, would avenge the act of disloyalty.[1] Others believe that it points to the covenant of circumcision undergone by Abraham.

4 Separate Son

Isaac is thought to have been forty years old at this time. Abraham wisely prevented his son from marrying a local Canaanite girl. Nor did he want him to physically leave the Promised Land to choose a wife from among his kindred, lest Isaac become tempted to settle in a distant land.

And the servant said to him, "Perhaps the woman will not be willing to follow me to this land. Must I take your son back to the land from which you came?" But Abraham said to him, "Beware that you do not take my son back there. The LORD God of heaven, who took me from my father's house and from the land of my family, and who spoke to me and swore to me, saying, 'To your descendants I give this land,' He will send His angel before you, and you shall take a wife for my son from there. And if the woman is not willing to follow you, then you will be released from this oath; only do not take my son back there." So the servant put his hand under the thigh of Abraham his master, and swore to him concerning this matter. Then the servant took ten of his master's camels and departed, for all his master's goods were in his hand. And he arose and went to Mesopotamia, to the city of Nahor. And he made his camels kneel down outside the city by a well of water at evening time, the time when women go out to draw water. Then he said, "O LORD God of my master Abraham, please give me success this day, and show kindness to my master Abraham." Genesis 24:1–12

1. a. In what three ways does the first sentence describe Abraham?

   b. Why do you think we need to know this about Abraham?

2. Describe the task Abraham gave to his oldest servant.

3. a. Recount how Abraham made his request.

   b. How do you think this made his servant feel?

4. Circle the word *take* and underline the word *not* in today's text. How do these words clarify the servant's task?

5. a. What promise did Abraham recall?

   b. Why do you think he remembered this promise at this point?

6. Describe the servant's caravan and its ultimate destination.

7. a. What time reference is given toward the end of this passage?

    b. Elaborate on its significance.

8. Upon arrival, what did the servant do?

LIVE OUT ...

9. Today we discovered that the Lord had blessed Abraham in "all things." Fill in the following chart to discover the significance of "all things" in Scripture.

SCRIPTURE	ALL THINGS
Mark 9:23	
Romans 8:32	
2 Corinthians 5:17	
Ephesians 1:11	
Philippians 4:13	

10. Abraham employed a trusted servant to complete an important commission. The Bible reveals that we, too, are called to be faithful servants. Rewrite the following passage into a personal prayer, swearing allegiance to your Master, Jesus.

    "He who loves his life will lose it, and he who hates his life in this world will keep it for eternal life. If anyone serves Me, let him follow Me; and where I am, there My servant will be also. If anyone serves Me, him My Father will honor." John 12:25–26

11. Abraham was called to separate his past from the future, from idols to the one true God, from his earthly father's land to His

LEARN ABOUT ...

9 Saint's Supply

Abraham had been blessed in "all things." Yet despite his blessedness, which means happiness, he experienced many troubles. He faced famine, fear, and failure. He fought marauders who kidnapped Lot. He was also a widower. The patriarch could be happy because "all things work together for good to those who love God" (Rom. 8:28).

10 Savior's Servant

Paul referred to himself as a "servant," a word frequently translated "slave." "Christians are not hired servants but slaves committed to service to Jesus. A slave does not manage his own life. The person who calls himself a slave of Christ acknowledges that the Savior has power over him."[2]

heavenly Father's Promised Land. Notice that separation is to be *from* one thing and joined *with* another. Under the appropriate columns list some of the things God asks you to separate from and join with.

SEPARATE FROM   **JOIN WITH**

∘ ∘ ● ∘ ∘

"I solemnly swear" might evoke images of kings commissioning knights to go on quests to capture fire-breathing dragons or rescue damsels in distress. We imagine the grandeur of the royal marriage as Prince Charming swears his undying love to his beloved. We picture the triumphant inauguration as the rightful heir finally receives the crown.

We know an oath is a solemn statement or promise. In biblical times, an oath was one of the following: (1) an appeal to God attesting to the truth, (2) a sworn covenant, (3) an imprecation or curse.[3] In those days, symbolic gestures were incorporated with oath taking. Some of these gestures included:

Raising the hand (Gen. 14:22)

Sacrificing animals (Gen. 21:28–31)

Touching the thigh (Gen. 24:2)

Standing before an altar (1 Kings 8:31)

By New Testament times oaths had become exaggerated and unbelievable. People began to swear *by* created things (the sun, moon, or stars) rather than *in* the Creator (God). Jesus repudiated this behavior, saying, "Do not swear *at all*: neither by heaven, for it is God's throne; nor by the earth, for it is His footstool; nor by Jerusalem, for it is the city of the great King. Nor shall you swear by your head, because you cannot make one hair white or black. But let your 'Yes' be 'Yes,' and your 'No,' 'No.' For whatever is more than these is from the evil one" (Matt. 5:34–37). In essence, Jesus expects our words and works to be our solemn oath to the King of Kings—no need for swearing.

LISTEN TO...

The servant of God has a good master.

—*Blaise Pascal*

DAY 2

The Wishing Well

Disney's Fantasyland is the place where fairy tales seem to come to life. Walking through this magical land, you'll see the whale that swallowed Pinocchio. Near a colorful carousel you'll discover the famed Excalibur, King Arthur's sword in the stone. Away from the hustle and bustle, you'll happen upon a peaceful waterfall. Sitting nearby you'll find Snow White's wishing well, where she made a wish to discover the man of her dreams. It's nice to visit the world of make-believe, but how does God work things out for His people in the real world? For Eliezer to find Rebekah, God's hand of providence moved to accomplish miraculous outcomes.

"Providence is God's subtle intervention in the affairs of humankind. Some skeptics would call providence coincidence. However, as Bill Moyers astutely commented, 'Coincidence is God's way of remaining anonymous.' In other words, providence is God incognito—a situation in which He leaves His fingerprints without revealing His hand. These situations may not involve parted seas, manna from heaven, or a star in the sky to guide your way. But they could mean a life-changing meeting or finding yourself with the exact resources to help someone in need."[4] In Genesis 24, Abraham's servant sat near a well to offer a prayer, not a wish. And in providential accuracy, each detail was fulfilled. As Christians, we don't have to wish for our dreams to come true. We turn to God in prayer. George MacDonald adds, "Anything large enough for a wish to light upon is large enough to hang a prayer on."

LIFT UP ...

Thank You, Lord, for answering me when I call on You. Help me to recognize answered prayer and to rejoice in the way You answer me. Amen.

LOOK AT ...

We've seen that Eliezer had been a faithful steward over Abraham's household. Therefore, Abraham believed he could be trusted to oversee an even greater task: escorting a virgin bride to Canaan. Eliezer exemplified Jesus' words, "He who is faithful in what is least is faithful also in much; and he who is unjust in what is least is unjust also in much" (Luke 16:10). So often we fail the test of the "little things." Jesus commends those who take care of the little details, do the small jobs, and continue doing those things that seem less important. True greatness is determined when we're faithful in the small things.

Now we see Eliezer meet Rebekah, a woman willing to serve a servant. No task was too small for Rebekah. During his brief encounter with her, she displayed humility, helpfulness, and honesty. Little did she know that by performing a random act of kindness for a perfect stranger, she would marry a rich and righteous man.

READ GENESIS 24:13–28.

"Behold, here I stand by the well of water, and the daughters of the men of the city are coming out to draw water. Now let it be that the young woman to whom I say, 'Please let down your pitcher that I may drink,' and she says, 'Drink, and I will also give your camels a drink'—let her be the one You have appointed for Your servant Isaac. And by this I will know that You have shown kindness to my master." And it happened, before he had finished speaking, that behold, Rebekah, who was born to Bethuel, son of Milcah, the wife of Nahor, Abraham's brother, came out with her pitcher on her shoulder. Now the young woman was very beautiful to behold, a virgin; no man had known her. And she went down to the well, filled her pitcher, and came up. And the servant ran to meet her and said, "Please let me drink a little water from your pitcher." So she said, "Drink, my lord." Then she quickly let her pitcher down to her hand, and gave him a drink. And when she had finished giving him a drink, she said, "I will draw water for your camels also, until they have finished drinking." Then she quickly emptied her pitcher into the trough, ran back to the well to draw water, and drew for all his camels. And the man, wondering at her, remained silent so as to know whether the LORD had made his journey prosperous or not. So it was, when the camels had finished drinking, that the man took a golden nose ring weighing half a shekel, and two bracelets for her wrists weighing ten shekels of gold, and said, "Whose daughter are you? Tell me, please, is there room in your father's house for us to lodge?" So she said to him, "I am the daughter of Bethuel, Milcah's son, whom she bore to Nahor." Moreover she said to him, "We have both straw and feed enough, and room to lodge." Then the man bowed down his head and worshiped the LORD. And he said, "Blessed be the LORD God of my master

Abraham, who has not forsaken His mercy and His truth toward my master. As for me, being on the way, the Lord led me to the house of my master's brethren." So the young woman ran and told her mother's household these things. Genesis 24:13–28

1. We start today with Abraham's servant in midprayer. Recount the main points of Eliezer's prayer.

2. Describe Rebekah in your own words.

3. a. When did Rebekah arrive at the well?

   b. What relevance do you see to the timeliness of her arrival?

4. Underline and list the words in Rebekah's actions that give the narrative a sense of urgency. What adjectives would you use to describe her actions and attitude?

5. Compare how Eliezer responded internally and externally to Rebekah's attentive service.

6. What else did Eliezer request of Rebekah, and how did she respond?

7. List the three persons mentioned in Eliezer's prayer. What compliments were connected with each individual?

8. Describe Rebekah's final response to this encounter.

LIVE OUT ...

9. Eliezer put bookends of prayer on his quest for Isaac's bride. One of the keys to experiencing God's providence is to pray both often

LEARN ABOUT ...

I Specific Prayer

Eliezer didn't pray in generalities but with great specifics. He believed in the promises of God. Now he saw God's providence fulfill His promises in detail. In the middle of his nonverbal prayer, a possible solution arrived. He "ran" to see if this was indeed the hand of God. His prayer involved both saying the words and seeing the fulfillment.

4 She's Prompt

John Phillips writes, "A camel will drink about five gallons of water, and the servant had ten of them. To draw some fifty gallons of water from the well and empty them into the trough in the heat of that climate was a big undertaking. Such a woman would make a very good wife."[5] Rebekah offered prompt assistance.

7 Seeing Providence

The word *providence* comes from two Latin roots: *pro-*, meaning "before," and *video*, meaning "I see." It literally means "foresight." In other words, God can see things before they happen. Through His providence He can orchestrate the details of lives, nations, and history. You might say that history is "His story."

and specifically. In light of this, match the Scripture reference to the admonition of how to pray:

2 Thessalonians 1:11	Pray fervently
1 Corinthians 14:15	Pray always
1 Thessalonians 5:17	Pray without ceasing
James 5:16	Pray with the Spirit

10. Rebekah was beautiful inside and out. What about you? In the appropriate column list your outward and inward attributes.

INNER BEAUTY	OUTER BEAUTY

11. The encounter between Rebekah and the servant Eliezer revealed God's hand of providence. Eliezer said, "Being on the way, the LORD led me" (Gen 24:27). Journal about a time God providentially moved in your life, leading you to the right place at the right time. Remember we often detect God's hand in the rearview mirror!

. . ● . .

If you want specific answers to prayer, you must make specific requests. Interestingly, some experts decided to test whether there was scientific evidence to prove that God answers prayer. They made their test specific to determine the "Positive Therapeutic Effects of Intercessory Prayer in a Coronary Care Unit Population." To accomplish this, they gathered cardiac patients from the San Francisco General Medical Center and randomly divided them (using a computer-generated list) into two groups. The names of the patients in the "test" group were given to a group of Christians who prayed for them while they were in the hospital. The "placebo" group received no prayer. Neither group of patients knew if they were receiving prayer. Likewise, the hospital staff, doctors, and nurses were "blinded" from knowing which patients belonged to which group. The results demonstrated that patients who were prayed for suffered "less congestive heart failure, required less diuretic and antibiotic therapy, had fewer episodes of pneumonia, had fewer cardiac arrests, and were less frequently intubated and ventilated."[7] Dr. Alexis Carrel once said, "As a physician, I have seen men, after all other therapy had failed, lifted out of disease and melancholy by the serene effort of prayer."

Eliezer's detailed prayer shows that, in addition to answering prayer *for* the heart, God also answers prayers *from* the heart. God can touch hearts physically, spiritually, and emotionally. You might say that He's the consummate heart doctor. Next we'll see that the Lord ignited Rebekah's heart to long for a man she didn't even know. When she met Isaac, God would cause their hearts to beat as one.

LISTEN TO...

The shortest distance between a problem and a solution is the distance between your knees and the floor.

—Charles Stanley

DAY 3

The Best Man?

Have you ever noticed that many fairy tales include a wedding? *Beauty and the Beast, Cinderella, Snow White, Sleeping Beauty,* and many others end as wedding bells peal in jubilation. Today, most weddings include a best man in the wedding party. To ensure that the couple enjoys their special day, the best man assumes some serious responsibilities, including the following:

- Overseeing the groomsmen by making sure they are on time for the ceremony, properly dressed, with boutonnieres on the left lapel.
- Ensuring that the groom is dressed and ready for the ceremony.
- Holding the wedding rings until the appropriate time in the ceremony.
- Writing and offering a toast at the wedding ceremony.
- Taking care of payment to the clergy and other financial needs after the ceremony.
- Ensuring that the groom has the marriage license and subsequently signing the document as a witness.
- Making sure travel arrangements have been made to transport the couple to the airport.[8]

Today we'll see Laban, Rebekah's brother, as he fulfilled some of the traditional responsibilities of a best man. He consented (bore witness) to the union. He also helped with travel accommodations for the wedding party by offering a bed for Eliezer and a barn for his camels. Rather than a toast, he offered a blessing over the bride-to-be. However, history may not consider him the best man in the truer sense of the word. One commentator calls him "a scheming, grasping person."[9]

LIFT UP ...

Lord, thank You that You are not a God of chance but a God who guides my life. Help me to trust in and surrender to Your headship. Amen.

Look at ...

We've seen Eliezer offer Rebekah a ring and bracelets of gold. The nose ring was tradition-ally worn through all parts of Arabia and Persia, particularly among young women. These large rings were generally worn on the left nostril, sometimes pierced through the cartilage in the central division of the nose, falling down over the mouth. Rebekah's weighed half a shekel, which is somewhat less than a quarter of an ounce. It was also traditional for women in the East to wear bracelets to adorn their arms or ankles. Often the arm, from the elbow to the wrist, was covered with bracelets of gold, silver, copper, or mother of pearl. These gifts were not intended as a betrothal gift, but as a reward for her kind service. Eliezer was honoring her behavior more than her beauty. Solomon warned, "A beautiful woman who lacks discretion is like a gold ring in a pig's snout" (Prov. 11:22 NLT). Thankfully, Rebekah acted both beautifully and discretely when Eliezer came into her home to meet her family.

READ GENESIS 24:29–49.

Now Rebekah had a brother whose name was Laban, and Laban ran out to the man by the well. So it came to pass, when he saw the nose ring, and the bracelets on his sister's wrists, and when he heard the words of his sister Rebekah, saying, "Thus the man spoke to me," that he went to the man. And there he stood by the camels at the well. And he said, "Come in, O blessed of the LORD! Why do you stand outside? For I have prepared the house, and a place for the camels." Then the man came to the house. And he unloaded the camels, and provided straw and feed for the camels, and water to wash his feet and the feet of the men who were with him. Food was set before him to eat, but he said, "I will not eat until I have told about my errand." And he said, "Speak on." So he said, "I am Abraham's servant. The LORD has blessed my master greatly, and he has become great; and He has given him flocks and herds, silver and gold, male and female servants, and camels and donkeys. And Sarah my master's wife bore a son to my master when she was old; and to him he has given all that he has. Now my master made me swear, saying, 'You shall not take a wife for my son from the daughters of the Canaanites, in whose land I dwell; but you shall go to my father's house and to my family, and take a wife for my son.' And I said to my master, 'Perhaps the woman will not follow me.' But he said to me, 'The LORD, before whom I walk, will send His angel with you and prosper your way; and you shall take a wife for my son

LEARN ABOUT ...

I Laban

Laban was an Aramean herd owner from Mesopotamia. According to custom, as Rebekah's brother, he and his father could consent to Rebekah's marriage. Eventually we'll see his shrewd business dealings with his nephew Jacob. Laban craftily switched his daughters on Jacob's wedding night to extract seven additional years of service from the groom.

from my family and from my father's house. You will be clear from this oath when you arrive among my family; for if they will not give her to you, then you will be released from my oath.' And this day I came to the well and said, 'O Lord God of my master Abraham, if You will now prosper the way in which I go, behold, I stand by the well of water; and it shall come to pass that when the virgin comes out to draw water, and I say to her, "Please give me a little water from your pitcher to drink," and she says to me, "Drink, and I will draw for your camels also,"—let her be the woman whom the Lord has appointed for my master's son. But before I had finished speaking in my heart, there was Rebekah, coming out with her pitcher on her shoulder; and she went down to the well and drew water. And I said to her, 'Please let me drink.' And she made haste and let her pitcher down from her shoulder, and said, 'Drink, and I will give your camels a drink also.' So I drank, and she gave the camels a drink also. Then I asked her, and said, 'Whose daughter are you?' And she said, 'The daughter of Bethuel, Nahor's son, whom Milcah bore to him.' So I put the nose ring on her nose and the bracelets on her wrists. And I bowed my head and worshiped the Lord, and blessed the Lord God of my master Abraham, who had led me in the way of truth to take the daughter of my master's brother for his son. Now if you will deal kindly and truly with my master, tell me. And if not, tell me, that I may turn to the right hand or to the left." Genesis 24:29–49

1. Today we are introduced to Rebekah's brother. In your own words, describe Laban by completing the following phrases:

   When he saw ...

   When he heard ...

   And he said ...

2. Describe the extent of Laban's hospitality. What do you think motivated him?

3. a. Explain what the servant refused and why.

   b. What does this teach you about his character?

4. List Abraham's possessions as described by the servant, and explain who would eventually inherit them.

5. In your own words, recap the task the servant was given and what occurred at the well.

6. In what ways did the Lord lead the servant?

7. What did the servant ask Rebekah's family to reveal about themselves, and what ultimatum did he give them?

8. Put yourself in Rebekah's sandals, and describe how you would react after discovering that you had been secretly tested and passed with flying colors.

LIVE OUT …

9. Any time we meet Laban in Scripture, we notice a struggle between the flesh and the Spirit. Read Romans 8:5–10 to learn more about these warring entities.

   a. What two lifestyles does Paul introduce, and where are they formulated?

   b. List the results of adhering to each of these lifestyles.

   c. How does a person know if he or she is "in the Spirit"?

   d. Have you had this experience? If so, how did it change your life?

LEARN ABOUT …

4 Legacy

Isaac would inherit both the promises and the possessions of Abraham. Like Abraham, he would marry a beautiful woman from Mesopotamia. Sadly, he would also inherit his father's legacy of lies: Isaac would say that Rebekah was his sister for fear of his enemies (see Gen. 26). His sin would be exposed while Rebekah's honor would be protected.

6 Leading

Matthew Henry wrote, "God's angels are ministering spirits, sent forth, not only for the protection, but for the guidance, of the heirs of promise."[10] Scripture confirms, "Are not all angels ministering spirits sent to serve those who will inherit salvation?" (Heb. 1:14 NIV). They often go unrecognized; "some have unwittingly entertained angels" (Heb. 13:2).

9 Lifestyle

Laban displayed carnality— one minute motivated by greed, the next by God. When he saw Rebekah's golden reward, he ran to impress the generous man, hoping to be rewarded. However, it backfired when Laban proclaimed Eliezer as blessed of God using the name "Jehovah," the covenant name for the Lord. Was Laban taking God's name in vain?

LEARN ABOUT ...

10 Hospitality

Hospitality was very important in Bible times. The Greek word literally means "love of strangers." Even today a traditional greeting to the guests among the Bedouin people of the Middle East is, "You are among your family."[11] Jesus promoted hospitality: "I was a stranger and you took Me in" (Matt. 25:35).

10. Laban offered a stranger typical Middle Eastern hospitality. Paul says that Christians should be "given to hospitality" (Rom. 12:13). Hospitality is gracious and generous reception and treatment toward guests.

a. Describe some ways you have given or received hospitality.

b. Determine to offer hospitality to someone this week. Who will it be? What will you do?

11. Eliezer refused to eat before completing his task. Job said of God, "I have treasured the words of His mouth more than my necessary food" (Job 23:12). What have you set aside so that you can obey God? Place a check in the appropriate box.

❏ Food   ❏ Sleep   ❏ Friendships
❏ Entertainment ❏ Hobbies   ❏ Finances
❏ Education   ❏ Sports   ❏ Other _____

o o ● o o

Throughout our study of the women in Genesis, we've encountered a number of angels. Angels are not mythical creatures from fairy tales; they are mysterious beings created by God. Abraham encountered them, and Eliezer attributed the success of his mission to them. The Bible teaches that they are spiritual beings that possess wings, are able to inhabit heaven, and are eternal. While they are not all-knowing or all-powerful, they are superior to humans in both strength and knowledge. We only know three of this vast company of angels by name: (1) Michael, who seems to have been given the special task of overseeing the nation of Israel; (2) Gabriel, who communicates special messages to God's servants like Mary, the mother of Jesus, and Zacharias, the father of John the Baptist; and (3) Lucifer (Satan), who was the chief architect in a rebellion against God. He was cast down with one-third of the other angels in his company, the fallen angels.

When manifesting themselves to people, angels often take on human form. Sometimes they cause great awe, as they did with the shepherds in Bethlehem. Other times they go undetected, as when Abraham offered hospitality to them unawares. *Nelson's Illustrated Bible Dictionary* states, "Angels are never known to appear to wicked people—only to those whom the Bible views as good, such as Abraham, Moses, David, Daniel, Jesus, Peter, and Paul. They are charged with caring for such people and serving them in times of need. They also guide and instruct good people. … Sometimes their guidance comes through human dreams."[12]

Have you ever wondered if you have an angel watching over you? The Bible tells us, "He will command his angels concerning you to guard you in all your ways" (Ps. 91:11 NIV).

LISTEN TO …

Angels guard you when you walk with Me. What better way could you choose?

—*Frances J. Roberts*

DAY 4

Showered with Blessings

There's one fairy-tale princess who was said to be showered with blessings at birth: Sleeping Beauty. Remember the story? At her christening, fairies came to bestow blessings upon the long-awaited child as a gesture of goodwill. One offered the gift of beauty, one the gift of charm, another the gift of song. However, a wicked fairy whom the king and queen had neglected to invite arrived unexpectedly. Angry, she cursed the princess with the fate of death at a spinning wheel when she reached adulthood. Thankfully, a good fairy was late to the event. Although she could not reverse the curse, she was able to bless the princess with the promise of not death but mere sleeping. She would awaken with the kiss of true love. Of course, when the princess awoke to her handsome prince, the couple would live happily ever after.

While Eliezer was not a fairy godfather, he did shower Rebekah with blessings at her betrothal. She received jewels of silver and gold as well as clothing. But the gift giving did not end with the bride-to-be. Rebekah's brother and mother also received precious gifts.

The word *jewelry* or *jewels* is better translated *vessels* or *instruments* of various kinds. Eliezer had already given Rebekah a nose ring and bracelets as a token of respect. The jewels or vessels bestowed in front of her family represented a dowry of sorts. The phrase "precious things" comes from a word that speaks of exquisite fruits, delicacies, precious plants, or exotic flowers. It is likely that these things refer to gifts that were inferior to the gifts given to Rebekah. All of the gifts together represent a picture of a modern-day wedding shower, complete with flowers, food, household gifts, and an elegant bridal trousseau.

LIFT UP ...

The greatest gift is the gift of the Holy Spirit. Thank You, Lord, for giving Him so freely and graciously. You are truly a generous God. Amen.

LOOK AT ...

We've seen Eliezer expound upon the vastness of his master's household and how Isaac would one day inherit everything. In addition to possessions, Isaac's dowry included greater riches still. The greatest was that he would be an heir to the promises of God. Abraham's covenant with God would one day be conferred upon him. He, too, would become one of Israel's patriarchs. Additionally, Isaac enjoyed the treasure of living with Abraham, the father of the faith. Just try to envision the inspiration Isaac received from witnessing his father's faithfulness. Imagine being able to eavesdrop on Abraham's conversations with God. In addition, consider the advice Isaac received during his upbringing, including advice about love and marriage. Today we'll see Rebekah as she made the decision to go to Isaac in the Promised Land and separate from her past.

READ GENESIS 24:50–60.

Then Laban and Bethuel answered and said, "The thing comes from the LORD; we cannot speak to you either bad or good. Here is Rebekah before you; take her and go, and let her be your master's son's wife, as the LORD has spoken." And it came to pass, when Abraham's servant heard their words, that he worshiped the LORD, bowing himself to the earth. Then the servant brought out jewelry of silver, jewelry of gold, and clothing, and gave them to Rebekah. He also gave precious things to her brother and to her mother. And he and the men who were with him ate and drank and stayed all night. Then they arose in the morning, and he said, "Send me away to my master." But her brother and her mother said, "Let the young woman stay with us a few days, at least ten; after that she may go." And he said to them, "Do not hinder me, since the LORD has prospered my way; send me away so that I may go to my master." So they said, "We will call the young woman and ask her personally." Then they called Rebekah and said to her, "Will you go with this man?" And she said, "I will go." So they sent away Rebekah their sister and her nurse, and Abraham's servant and his men. And they blessed Rebekah and said to her: "Our sister, may you become the mother of thousands of ten thousands; and may your descendants possess the gates of those who hate them."
Genesis 24:50–60

Learn About ...

I Heaven Sent

Rebekah's family confirmed that this match "comes from the LORD" (Gen. 24:50). They saw the evidence of God's hand on the union. According to ancient customs, perhaps in imitation of Father God providing Adam with a wife, Eastern fathers considered it their duty to obtain wives for their sons. Sometimes the father of the girl made the proposal.[13]

2 Humble Servant

Bowing down meant more than bending the knee. It also involved prostration, the practice of falling upon the knees, gradually inclining the body, and touching the forehead to the ground. In Bible times such practices were intended to convey an attitude of reverence, respect, and humility, paying homage to others.[14]

6 Wholly Surrendered

Sensing God's hand, Rebekah agreed to the marriage and the timetable without hesitation. Sight unseen she said, "I will" to her future bridegroom. It can be the same with our Bridegroom, Jesus, "whom having not seen you love. Though now you do not see Him, yet believing, you rejoice with joy inexpressible and full of glory" (I Peter 1:8).

1. How did Laban and Bethuel respond to the servant's request and why?

2. a. What action did Eliezer take in response to this answer?

   b. Review this week's lesson, and record how many times Eliezer repeated this action.

3. a. We know the groom showered Rebekah's family with many gifts. Why do you think Abraham and Isaac were so generous?

   b. How might this have influenced Rebekah's family?

4. Next we see a conversation to negotiate the timing of Rebekah's departure. Recount each party's position and why they reasoned as they did.

5. What solution did the family offer to decide the timing of Rebekah's departure?

6. a. How did Rebekah respond to this proposal?

   b. What does this teach you about her character?

7. Describe the farewell blessing Rebekah's family gave her. How did this line up with God's promises to Abraham?

Live Out ...

8. Eliezer repeatedly bowed to worship the Lord. Using BOW as an acrostic, list some praiseworthy things about God. Then take time to bow before your King and proclaim these words of adoration.

B (ex. beneficent)

O

W

LEARN ABOUT ...

8 Bow Down

Sadly, there are many instances in the Bible where people bowed down to idols instead of God. Yet this behavior was strictly forbidden: "You shall not make mention of the name of their gods, nor cause anyone to swear by them; you shall not serve them nor bow down to them" (Josh. 23:7).

10 Heart and Soul

Rebekah and Sarah treated their husbands with respect and obedience. Their hearts cried, "I will," rather than, "I won't." Lockyer says, "Through the marriage of Isaac and Rebekah, Abraham saw that day of Christ in which the church should become the Bride of Christ." [15] Have you given Jesus your heart and soul by saying, "I will"?

9. Rebekah's family wanted to hold on to her for a few more days rather than letting her move toward the future. Think about a time when you knew you needed to let something go but wanted to hold on to it longer. Journal about when you let it go and any blessings the Lord gave in return for your obedience.

10. Rebekah's words *I will* are reminiscent of wedding vows. Recite the following wedding vows out loud to Jesus. Then write a prayer surrendering your will to His.

> Will you, _____, take Jesus to be your God-given husband in this covenant of marriage? Will you love Him? Will you honor Him? And forsaking all others live only unto Him for all of eternity?

○ ○ ● ○ ○

A precocious little boy named Jimmy was the ring bearer in a wedding. At the rehearsal, the wedding planner asked the pastor when the couple's special song would play. The pastor replied, "After the vows." She asked, "What are the vows? I need a cue." Jimmy couldn't believe the adults didn't know the answer, so he chimed in, "The vowels are A-E-I-O-U. Q isn't a vowel!"

Sometimes people enter into marriage like it's a game of *Wheel of Fortune.* They'll take an "I" but not realize that the vows include "we." In marriage, two people become one. It's a mystery ordained by God as a portrait of Christ and the church. How often do we fail God when we neglect our vows or selfishly focus on what "I" can get out of my marriage?

Rebekah willingly entered into the marriage covenant, seeing it as a gift from the Lord. She bravely set out for a land she had never seen to become permanently linked to a man she had never met. And the Lord blessed her with Isaac. We can learn from this couple that when we act in faith, our feelings will follow. Rebekah trusted God to give her the husband He had chosen for her. When she followed His plan for her life, she discovered that He had chosen perfectly.

LISTEN TO ...

There's a great deal of difference between go and let's go.

—*Luc de Clapiers, Marquis de Vauvenargues*

DAY 5

Happily Ever After

We've been looking at Rebekah's true story as if it were a fairy tale. After all, she had a faithful servant come to her aid much like the happy forest animals that helped out Snow White. There's the hint of a greedy brother—Laban—who was similar to Cinderella's wicked stepsisters. And what would a fairy tale be without Prince Charming? Today we'll see Rebekah meet the man of her dreams—Isaac.

You could say that Isaac really was a prince of a man because he carried royal blood in his veins. Through his lineage, "the Lion of the tribe of Judah" (Rev. 5:5) would come into the world. In Matthew we read that "Abraham begot Isaac, Isaac begot Jacob, and Jacob begot Judah" (Matt 1:2). Judah's line led to King David, King Solomon, and ultimately the King of Kings, Jesus Christ. Isaac foreshadows or portrays Jesus. Remember how God told Abraham, "Take now your son, your only son Isaac, whom you love, and go to the land of Moriah, and offer him there as a burnt offering" (Gen. 22:2)? Isaac willingly climbed onto the altar, but just in the nick of time God provided a ram in the thicket.

Today we learn how Isaac and Rebekah finally met and had their wedding. The Bible makes it clear that for both it was love at first sight. The maiden rushed to meet her fiancé. The groom was thrilled to meet his bride. Surely they would live happily ever after, wouldn't they?

LIFT UP ...

Father, You are my first love. Thank You for giving of Yourself so freely. Forgive me for the times when I am unlovable. Help me to walk in love knowing that You are with me. Amen.

LOOK AT ...

We've seen Rebekah leave her family in Mesopotamia and move forward to become a part of the covenant people. Abraham made sure that Isaac's wife was descended from his own family line—that of his brother Nahor. Her willingness to turn her back on her people showed a willingness to leave not only her people but also the many gods worshipped by

LEARN ABOUT ...

2 Destination

Beer Lahai Roi is the well where Hagar had fled from Sarah. It is known as "the well of the One Who Sees Me." Isaac is often identified with wells (Gen. 24:62; 25:11; 26:17–33). It's fitting that Rebekah, who was discovered at a well, would see her groom coming from a well.

3 Meditation

Meditation is a private devotional act in which one reflects and prays about spiritual truth. Often, it ends in decisions concerning future conduct or results in answered prayer or providential responses. Meditation should bring delight: "His delight is in the law of the LORD, and in His law he meditates day and night" (Ps. 1:2).[16]

---

those in the area of Ur of the Chaldees. But the covenant promises brought a command to cleave to God. Isaac would need to help his bride separate from her people. Together they would learn to live holy lives, separate from the Canaanites among whom they dwelled. Paul encourages all of God's children, "Come out from among them and be separate, says the Lord. Do not touch what is unclean, and I will receive you. I will be a Father to you, and you shall be My sons and daughters, says the LORD Almighty" (2 Cor. 6:17–18).

READ GENESIS 24:61–67.

Then Rebekah and her maids arose, and they rode on the camels and followed the man. So the servant took Rebekah and departed. Now Isaac came from the way of Beer Lahai Roi, for he dwelt in the South. And Isaac went out to meditate in the field in the evening; and he lifted his eyes and looked, and there, the camels were coming. Then Rebekah lifted her eyes, and when she saw Isaac she dismounted from her camel; for she had said to the servant, "Who is this man walking in the field to meet us?" The servant said, "It is my master." So she took a veil and covered herself. And the servant told Isaac all the things that he had done. Then Isaac brought her into his mother Sarah's tent; and he took Rebekah and she became his wife, and he loved her. So Isaac was comforted after his mother's death. Genesis 24:61–67

1. a. Who accompanied Rebekah on her journey?

   b. How did they travel?

2. From where did Isaac come and why?

3. a. What was Isaac doing in the fields?

   b. What does this activity reveal about Isaac's spiritual life?

4. What did Isaac and Rebekah seem to do at the same time?

5. a. What did Rebekah do when she learned the identity of the man in the field?

 b. Why do you think she did this?

6. What last task did the faithful servant perform?

7. Isaac brought his wife home and "loved her." How does this exemplify what you've learned about God's hand of providence?

Live Out ...

8. a. Rebekah left her home and family with only her maidservants to accompany her. What emotions do you think she might have been feeling?

 b. Look back to Day 1. Who was accompanying the caravan (other than Eliezer) who could offer comfort?

 c. Describe a time you felt far away from home and lonely. Who or what comforted you?

9. We saw Isaac in meditation as he waited for his bride. Many Christians believe meditation is not biblical—but it is!

 a. Describe the things we should meditate upon based on the following passages:

 Joshua 1:8

 Psalm 4:4

Learn About ...

5 Identification

While some Eastern women were heavily veiled and concealed, Jewish women did not adopt this practice. However, Rebekah may have put on a veil or cloak to identify herself to Isaac as a woman who was pure and modest. It is also possible that she put on a wedding veil to identify herself as Isaac's intended.

7 Connection

The word *love* first appears in Scripture when Abraham took Isaac "whom he loved" in obedience to God, speaking of a father's love for a son. The second time love appears is concerning a husband's love for his wife. The typology is clear. Just as God the Father loved the Son, Christ the Bridegroom loves His bride, the church.

8 Consolation

Whether we're surrounded by people or isolated at home, it's possible to feel absolutely alone without the presence of God. The living God is Spirit, unlimited and capable of being everywhere at one time. The theological term is omnipresence. Jesus promised, "Lo, I am with you always, even to the end of the age" (Matt. 28:20).

LEARN ABOUT ...

9 Contemplation

Meditation leads to transformation. Paul wrote, "Whatever things are true, whatever things are noble, whatever things are just, whatever things are pure, whatever things are lovely, whatever things are of good report, if there is any virtue and if there is anything praiseworthy—meditate on these things" (Phil. 4:8).

Psalm 145:5

Malachi 3:16

b. Now take some time—real time—to meditate upon one of these things. Take the phone off the hook, turn off any electronic devices, and really engage in deep thought and prayer about the Law, the glorious splendor of God's majesty, or whatever thing you chose. Then record what God spoke to your heart as you meditated.

○ ○ ● ○ ○

Most fairy tales end with the bride and groom riding off into the sunset and the words AND THEY LIVED HAPPILY EVER AFTER written across the page. It's lovely to think that life is a fairy tale. But God wrote the true and living Word not as a fairy tale but as true life so that we can learn eternal lessons and apply them to our lives.

Isaac and Rebekah were married. They loved each other. But Isaac could only wish that his mother had lived to see his bride. Isn't true life that way? So this chapter ends and another chapter begins. And there were times of trouble. Theirs stemmed from infertility and sibling rivalry between their sons. Jacob was born grasping the heel of his older twin, Esau. Jacob usurped the birthright from his older brother with the help of his mother, Rebekah. Clearly, there was some conflict in the home.

Writer's today argue about whether every romance needs an HEA (Happily Ever After) ending. The Romance Writers of America explain, "Two basic elements comprise every romance novel: a central love story and an emotionally satisfying and optimistic ending." But romance authors and publishers agree that though the "happy ending" is one component, a romance novel must include other elements to be publishable: conflict, growth, and resolution.[17]

Despite any conflict, we follow the God of Abraham, Isaac, and Jacob, the patriarchs whose lineage sent us the perfect Bridegroom, Jesus Christ. Our love story with Him will bring spiritual growth and ultimate resolution when we meet Him face-to-face.

LISTEN TO ...

Genuine love is so contrary to human nature that its presence bears witness to an extraordinary power.

—John Piper

Rachel and Leah— He Loves Me; He Loves Me Not

Genesis 29

Do cheerful daisies make your day? Maybe you gaze at them and long to pluck away the petals while saying, "He loves me; he loves me not," to determine whether the one who holds your fancy feels the same way you do.

Have you ever wondered where the daisy custom began? No one really knows when people began acting out the ritual, but the German poet Goethe immortalized the activity when he wrote an opera depicting the naive Marguerite, in a desire to know whether Faust really loves her, pulling away daisy petals and chanting, "He loves me. He loves me not." There's a less familiar ritual that takes place using the daisy to predict when marriage might occur. The petals are plucked as the spouse-to-be chants, "This year, next year, sometime, never."

Our lovers find themselves in a complex situation this week. Jacob—Isaac and Rebekah's son—followed his family's path to seek a bride. He went to the land of his fore-fathers in Haran just as Eliezer had sought Rebekah there on behalf of Isaac. There he met the love of his life—Rachel, one of Laban's daughters. If Rachel had played the daisy game, she would no doubt have landed on "He loves me." However, Rachel had a sister, Leah. Leah also fell in love with the man from Canaan. According to Eastern custom, as the eldest daughter she got first rights to a marriage proposal. Would Jacob ever get to marry Rachel? In their case, the daisy game would play out "Not this year, not next year, maybe sometime, fourteen years later."

Day 1: Genesis 29:1–6   **LONG-LOST RELATIVES**

Day 2: Genesis 29:7–12   **LOVE AT FIRST SIGHT**

Day 3: Genesis 29:13–19   **FATHER OF THE BRIDES**

Day 4: Genesis 29:20–27   **LOVE'S LABOURS LOST**

Day 5: Genesis 29:28–35   **FIRST COMES LOVE?**

DAY 1

Long-Lost Relatives

LIFT UP ...

Father, thank You for leading me every step of my journey. I ask You to guide me everywhere You want me to go and help me to ask the right questions when I get there. Amen.

LOOK AT ...

Today we meet two of the characters in this week's love triangle: Rachel and Jacob. Jacob was his mother Rebekah's favorite son. God spoke to her during her pregnancy. Rebekah carried the twins Esau and Jacob in her womb, and God told her that "the older shall serve the younger" (Gen. 25:23). Rebekah ensured that the prophecy would come true by helping Jacob deceive his father. She dressed Jacob up as his older brother, Esau, and sent him into Isaac's tent with a pot of stew to seek his blessing. Having received the blessing, he was forced to flee from Esau's wrath. Later Isaac told him, "You shall not take a wife from the daughters of Canaan. Arise, go to Padan Aram, to the house of Bethuel your mother's father; and take yourself a wife from there of the daughters of Laban your mother's brother" (Gen. 28:1–2).

READ GENESIS 29:1–6.

So Jacob went on his journey and came to the land of the people of the East. And he looked, and saw a well in the field; and behold, there were three flocks of sheep lying by it; for out of that well they watered the flocks. A large stone was on the well's mouth. Now all the flocks would be gathered there; and they would roll the stone from the well's mouth, water the sheep, and put the stone back in its place on the well's mouth. And Jacob said to them, "My brethren, where are you from?" And they said, "We are from Haran." Then he said to them, "Do you know Laban the son of Nahor?" And they said, "We know him." So he said to them, "Is he well?" And they said, "He is well. And look, his daughter Rachel is coming with the sheep." Genesis 29:1–6

LEARN ABOUT ...

1 Bethel

At Bethel, "the house of God," Jacob had a personal encounter with God that was life changing. Previously God was the God of his fathers. Now God was *his* God. God made personal promises to Jacob concerning his future. These were the same promises Abraham and Isaac had received. Now they were promises Jacob could cling to.

2 Behold

Whenever you see the word *behold* in Scripture, you can be sure that a momentous encounter is about to take place. It means to take a good look or regard intently. As a shepherd, Jacob would recognize the signs of sheep nearby. His eyes were probably intently seeking a well.

6 Beloved

Rachel, whose name means "lamb," came to the well to tend the family's sheep. The shepherds pointed out a beautiful little lamb bringing her sheep behind her. Warren Wiersbe said, "I get the impression that when Jacob saw Rachel, it was love at first sight." "Tell me, O you whom I love, where you feed your flock" (Song 1:7).

1. Review Genesis 28:10–18, and explain how you think God was preparing Jacob for this journey.

2. Describe what caused him to stop and look.

3. a. Refer back to last week's lesson, and describe the similarities to how Jacob's father, Isaac, found a bride.

   b. How did that situation differ from this one?

4. What was Jacob trying to discover with his questions?

5. Do you think the men gave him any insight into Laban? What makes you say that?

6. How did this encounter end?

LIVE OUT ...

7. We saw that Jacob had a personal encounter with God where he acknowledged the Lord as his own personal God. Describe the time you came to know Jesus as your personal Lord and Savior. If you have not, search your heart to see if God is calling you to turn to Him now.

8. We learned today that the word *behold* is used in Scripture to draw our attention to important events. Fill in the following chart to discover some things we should be on the lookout for.

SCRIPTURE	BEHOLD
2 Corinthians 6:2	
Hebrews 8:8	

1 John 3:1

Revelation 1:7

9. a. The shepherds drew Jacob's attention to Rachel. Clearly, Jacob was in the right place at the right time to meet this special person. What word did you learn in last week's lesson to describe God's leading a person by His good hand to a divine appointment?

    b. Describe a time when you were in either the right place at the right time or the wrong place at the wrong time. How did God work everything out for your good and His glory?

○ ○ ● ○ ○

LEARN ABOUT ...

7 Bequest

In the family of God, there are only children, not grandchildren. What does that mean? We cannot bequeath our personal faith to others. They must have a personal encounter with Christ and embrace Him as their Lord and Savior. What we can do is share the gospel message and pray for their spiritual enlightenment.

8 Believe

How do you know if Jesus is *your* Lord? "If you confess with your mouth the Lord Jesus and believe in your heart that God has raised Him from the dead, you will be saved" (Rom. 10:9). A heartfelt belief in Christ's life, death, and resurrection and public profession of faith in Him are beautiful to behold.

Human beings are trying to make the dating scene easier and safer with a device called "the Love Detector." Richard Parton, chief executive of V Worldwide said that the Love Detector utilizes layered voice analysis to assess levels of emotion, embarrassment, concentration, and whether what is said reflects certainty, uncertainty, or outright lies.

Ironically, it depicts the love level as a digital daisy flower that progresses from a wilting stem to an upright bloom with up to five petals. The goal is to develop a high-tech version of "loves me–loves me not." Eventually the device will fit onto a pair of sunglasses so that singles can immediately tell whether the one they meet loves them or not.

The *New York Times* reports that Abigail Ramble, a sophomore majoring in psychology at Judson College, in Elgin, Illinois, borrowed the detector from a friend and tried it at a coffeehouse. She said, "With a close friend, the onscreen flower showed a few petals, indicating I really liked her as a friend, and the embarrassment level was low because I was open and comfortable talking to her. But when I was talking with one guy, the embarrassment level was high; I didn't know him all that well, and here I was talking to him on this Love Detector!"[2]

Jacob's courtship with Rachel would not be easy, but he had an inward "love detector." His heart immediately went out to the beautiful shepherdess who came to the well. However, he may have wished he had a lie-detecting device when it came to dealing with his wily uncle Laban.

LISTEN TO ...

Life minus love equals zero.

—*Rick Warren*

DAY 2
Love at First Sight

Reuters news wrote, "Disbelievers in love at first sight may have to think again because new research shows it only takes half a second to decide if someone is attractive and a potential mate." Psychologist Jon Maner of Florida State University noted, "People are attuned to physical attractiveness whether looking for mates or guarding their mates from potential rivals."

Maner and his team studied the reactions of people to attractive faces. They found that people could decide in half a second if someone was eye-catching. They also noticed that people fixated on attractive faces half a second longer than the one-second time limit. So if you're looking for a potential mate, the next time someone asks, "Got a second?" you may want to take the time.[3]

Isaac and Rebekah experienced love at first sight. Jacob went to Haran, desiring the same experience. James Montgomery Boice wrote, "Is there love at first sight? There seems to be, and the Bible seems to recognize it in this passage."[4] Rachel's inner and outer beauty instantly captured and held Jacob's heart his whole life. Even after seventy years, Jacob thought of Rachel instead of Leah on his deathbed as he recalled, "But as for me, when I came from Padan, Rachel died beside me in the land of Canaan on the way, when there was but a little distance to go to Ephrath; and I buried her there on the way to Ephrath (that is, Bethlehem)" (Gen. 48:7).

LIFT UP ...

Father, I know that You are working in my life today. Help me to recognize and rejoice in the people You send my way. Amen.

LOOK AT ...

Yesterday we learned about Jacob, one of the patriarchs of the Hebrew people. We discovered that he had deceived his father, Isaac, to obtain his blessing and was forced to flee from his angry brother, Esau. Nevertheless, God met him in the wilderness and began a long process that would change Jacob into the man of faith he was intended to be.

LEARN ABOUT ...

1 Comfortable Conversation?

Jacob's name means "heel catcher" or "supplanter." Often, biblical names indicate a personality trait. It could be that Jacob's tendency to take command of a situation was exhibited here when he questioned the shepherds. Some look at this as a breech of etiquette, while others regard it as a sign of camaraderie and strength.

3 Rolling Stone

Last week we saw that Isaac was associated with wells. It may be this was the same well where Eliezer met Rachel and she watered the camels. Now we see Jacob roll away the stone to water Rachel's flock. Wells are often associated with divine blessing. Laban's flocks would prosper under Jacob's care.

4 Kissing Cousins

Some attribute Jacob's break with his family, encounter with God, and long journey to his emotional outburst. Others say that kissing relatives was a proper Eastern greeting and that Jacob had every right to treat Rachel in this manner. A kiss was seen as a sign of respect, affection, reverence, and subjection.

Isn't that how God works with all of us? We all experience ups and downs on our spiritual journeys through life. We all have moments we're not proud of—wilderness experiences. Oftentimes, God meets us in the proverbial wilderness and reveals Himself to us personally, calling us to a relationship with Himself. After the wilderness God propels us forward to the next phase in our spiritual walk. For Jacob, the next phase was meeting Rachel, the love of his life. Let's see how he reacted when he met the beautiful shepherdess.

READ GENESIS 29:7–12.

Then he said, "Look, it is still high day; it is not time for the cattle to be gathered together. Water the sheep, and go and feed them." But they said, "We cannot until all the flocks are gathered together, and they have rolled the stone from the well's mouth; then we water the sheep." Now while he was still speaking with them, Rachel came with her father's sheep, for she was a shepherdess. And it came to pass, when Jacob saw Rachel the daughter of Laban his mother's brother, and the sheep of Laban his mother's brother, that Jacob went near and rolled the stone from the well's mouth, and watered the flock of Laban his mother's brother. Then Jacob kissed Rachel, and lifted up his voice and wept. And Jacob told Rachel that he was her father's relative and that he was Rebekah's son. So she ran and told her father. Genesis 29:7–12

1. a. What did Jacob ask the men at the well to do for the sheep and why?

   b. What do you think this reveals about Jacob's personality?

2. a. How did the men respond?

   b. Do you think this was reasonable? Please explain.

3. a. Describe how Jacob's actions mirrored the actions of his mother, Rebekah, when he saw Rachel (see Gen. 24:18).

b. Why might he have acted this way?

4. a. What physical and emotional responses did Jacob exhibit?

b. Do you think this was appropriate? Please explain.

5. How was Jacob linked to Rachel's family?

6. a. How did Rachel respond to this explanation?

b. Why do you think she reacted this way?

LIVE OUT ...

7. a. Depending upon who met him, Jacob could have come across as either conscientious or conniving. When people meet you for the first time, how do you think you come across?

b. Read Galatians 5:22–23, and determine what godly attribute God is working on in your life. How is He using your present circumstances to go about it?

8. We saw that Jacob kissed his cousin Rachel as a sign of affection. Read Psalm 2:11–12, and describe who you can kiss as a sign of affection and reverence. In what ways will you accomplish this?

9. Rachel ran to her father when she needed direction regarding her personal relationships. Journal a prayer to your heavenly Father about a relationship that is troubling you. Ask Him to give you

LEARN ABOUT ...

6 Dutiful Daughter

As welcome as Jacob's attentions might be, Rachel was honor bound to immediately alert her father to his presence. A modest girl would not accept the attention of any man, even one whom she might marry. In the patriarchal system of Old Testament days, the father's word was law.

7 Fruit of the Spirit

Jacob acted deceitfully to his father when he dressed up as his brother, Esau, and received his blessing. He also acted unfaithfully when he used the Lord's name to further his plans and continue the deception (see Gen. 27:7). God would use the time in Padan Aram to help Jacob develop patience and faith, among other things.

8 Kiss the Son

Here the word *kiss* means to come to subjection and friendship. The word *son* is not the Hebrew word *ben* but the Chaldee word *bar*. It could be that the influence of Rebekah, Rachel, and Jacob living in Haran passed through the generations and led to the prophetic psalm encouraging all of us to worship the Son.

wisdom and guidance. (Please note, this does not have to be a prayer about a "love" relationship—God cares about every relationship in your life.)

o o • o o

Over the past few decades our culture has promoted the idea that "real men don't cry." Somehow the idea of the rough-and-tough macho man has gotten a grip on the male psyche. It could be a holdover from Western movies. Those were the days when everyone was ready to "shoot 'em up" and "ride 'em, cowboy!" It could be a residue from the world wars and the cold war, when our nation banded together to fight the growing menace of the "isms": facism, Nazism, communism, terrorism, etc. Whatever the reason, it was not cool for men to show their emotions on the surface.

However, the Bible seems to have a different opinion of what makes a real man. We saw Jacob burst into tears at the sight of his bride-to-be. Was Jacob a man who lacked courage? Absolutely not! In those days men were rough and tough like cowboys in the old West. And like soldiers, they were strong enough to fight wild animals. Remember David, who killed a lion and a bear (1 Sam. 17:34–35)? And don't forget that Jacob rolled the massive stone away by himself. Jacob reminds us of another strong man who was tender enough to cry—Jesus Christ. Jesus' visit to the tomb of his dear friend Lazarus gives us the shortest verse in the Bible: "Jesus wept" (John 11:35).

Real men *do* cry. The Man who can raise the dead, the Man who rolled the stone from the grave, the Man who conquered sin and death so we can live eternally was man enough to cry. He's the type of Man we can run to in a crisis.

LISTEN TO ...

Respect is what we owe; love is what we give.

—*Philip James Bailey*

DAY 3

Father of the Brides

Let's face it; planning a wedding can be stressful for everyone involved. The bride may have been dreaming of this day since childhood. The mother of the bride probably wants to be involved in every detail of the planning. And the father of the bride has quite a few duties he must undertake. He is responsible for paying for the wedding and reception. People look to him to be the calm in the midst of the storm. And last but certainly not least, he must walk his little girl down the aisle and give her away whether he likes it or not. When the pastor or officiant of the ceremony asks, "Who gives this woman in marriage to this man?" the father, usually with a lump in his throat, responds, "I do."

This ritual probably hearkens back to the times when marriages were arranged between families. In the case of the Hebrews, the father, as God's representative on earth, made an alliance for the well-being of his clan, his tribe, and the nation. The young people agreed as though God were speaking through their fathers. As we've seen, especially in the case of the patriarchal progeny, the bloodline was particularly important. At this time, God did not want the bloodline tainted with that of the Canaanites (although later, Rahab, the Canaanite harlot, would be grafted into the family tree when the Israelites conquered Jericho). Thus Jacob, like his father before him, went to Padan Aram in the land of Haran to meet the father of the bride. Little did he know there would be two brides.

LIFT UP ...

Lord, You embrace me as beautiful. I know that nothing can separate me from Your love. Please empower me to love others with the strength and purity of Your love. Amen.

LOOK AT ...

Jacob traveled far to find his bride. When he found her, he revealed that he was her long-lost relative, exultantly kissing her and weeping. In ancient Israel and other Near Eastern

LEARN ABOUT ...

2 Warm Welcome

Near Eastern cultures were given to hospitality. Any relative was welcomed warmly. Even strangers were welcomed with open arms. In addition, Laban's sister, Rebekah, was given a large *mohar* from Abraham when his servant Eliezer came to Haran to seek a bride for Isaac. With two unmarried daughters, this might have crossed Laban's mind.

cultures, the fathers of the bride and groom entered into marriage arrangements. They negotiated to have their children marry each other and agreed upon a bridal price known as a *mohar*. The *mohar* would be agreed upon and paid by the bridegroom and his family to the father for the loss of his daughter.

The *mohar* was paid either in money or services. The loss of a daughter could be costly for a tribe. For instance, Rachel was very valuable to her father as a shepherdess. To lose her meant Laban would be forced to replace her with another. But Jacob had no relatives present, so he had to negotiate for himself.

READ GENESIS 29:13–19.

Then it came to pass, when Laban heard the report about Jacob his sister's son, that he ran to meet him, and embraced him and kissed him, and brought him to his house. So he told Laban all these things. And Laban said to him, "Surely you are my bone and my flesh." And he stayed with him for a month. Then Laban said to Jacob, "Because you are my relative, should you therefore serve me for nothing? Tell me, what should your wages be?" Now Laban had two daughters: the name of the elder was Leah, and the name of the younger was Rachel. Leah's eyes were delicate, but Rachel was beautiful of form and appearance. Now Jacob loved Rachel; so he said, "I will serve you seven years for Rachel your younger daughter." And Laban said, "It is better that I give her to you than that I should give her to another man. Stay with me." Genesis 29:13–19

1. a. How did Laban respond upon hearing about Jacob's arrival?

   b. How was this appropriate?

2. Review Lesson 6 about Rebekah. Why do you think Laban welcomed Jacob so warmly?

3. What did Jacob report to Laban? Based on what you know of Jacob's past, what do you think Jacob included in his report?

4. a. What conclusion did Laban reach about their family relationship, and how long did it take before he began to negotiate wages?

   b. What do you think this shows about Laban's character?

5. Describe Laban's daughters.

6. a. What did Jacob offer Laban for Rachel?

   b. Why do you think he made this offer?

7. How did Laban respond to this offer and why?

Live out ...

8. It seems that Laban expected Jacob to bring a large bride-price for a marriage with one of his daughters.

   a. Describe a time when you expected something from someone but did not receive it. How did you respond? How did things turn out?

   b. According to Psalm 62:5–6, what spiritual principle can you glean to help you the next time you're in such a situation?

9. Today we again saw the importance of offering hospitality to friends, relatives, and strangers. Abraham and Lot entertained angels, and Laban welcomed his nephew.

Learn About ...

5 Different Daughters

Leah had "delicate eyes." Some think this means her eyes were weak, or had bad vision. Others believe her eyes were pale, lacking luster and sparkle. Ancient rabbis believed Leah's eyes were delicate from weeping, because as the older daughter she thought she was destined to marry Esau. Rachel, on the other hand, was beautiful to behold.

7 Marriage Mentioned

Jacob offered to work for his wage and the bride-price for his beloved Rachel. However, Laban did not fully commit to the marriage. Did Jacob hear what he wanted to hear, or did Laban lead him on? How much better to "put away from you a deceitful mouth, and put perverse lips far from you" (Prov. 4:24).

8 Monetary Motives

God sees the heart and knows exactly what motivates us. Would you do for God what you'd do for gold? Jesus warned, "No one can serve two masters; for either he will hate the one and love the other.... You cannot serve God and mammon [wealth]" (Matt. 6:24).

a. Fill in the following chart to discover others who offered the gift of hospitality.

SCRIPTURE	WHO OFFERED HOSPITALITY TO WHOM
2 Samuel 6:18–19	
2 Kings 4:8–10	
Acts 16:14–15	

b. How has God blessed you when you welcomed others into your home and heart?

10. Journal about which of the two sisters you most relate to and why.

o o ● o o

Jacob offered to work seven years to pay the bride-price, or *mohar,* to Laban. Jacob, the son who was prone to getting his own way quickly, showed that he was willing to wait and work for the one he loved. More well-known to us than the practice of *mohar* is the marriage custom known as the dowry. This is a reverse bride-price where the bride's family pays money or goods so the couple can set up housekeeping. To the modern reader, this may seem archaic. We don't typically bring dowries into our marriages. Generally, we prepare for married life when friends and families bestow wedding gifts at showers or the wedding reception. But some see the cost of the wedding as a "dowry" of sorts. Most parents believe that the bride and groom will receive gifts equal to the price of the wedding.

However, in the Middle Ages, the father of the bride was responsible for paying his daughter's dowry. The story is told of one father in Myra, Turkey, who was so poor that he could not afford to provide a dowry for his three daughters. A man named Nicholas heard of the family's plight and was filled with compassion. So he decided to come to their aid.

When the eldest daughter reached marriageable age, he sneaked by the house in the dark of night and threw a stocking full of money into an open window. He repeated this action for each of the girls. Thus began the tradition of tacking stockings onto the fireplace at Christmas to be filled by St. Nicholas. You see, Nicholas became known as St. Nicholas, the model for Santa Claus, a real man who believed in the power of love.

LISTEN TO ...

God's fingers can touch nothing but to mould it into loveliness.

—George MacDonald

DAY 4

Love's Labours Lost

One of William Shakespeare's earlier plays, *Love's Labours Lost,* builds on some of the themes found in the love story of Rachel and Jacob. In the play, King Ferdinand of Navarre makes a contract with three of his lords. One of the conditions is that the men give up women in order to pursue knowledge. The lords, wanting to please their king, agree. In Shakespearean fashion, the beautiful princess of France arrives on a diplomatic mission to discuss a financial matter. She brings three lovely attendants along. Of course, the king's lords fall in love with the maidens and violate the contract, as does the king himself.

Usually in Shakespeare's romantic comedies the characters live happily ever after. However, this play ends differently. The princess finds out that the king and his lords have broken a vow. She also learns that her father has died. So she proclaims that she and her ladies will not entertain proposals from the men for a year. One must go to a hermitage to grow spiritually. One must go to bring joy to people in hospitals. Two others are commissioned to become thoughtful and mature in the year they are given. Two key themes emerge from this play: True love is tested in the crucible of time, and true character is developed when love is put to the test.

Today we'll see that Jacob agreed to labor seven long years to win the hand of his true love only to be deceived by Laban on his wedding night. How would his character be shaped by the events that unfolded?

LIFT UP ...

God, although we live in a world filled with the lies of deceitful men, I take comfort in knowing that You will never deceive me. Your Word is truth, and I will hold it in my heart. Help me to forgive the people whose lies or deceptions have hurt me. Amen.

LOOK AT ...

Jacob believed he made a contract with Laban to work seven years in return for Rachel's hand in marriage. But Laban had different plans for Jacob as well as his two daughters. Some people view the Laban-Jacob agreement in light of Hurrian laws discovered in the Nuzi area of northern Mesopotamia. Because the biblical laws hadn't yet been written down, Laban may have adhered to these codes.

Laban seems to have had no male heir at this point and might have considered his agreement with Jacob an adoption-marriage contract. Typically, the adopted son would work to pay the bride-price. The bride and any children would become the father's property. However, years later Laban had sons of his own, and their inheritance was jeopardized by the presence of Jacob's family (see Gen. 31:1). Rachel and Leah began to be treated badly by their family, so Jacob decided to go home (see Gen. 31:15).Viewing Laban's life in light of the Hurrian tablets helps us understand why Laban would want Jacob to marry his daughters.[5]

READ GENESIS 29:20–27.

So Jacob served seven years for Rachel, and they seemed only a few days to him because of the love he had for her. Then Jacob said to Laban, "Give me my wife, for my days are fulfilled, that I may go in to her." And Laban gathered together all the men of the place and made a feast. Now it came to pass in the evening, that he took Leah his daughter and brought her to Jacob; and he went in to her. And Laban gave his maid Zilpah to his daughter Leah as a maid. So it came to pass in the morning, that behold, it was Leah. And he said to Laban, "What is this you have done to me? Was it not for Rachel that I served you? Why then have you deceived me?" And Laban said, "It must not be done so in our country, to give the younger before the firstborn. Fulfill her week, and we will give you this one also for the service which you will serve with me still another seven years." Genesis 29:20–27

1. Describe the seven years Jacob spent working for Rachel's hand.

2. What did Jacob ask of Laban?

3. What did Laban do to make Jacob think he was complying with his request?

LEARN ABOUT …

1 Working Fast

Time seemed to fly as Jacob worked seven years, the number he had set to work for his bride. Seven is a sacred number to the ancient Hebrew people. The word is used often in the Bible to symbolize perfection, fullness, abundance, rest, and completion. Jacob believed he worked a perfect amount of time to obtain true love.

---

2 Wanting a Wife

Jacob the deceiver was truly deceived. Perhaps he made the grave mistake of not being specific enough. He said, "Give me my wife," to Laban rather than, "Give me Rachel." We don't know when Laban made the plan to replace Leah with Rachel, but the door opened at that moment, and the trap was sprung.

LEARN ABOUT ...

5 Waking Furious

Leah probably appeared in the dark of the night, heavily veiled. She may have had some similar physical characteristics to her sister Rachel. It could be that Jacob had overindulged at the wedding feast. Whatever the reason, he did not recognize the deception until the marriage was consummated and the light of day came.

7 Well-Spent Time

We measure time in seconds, hours, days, weeks, months, and years. Biblically, God exists eternally, while humans exist in the time-space framework. Solomon declared, "There is ... a time for every purpose under heaven" (Eccl. 3:1).[6] Are you using your time for God's good, or are you wasting time?

9 Words of Comfort

Laban justified his deceitful actions by saying he sent Leah because it was the custom. Jacob accepted this and moved forward rather than looking backward. Our heavenly Father only speaks the truth. Solomon wrote, "Let not mercy and truth forsake you; bind them around your neck, write them on the tablet of your heart" (Prov. 3:3).

4. How did Laban dupe Jacob, and who might have helped him?

5. Describe when the deception was discovered and how Jacob responded.

6. How did Laban explain his actions, and what did he offer to Jacob?

LIVE OUT ...

7. We saw that time flew for Jacob when he thought he was working toward the goal of marrying Rachel. Which of the following time statements reflects your personal views and why?

   ❏ Time is on my side.
   ❏ Time waits for no one.
   ❏ There's no time like the present.
   ❏ Time is money.
   ❏ Redeeming the time, for the days are evil.
   ❏ Other _____

8. Leah dressed up as her sister, Rachel and went into Jacob's tent. We don't know the motive, but we know the result—Jacob was shocked. Sometimes we do the same thing and "dress up" as Christians. In what ways, past or present, have you perhaps looked like a Christian without really being one?

9. Jacob asked Laban, "What have you done to me?" Describe a time you felt deceived by someone. How did the person justify his or her actions?

○ ○ ● ○ ○

In March 1925, an editor in Anacostia grew tired of being called a liar. He decided to write only the whole truth about everything. One wedding announcement read as follows:

> Married: Miss Sylvan Rhodes and James Collins, last Saturday at the Baptist parsonage, by Rev. J. Gordon. The bride is a very ordinary town girl, who doesn't know any more about cooking than a jack rabbit, and never helped her mother three days in her life. She is not a beauty by any means, and has a gait like a duck. The groom is an up to-date loafer. He has been living off the old folks at home all his life; and is not worth shucks. It will be a hard life.[7]

What if the editor of the *Haran Herald* printed the truth about Jacob and Leah's wedding?

> Married: Leah and Jacob last night at the home of Laban after a seven-year engagement. The bride has weak eyes and is not as beautiful as her sister Rachel. She was attended by her handmaid Zilpah. The groom is a hard worker but prone to deception. He probably got what he deserved when his father-in-law deceived him into thinking he could marry Rachel. The three will not have it easy.

Two ironies should be noted before we leave the wedding scene: (1) Jacob deceived his father and was in turn deceived by his father-in-law; (2) Jacob deceived his father dressed in Esau's clothes, and Leah deceived Jacob dressed in Rachel's clothes. "Do not be deceived, God is not mocked; for whatever a man sows, that he will also reap" (Gal. 6:7).

Listen to ...

O what a tangled web we weave, when first we practice to deceive!

—*Walter Scott*

DAY 5

First Comes Love?

Do you remember singing the playground rhyme K-I-S-S-I-N-G when jumping rope?

> Harry and Sally,
> Sittin' in a tree,
> K-I-S-S-I-N-G
> First comes love,
> Then comes marriage,
> Then comes Harry with a baby carriage!

The silly rhyme describes the proper sequence of events for thriving families: (1) love, (2) marriage, and then (3) children. Sadly, Jacob and Leah didn't exactly follow the schedule defined by the rhyme. While marriage and childbirth followed each other, love in the relationship was tragically one sided. Leah truly loved Jacob, but her love was not reciprocated, for Jacob loved Rachel, Leah's sister, throughout their lives. One can't help but pity Leah. And that seems to be the godly response, for God "saw that Leah was unloved" (Gen. 29:31). Therefore, He opened her womb and gave her multiple children. "The unattractive Leah may have repelled others, but God was attracted toward her because of an inner beauty which the lovely Rachel lacked," wrote Herbert Lockyer.[8] The names that Leah gave her children testify of her intimate relationship with the Lord. Scripture records that Rachel used "Elohim," the mere word for God when addressing the Life-Giver, while Leah used "Jehovah," God's intimate covenant name at the birth of her first four sons.

Leah's testimony serves to comfort modern female counterparts who may feel neglected or despised by their husbands. If her story parallels yours, may it have the same results. Unloved by a man, she fell in love with the Lord. She went from desperately trying to gain her husband's affection to basking in God's goodness and grace.

Lift up ...

Lord, I confess that there have been times when I have felt unloved and unwanted. Thank You for loving me unconditionally and showering me with Your favor. Amen.

Look at ...

Jacob woke up completely shocked to find he was married to Leah instead of Rachel. Laban, rather than apologizing, offered a compromise: Work seven more years and marry Rachel as well. Despite the example of monogamy in his parents' marriage, Jacob accepted the offer and agreed to Laban's plan, thus following the local custom of marrying more than one woman.

Jacob never criticized Leah for her part in the subterfuge. Over the years he performed a husband's duties to her. It's possible that Leah experienced unrequited love for Jacob. It was always obvious that Jacob loved Rachel most. In the Old Testament, the word used concerning marriage comes from the word *checed,* which is translated loving-kindness. This type of love speaks of a strong and steadfast love. However, when it is said that Jacob "loved" Rachel, the word *ahab* is used, implying an affectionate sexual love. Thus, Jacob loved Rachel passionately and Leah persistently.

Read Genesis 29:28–35.

Then Jacob did so and fulfilled her week. So he gave him his daughter Rachel as wife also. And Laban gave his maid Bilhah to his daughter Rachel as a maid. Then Jacob also went in to Rachel, and he also loved Rachel more than Leah. And he served with Laban still another seven years. When the LORD saw that Leah was unloved, He opened her womb; but Rachel was barren. So Leah conceived and bore a son, and she called his name Reuben; for she said, "The LORD has surely looked on my affliction. Now therefore, my husband will love me." Then she conceived again and bore a son, and said, "Because the LORD has heard that I am unloved, He has therefore given me this son also." And she called his name Simeon. She conceived again and bore a son, and said, "Now this time my husband will become attached to me, because I have borne him three sons." Therefore his name was called Levi. And she conceived again and bore a

son, and said, "Now I will praise the L<small>ORD</small>." *Therefore she called his name Judah. Then she stopped bearing.* Genesis 29:28–35

LEARN ABOUT ...

3 Unloved

God loved Leah as much as He loved Rachel regardless of how Jacob felt. Therefore, He took action to rectify the situation by allowing Jacob's beloved to experience infertility and Jacob's unloved to be fruitful. Sons were essential to a man's societal standing. Perhaps God hoped that Jacob would learn to value Leah, since he valued the sons she bore him.

---

4 Unfruitful

Barrenness means the inability to bear children. It was viewed as a curse or punishment from God. "In the Bible, the term is also applied figuratively to anything that is unproductive, such as land (2 Kings 2:19) or a nation (Isa. 54:1)."[9] Biblical figures who suffered from infertility were Sarah, Rebekah, and Hannah.

---

7 Unburdened

Judah's name meant praise. We see Leah praising the Lord rather than pining for her husband upon the child's birth. God honored her for putting His love above Jacob's. Judah's offspring would become the kingly line from which the Messiah would one day be born. Leah found an outlet for her great love!

1. What was Jacob doing at the beginning of this passage of Scripture?

2. How did Laban reward Jacob's labor?

3. In what way does this passage compare Jacob's love for his two wives?

4. Describe what the Lord saw and how He responded.

5. Put yourself in the place of each sister. Describe briefly how each would feel based on Jacob's and God's reactions.

   Leah

   Rachel

6. Leah had four sons in the beginning. List their names and why she named them as she did.

7. How do we leave Leah?

LIVE OUT ...

8. Today we observed a contrast between the love of God and human love. God loves unconditionally, while people often place conditions on their love. Place the following Scripture references in the column that best describes the type of love displayed: 1 Samuel 1:5; 1 Samuel 18:1–3; 2 Samuel 13:1, 14–15; 1 Kings 11:1–2; John 3:16, 19.

UNCONDITIONAL   **CONDITIONAL**

LEARN ABOUT …

8 Loved

There are several words in Greek for the English word *love*. The word *phileo* describes a love that shows ardent affection or feeling. It is an impulsive and inconsistent love. The word *agapao* means to possess high esteem or regard. It is the opposite of selfishness. Its absence invalidates one's claim to being a Christian.

---

9 Fruitful

Biblically, fruit is often literal as in figs or grapes. Sometimes it is used figuratively to describe human beings, their attributes, or the outcome of their actions. God made Sarah's womb fruitful even in old age. But if you are not blessed with physical children, perhaps God will bless you with spiritual children to love.

9. The Lord's hand was behind Leah's fruitfulness and Rachel's infertility. Name an acquaintance who is going through the pain of infertility. Rewrite the following Scripture into a personal prayer on her behalf.

> "Abide in Me, and I in you. As the branch cannot bear fruit of itself, unless it abides in the vine, neither can you, unless you abide in Me. I am the vine, you are the branches. He who abides in Me, and I in him, bears much fruit; for without Me you can do nothing." John 15:4–5

10. Scripture uses the word *fruit* to describe more than agricultural produce. Place a check in the box to indicate the kind of fruit that has grown in your life.

❏ "fruit of the womb" (Gen. 30:2)
❏ "fruit of the arrogant heart" (Isa. 10:12)
❏ "fruit of lies" (Hos. 10:13)
❏ "fruit of their own way" (Prov. 1:31)
❏ "fruit of the Spirit" (Gal. 5:22–23)
❏ "fruits of righteousness" (Phil. 1:11)

∘ ∘ ● ∘ ∘

Leah was considered the homely sister, while Rachel was considered the beautiful one. Unfortunately, like all humans, they were both flawed.

Throughout their marriage to Jacob, they vied for his affection, even drawing their servants into the mix.

You might think they would have learned from their forefather Abraham the consequences of bringing children into the picture through helpless handmaidens. But Rachel's infertility made her desperate for children. And Leah's jealousy made her eager to get back at her sister through the arms of another woman. They enlisted their maidservants, Zilpah and Bilhah, as surrogates to produce offspring for Jacob. Thus, the twelve tribes of Jacob came into being through the shortcomings and sinful wranglings of desperate women.

Jacob's family multiplied steadily while they lived in Padan Aram. When he arrived, he brought with him only a simple shepherd's rod as he fled from his brother Esau's wrath. Over the twenty-year period he resided in Haran, he acquired wives and children in abundance—twelve sons and one daughter. His deal with Laban ensured that he left Haran a wealthy man—he "became exceedingly prosperous, and had large flocks, female and male servants, and camels and donkeys" (Gen. 30:43). But his freedom came at a high price: His family was divided. The future in the Promised Land was unforeseen. But God's sure hand of providence beckoned Jacob and his family home. There they would face more hardship: death, sorrow, and pain. What would it take to unite the tribes of Israel?

LISTEN TO ...

Grace is the love that gives, that loves the unlovely and the unlovable.

—*Oswald C. Hoffmann*

Dinah—True Love Waits

Genesis 34

If we could protect them every day, every minute, every second of their lives, we would. We would watch their every move and guard them from harm. But our daughters grow up and spread their wings. Like little birds they want to fly from the nest. As parents, our job is to teach them to soar safely. They go to school. To work. To play. They develop friendships. They have places to go, people to see, and things to do. And in a fallen world, bad things sometimes happen to good girls.

The numbers are staggering. According to the 2003 Department of Justice Report, *Acquaintance Rape of College Students*, it is estimated that one out of four college women has been a victim of rape or attempted rape since the age of fourteen. Kelli Mahoney of about.com reports that Christian teen girls in college are most susceptible to rape during the first few weeks of their freshman and sophomore years. Also, teens between the ages of sixteen and nineteen are 3.5 times more likely than older women to be victims of rape or attempted rape. Fifty percent of rape victims are under the age of eighteen. The actual number of rape victims is unknown because fewer than 5 percent report the crime.[1]

"Date rape" and "acquaintance rape" are terms coined in the late 1980s by Robin Warshaw in her book *I Never Called It Rape*. She helped break the silence on many women's secret shame and sorrow. By bringing this subject to light, she took a step toward helping society realize that no means no, whatever the circumstance.

This week we'll see that Jacob's daughter, Dinah, was the victim of rape. But when her family learned about the situation, they didn't comfort her or seek God's help—they sought revenge.

Day 1: Genesis 34:1–4   **TOO CLOSE FOR COMFORT**

Day 2: Genesis 34:5–12   **TOO LITTLE, TOO LATE**

Day 3: Genesis 34:13–18   **TWO CAN PLAY THAT GAME**

Day 4: Genesis 34:19–24   **TOO GOOD TO BE TRUE**

Day 5: Genesis 34:25–31   **TOO MUCH TO ASK**

DAY 1

Too Close for Comfort

LIFT UP ...

Father, You're the one who watches over me wherever I go. Thank You for being with me even in the most difficult times. Amen.

LOOK AT ...

After twenty years in Haran, Jacob separated from Laban. He and his large family left Haran to return to the Land of Promise. They must have been an imposing force making their way to Canaan. The journey was surely eventful. Jacob encountered God in human form (a theophany) and wrestled with Him all night. By morning neither had prevailed, so the Man put Jacob's hip out of joint. But Jacob would not let go of the God-man without a blessing. So God renamed Jacob "Israel" and blessed him (see Gen. 32:22–31). Next Jacob had a tearful reunion with his estranged brother, Esau (see Gen. 33:4), then "came safely to the city of Shechem, which is in the land of Canaan" (see Gen. 33:18). Most believe Jacob pitched his tent too close to the idolatrous city.

Almost thirty years have passed since Jacob went to Padan Aram. Jacob purchased land in Shechem instead of returning to Bethel and his father's house as he promised God when he left the Promised Land (see Gen. 33:18–19). Now we meet Jacob's daughter, Dinah. The Bible doesn't shield us from the harsh reality of Dinah's story; rather, it shows us how things can go terribly wrong for a young girl out on her own.

READ GENESIS 34:1–4.

Now Dinah the daughter of Leah, whom she had borne to Jacob, went out to see the daughters of the land. And when Shechem the son of Hamor the Hivite, prince of the country, saw her, he took her and lay with her, and violated her. His soul was strongly attracted to Dinah the daughter of Jacob, and he loved the young woman and spoke kindly to the young woman. So

LEARN ABOUT ...

2 To See

Dinah, who was between twelve and fifteen years old, left her family's home, apparently without a chaperone. She wanted to see how the girls "of the land" lived. The historian Josephus records that Dinah went to a Canaanite festival of nature worship. As a young, single Hebrew girl, she would have been forbidden to attend this pagan festival.

4 To Be Seen

Apparently Dinah was a beautiful young girl who attracted the attention of Prince Shechem. We know he *saw* her. This means he gazed or beheld her, perhaps even spied on her. One definition of the word, according to *Strong's Hebrew Dictionary*, compares this to the sight of a bird of prey, probably a vulture known for being sharp sighted.[2]

5 To Sully

Some commentators believe that Shechem seduced Dinah into submitting to his advances. However, the original language does not lend itself to this idea. The Hebrew words used are strong and speak of rape: He "took her" implies that he carried her away; "lay with her" means he had intercourse with her; "violated her" means he dealt harshly or exercised force.

Shechem spoke to his father Hamor, saying, "Get me this young woman as a wife." Genesis 34:1–4

1. Who were Dinah's parents?

2. Where did Dinah go?

3. Put yourself in her young teenage shoes. What do you think she was in search of as she went out?

4. Who saw her, and what did he do to her?

5. a. Following the violation, how did Shechem feel and act toward Dinah?

   b. Do you think this is common in this type of situation? What makes you say that?

6. What did Shechem ask his father to do?

LIVE OUT ...

7. Dinah supposedly went out "to see" the religious rites of the pagan Canaanites and socialize with the girls of the city. Describe a time when you socialized with the wrong people. How did it make you feel, and what were the consequences?

8. a. Shechem saw Dinah walking among the townsfolk and like a bird of prey swooped in on her when she was vulnerable. Fill in the following chart to discover how we are to walk in these dangerous days.

SCRIPTURE

HOW TO WALK

Deuteronomy 10:12

Psalm 84:11

Psalm 101:2

Ephesians 5:15

LEARN ABOUT ...

7 To Socialize

We don't know if Dinah had permission to visit the daughters of the land. There's no mention of where Leah was while Dinah was out socializing. Perhaps Dinah slipped away from the care of her servants. Historically, most Hebrew girls were not permitted to go out unsupervised. She was vulnerable and running with the wrong crowd.

b. How can you improve your spiritual walk?

c. How will you help your children learn to walk carefully?

9. a. Shechem claimed to love Dinah after he violated her. Read 2 Samuel 13:7–15, and describe how Amnon treated his sister Tamar after forcing her to have sex with him.

b. According to Jesus in Mark 7:21–23, why do men become capable of defiling women?

6 To Seek

The phrase "get me" leads us to believe that Shechem viewed Dinah as a possession to purchase, not a woman to woo. Only after raping her did he seek her heart and hand. He may have been trying to make amends for his abominable behavior. Samson used similar language: "Get her for me" (Judg. 14:3).

c. According to 1 Corinthians 6:11, how can we be cleansed?

o o ● o o

Most counselors agree on ways to protect single girls against acquaintance rape:

8 To Stroll

Some of us treat our spiritual journeys as a stroll in the park until something dreadful happens. That's when we turn to the Lord for protection and direction. Thankfully, God never leaves our side. The psalmist wrote, "Though I walk in the midst of trouble, You will revive me" (Ps. 138:7).

- Set boundaries early.
- Go on group dates rather than alone.
- Don't drink alcohol, because it can lower inhibitions and make the situation volatile.
- Carry a cell phone in case of emergency.
- Use your voice. Say no loudly.
- Drive your own car, or have money for a taxi if necessary.
- Pour your own beverage, and never let it leave your sight so it can't be tampered with.

Even Christian girls can fall victim to date rape. The date rape pill Rohypnol is widely available on the black market. Like alcohol, "roofies" make some people highly aggressive. The more frightening effect is blackouts and complete loss of memory. *Newsweek* reported about the high incidence of rape in Broward County, Florida. Prosecutor Bob Nichols said that rape cases involving roofies are difficult to prosecute because the victim usually can't remember any details of the crime. He did get lucky in the case of Mark Perez, a satellite-dish installer from Pembroke Pines, Florida. Perez boasted to friends that he had drugged and raped a dozen women, most of whom he had picked up in bars. He pleaded no contest to one count of sexually battering a helpless person and received an eight-year prison sentence.[3]

No doubt Dinah carried the memories of being violated throughout her life. With love, prayer, and forgiveness, the victim of rape can move from surviving to thriving. The most helpful thing you can do as a friend or family member is to remind the victim that it wasn't her fault.

LISTEN TO ...

Sin is the dare of God's justice, the rape of his mercy, the jeer of his patience, the slight of his power, and the contempt of his love.

—*John Bunyan*

DAY 2

Too Little, Too Late

Nancy Gibbs of *Time* gives us some insight into the history of rape: "Rapes have been divided between those that mattered and those that did not. For the first few thousand years, the only rape that was punished was the defiling of a virgin, and that was viewed as a property crime." Throughout time, women have been viewed as property or assets. Many times, rapists were not sentenced to prison but ordered to pay a price for a girl's loss of virtue. William the Conqueror did impose penalties: castration and loss of both eyes. But he did allow the woman the option of marrying her attacker. There's also historical precedent for men "stealing an heiress" or literally "taking a wife."[4]

While rape victims may feel like they don't matter to the justice system or to a male-dominated society, we know that victims of rape matter to God. He is the God who catches our tears in a bottle and counts the number of hairs on our heads. When God established the Levitical law, He made sure that innocent women were not punished, but rather cared for and protected. In the book of Exodus, God decreed that if a man "enticed" a woman who was not betrothed, he was responsible for paying the bride-price and marrying the girl (see Ex. 22:16). If a man forced an engaged virgin girl to have sex with him, God pronounced the death penalty upon the man. But He proclaimed, "You shall do nothing to the young woman; there is in the young woman no sin deserving of death" (Deut. 22:26).

Shechem may have been following the conventions of the day in offering to marry Dinah. Maybe he was "taking a bride" in order to gain her wealth. He probably thought she didn't matter. His offer might have been too little, too late.

LIFT UP ...

God, thank You for including me in Your family circle. I'm so grateful that You love and protect women with Your love and in Your Law. Help me to stay in Your perfect will. Amen.

LOOK AT ...

Yesterday we saw Dinah fall victim to Shechem, the prince of the land. Some commentators believe Dinah visited the "daughters of the land" on several occasions and made the acquaintance of Shechem prior to this. Others see Shechem as an aggressive young male who exercised power over a naive young girl visiting the city for the first time. The Bible does not explain what happened beforehand, so it's better to take the incident at face value: Dinah went to town and was raped by the prince. Shechem was drawn to Dinah, even claimed to love her, and proposed marriage. Today we see Jacob learn what happened to his daughter. We also see Shechem approach Jacob and his sons with his proposal.

We know Dinah was in the wrong place at the wrong time. Could it be she was there partially because of Jacob's choices? He bought property in the land God promised to give him by faith. He built a dwelling place in close proximity to a pagan city. There is no mention of God in this chapter. Warren Wiersbe said, "When we disobey the Lord, we put ourselves and our loved ones in danger."[5]

READ GENESIS 34:5–12.

And Jacob heard that he had defiled Dinah his daughter. Now his sons were with his livestock in the field; so Jacob held his peace until they came. Then Hamor the father of Shechem went out to Jacob to speak with him. And the sons of Jacob came in from the field when they heard it; and the men were grieved and very angry, because he had done a disgraceful thing in Israel by lying with Jacob's daughter, a thing which ought not to be done. But Hamor spoke with them, saying, "The soul of my son Shechem longs for your daughter. Please give her to him as a wife. And make marriages with us; give your daughters to us, and take our daughters to yourselves. So you shall dwell with us, and the land shall be before you. Dwell and trade in it, and acquire possessions for yourselves in it." Then Shechem said to her father and her brothers, "Let me find favor in your eyes, and whatever you say to me I will give. Ask me ever so much dowry and gift, and I will give according to what you say to me; but give me the young woman as a wife." Genesis 34:5–12

1. a. When Jacob heard about Dinah's defilement, how did he respond and why?

   b. Explain whether you think this was the right thing to do.

2. Describe how the sons of Jacob felt and why.

3. Talk about the man who came to "fix" the situation and why you think he pleaded his son's case.

4. What did Hamor offer the Israelites …

   socially?

   territorially?

   financially?

5. What did Shechem ask Jacob for?

6. What did Shechem offer?

LIVE OUT …

7. Jacob seemed to abdicate his role as father where Dinah was concerned. Fill in the following chart to discover the duties of a dedicated dad.

SCRIPTURE	DEDICATED DAD
Deuteronomy 11:18–21	
Ephesians 6:4	
1 Thessalonians 2:10–12	
Hebrews 12:7	

LEARN ABOUT …

1 Daughter Defiled

When Jacob heard his daughter had been defiled, he "held his peace" until his sons came home. Apparently he forgot what he promised at Bethel, "[If] I come back to my father's house in peace, then the LORD shall be my God" (Gen. 28:21). He should have prayed to his heavenly Father for wisdom and peace.

4 Nuptial Negotiations

Hamor used placating language to negotiate with Dinah's stunned father and angry brothers. Though he did not apologize, he used the word please when he asked for Dinah's hand in marriage. John Phillips said, "Had Jacob accepted the offer it would have wiped out the patriarchal line in a single generation."[6]

6 Find Favor

Whether it was passion or true love, Shechem interrupted his father's meeting with an offer to give any amount to have Dinah as his wife. Perhaps asking for "favor" was his way of offering an apology. Interestingly, he never referred to her as anything but the "young woman."

LEARN ABOUT …

7 Faithful Father

Since the first family in Eden, the father has been responsible for the family's spiritual well-being. Abraham functioned as priest for his family, building an altar and making sacrifices on their behalf. Throughout the ages, the father's role was to be the religious leader in the home. The father was also looked to as protector and provider.

8 Corrupt Canaanites

The Canaanites were a sexually immoral people who worshipped a fertility goddess and participated in lewd acts with temple prostitutes. Their religion appealed to the most sordid instincts in people. They did not understand the Hebrews' desire for purity and holiness.

8. According to Genesis 24:1–4 and Genesis 28:1, what did God warn Jacob and Isaac against?

9. Based on what you've learned, why did He warn against this? How would you apply this to a Christian?

○ ○ ● ○ ○

Love-struck Prince Shechem was willing to pay any price to get the object of his affections. Apparently, he was in the habit of getting what he wanted—and he wanted Dinah. His father, a ruler in the land, thought he made Jacob an offer he couldn't refuse. He could provide wives for all of his sons. Business opportunities galore. And land. There was enough land for all of them—so he said. Hamor dangled the carrot. Would Jacob take the bite?

You can almost hear the wheels turning in Jacob's mind. If it were modern times, these might have been his thoughts: *Let's face it, Dinah has been ruined. She might as well marry the boy.*

Then another thought flew swiftly by: *What will her mother say?*

And another: *What church will they go to?*

Then this: *What about children?*

If Dinah didn't marry, she would wind up an old maid. If she did marry Shechem, she might turn to the Canaanites' religion. What was a father to do?

The reality of the situation was that God gave the land to Abraham and his descendants. No one, including Hamor, could give Jacob the inheritance he had already been promised from God. It was a done deal. But Jacob and his family got caught up in the emotion of their situation and failed to look to God for guidance. They listened to the words of men rather than stopping to wait on God. What's a father to do? Turn to the heavenly Father.

LISTEN TO ...

Becoming a father is easy enough, but being one can be very rough.

—*Wilhelm Busch*

DAY 3

Two Can Play That Game

Dwight D. Eisenhower became president of the United States in 1953. He was a popular president, mostly because of his military success in World War II. Raised in rural Kansas, he was one of seven boys. President Eisenhower described his mother as a smart and godly woman. The story is told how one night on the farm Mrs. Eisenhower played a card game called Flinch with her boys. He said, "Mother was the dealer, and she dealt me a very bad hand. I began to complain. Mother said, 'Boys, put down your cards. I want to say something, particularly to Dwight. You are in a game in your home with your mother and brothers who love you. But out in the world you will be dealt bad hands without love. Here is some advice for you boys. Take those bad hands without complaining and play them out. Ask God to help you, and you will win the important game called life.'" The president added, "I've tried to follow that wise advice always."[7]

In the game of life, Dinah was dealt a bad hand when she was taken by Shechem and lost her purity. Hamor tried to win political and personal advantage through his son's sin by raising the stakes and offering the tribe of Israel great financial gain. Jacob folded his hand. But his sons decided that they could play the game by cheating and lying.

LIFT UP ...

Lord, I know that Your Word is truth, and in it there is no deceit. Help me to speak truth to those I encounter. I pray for wisdom and mercy when I deal with the world. Amen.

LOOK AT ...

Yesterday we saw Jacob field Hamor's offer of marriage for Dinah as well as brides for Jacobs's boys, land for the tribe, and trade for the people. Could it be he was trying to buy the family's favor? Impetuously, Shechem offered Jacob whatever he asked for Dinah's hand. Jacob seemed to be at an impasse, unsure of what to do.

Today we'll see that Dinah's brothers entered into the negotiations with their father. Though we have seen that Jacob had made great spiritual progress and gave up his deceitful

ways, his sons were devious. Like Laban who bargained on behalf of his sister Rebekah, Jacob's sons took it upon themselves to strike a deal using their religious practices to achieve their ends. We know they had no intention of allowing Dinah to marry Shechem. To their everlasting shame, they used hypocritical spiritual means to settle the score.

READ GENESIS 34:13–18.

But the sons of Jacob answered Shechem and Hamor his father, and spoke deceitfully, because he had defiled Dinah their sister. And they said to them, "We cannot do this thing, to give our sister to one who is uncircumcised, for that would be a reproach to us. But on this condition we will consent to you: If you will become as we are, if every male of you is circumcised, then we will give our daughters to you, and we will take your daughters to us; and we will dwell with you, and we will become one people. But if you will not heed us and be circumcised, then we will take our daughter and be gone." And their words pleased Hamor and Shechem, Hamor's son. Genesis 34:13–18

1. As Jacob's sons took over the negotiations, how did they speak and why?

2. What would the brothers consider a reproach? Did this reasoning make sense?

3. What condition did they require for giving their consent? Do you think they believed Shechem and Hamor would agree to this condition?

4. What four things did they promise to do if the men were circumcised?

5. What did they threaten to do if the men did not agree?

LEARN ABOUT …

I Deceitful

It doesn't appear that Jacob was in on his sons' scheme. They may have come up with their plan while their father was negotiating with Hamor. Perhaps living with the deceitful Laban and hearing about their father's deceit affected them. Or perhaps they thought that the end justified the means. But deceit is never right.

2 Reproachful

Ancient Eastern cultures believed that brothers were more deeply disgraced by a sister's fall than that of a wife because the wife could be divorced but a sister could not. Here Dinah's brothers believed the rape was a reproach or insult to themselves: "We have become a reproach to our neighbors, a scorn and derision to those who are around us" (Ps. 79:4).

LEARN ABOUT ...

6 Agreeable

The Canaanites apparently viewed circumcision as a marriage ritual rather than a covenant relationship. They readily agreed to the condition the brothers set. We don't know if this was a surprise or if the brothers expected this. We do know that biblically, circumcision was intended to be an outward sign of an inward change of heart.

7 Deliver from Deceit

God hates deceit because it is one of Satan's tools. Jesus said, "He is a liar and the father of it" (John 8:44). Anytime we use deceit to get our way, we become like the Enemy. Trying to do the right thing the wrong way is never an excuse. Wanting justice for Dinah was no excuse for unjust behavior.

8 Reproach Removed

In the Old Testament, infertile and unmarried women felt disgrace and reproach because the society highly valued marriage and children. Dinah's reproach must have felt even more profound. But like Elizabeth, John the Baptist's mother, when we seek God's help, we can say, "He looked on me, to take away my reproach among people" (Luke 1:25).

6. How did Hamor and Shechem respond?

LIVE OUT ...

7. Dinah's brothers spoke deceitfully to Shechem and Hamor. Fill in the following chart to discover how God views lies and deceit.

SCRIPTURE	GOD'S VIEW OF LIES AND DECEIT
Psalm 24:3–4	
Psalm 52:2–5	
Psalm 101:7	
Proverbs 12:20	

8. Today we saw that Dinah's brothers were concerned about the reproach they would experience because of what happened to Dinah. Talk about a time you felt you might suffer socially because of another person's actions, or describe a time someone made you feel guilty for something that happened to you.

9. If you are carrying a sense of reproach for something that happened in the past or for something that happened to a family member, rewrite the words of Psalm 119:22–24 into a personal prayer. Know that the Lord loves you and will hear the cries of your heart.

> Remove from me reproach and contempt,
> For I have kept Your testimonies.
> Princes also sit and speak against me,
> But Your servant meditates on Your statutes.
> Your testimonies also are my delight
> And my counselors. Psalm 119:22–24

○ ○ ● ○ ○

We may think that Dinah's brothers are relics of a different time and more brutal age. But the sad truth is that the concept of "family honor" taken to such a deadly extreme is alive and well. Two sisters in Lewisville, Texas, were found shot to death in their father's taxi because he believed their dating brought shame to Islam. The Egyptian-born Yaser Abdel Said remains at large and is suspected of murdering his own daughters.

The United Nations Population Fund estimates that 5,000 honor killings take place every year. These murders are committed by close family members, usually a father or brother, who believe the female has brought disgrace to her family because of her activities. Many women are murdered because they have refused an arranged marriage, were sexually assaulted, were sexually promiscuous, or are otherwise perceived to be "out of control." Many of the killings have taken place in Southeast Asia or the Middle East among Muslims, Hindus, and Sikhs.[8] But there are also instances in America.

Jesus is in the business of restoration not reproach. He asks us to reach out in love to the wounded women we know and love. The psalmist wrote, "Reproach has broken my heart, and I am full of heaviness; I looked for someone to take pity, but there was none; and for comforters, but I found none" (Ps. 69:20). Thank heaven we have a God who *is* the God of all comfort and takes away our reproach. His Word says that "the reproaches of those who reproached You fell on Me" (Rom. 15:3).

LISTEN TO ...

To forbear replying to an unjust reproach, and overlook it with a generous or, if possible, with an entire neglect of it, is one of the most heroic acts of a great mind.

—*Joseph Addison*

DAY 4

Too Good to Be True

You've probably heard the saying "If something seems too good to be true, it probably is." Some things really are too good to be true. If you google the phrase "too good to be true," you'll discover many scams that are in the realm of impossibility.

One woman in Britain was diagnosed with cancer and decided to spend the end of her life recording every type of music on the piano. When she submitted her pieces, the music industry was stunned by the brilliance of her work. Too good to be true? Indeed! It turned out she had pieced together recordings of great artists from around the world and submitted the music as her own.

Or how about the drink that claims to burn calories and help us lose weight? It's too good to be true! Scientists tell us the best way to lose weight is to eat less and exercise more.

A physicist claims to be able to turn tiny amounts of water into near-limitless power at a cost of virtually nothing. But scientists agree this is probably too good to be true.

You get the idea—as grandmothers throughout the ages have put it, "If it looks like a fish and smells like a fish, it might be fishy."

Jacob's sons proposed something really fishy to Shechem and Hamor, and the Canaanites took the bait hook, line, and sinker.

LIFT UP ...

Father, help me to treat others with grace as You've treated me. Please help me to speak truth and grace to those around me, especially to those who do not know You. And speak to me today as I study Your Word. Amen.

LOOK AT ...

Yesterday we saw Jacob's sons make empty promises to Shechem and Hamor as they used their religious rite of circumcision as the condition for marriage. Circumcision was initiated with the Abrahamic covenant and was performed on the eighth day after every male birth (Gen. 17:12). Circumcision was seen as a visible sign of God's covenant with His chosen people. Circumcision was so important that "the uncircumcised male child, who is not circumcised in the flesh of his foreskin, that person shall be cut off from his people" (Gen. 17:14).

Today we see Shechem and Hamor convincing the men of the city to participate in a mass circumcision to benefit themselves. They did not persuade them based on covenant reasons or religious reasons. They offered financial gain as their incentive. They would concede to a religious ritual without a relationship with God. As you study this lesson, ask yourself why you conduct the rituals you perform—do you go through the motions, or are they full of meaning?

LEARN ABOUT ...

2 More Honorable?

Shechem did not act honorably toward Dinah, so how could he be described as honorable? Some believe it was because he offered to marry the young woman. Others say this description was due to Shechem's social standing. In other words, he did not have personal honor but held a place of honor in the community.

READ GENESIS 34:19–24.

So the young man did not delay to do the thing, because he delighted in Jacob's daughter. He was more honorable than all the household of his father. And Hamor and Shechem his son came to the gate of their city, and spoke with the men of their city, saying: "These men are at peace with us. Therefore let them dwell in the land and trade in it. For indeed the land is large enough for them. Let us take their daughters to us as wives, and let us give them our daughters. Only on this condition will the men consent to dwell with us, to be one people: if every male among us is circumcised as they are circumcised. Will not their livestock, their property, and every animal of theirs be ours? Only let us consent to them, and they will dwell with us." And all who went out of the gate of his city heeded Hamor and Shechem his son; every male was circumcised, all who went out of the gate of his city. Genesis 34:19–24

1. How did Shechem respond to the proposal and why?

2. The text says Shechem was "more honorable than all the household of his father." As he had committed rape, what does this reveal about his father's people?

3. Shechem and Hamor went to the city gate, the usual place for

LEARN ABOUT ...

4 One People?

The Hebrew people are known as the chosen people, a people intended to be set apart from the world and the things of the world. It was presumptuous at best for Hamor and Shechem to try to assimilate God's people into their people. Isaac commissioned Jacob to "be an assembly of peoples" (Gen. 28:3).

5 True Colors

Hamor showed his true colors by revealing he was motivated by greed. He wanted to control their property, their livestock, and their land. He encouraged his people to pay the price in pain to make sure he gained what he wanted. "The wicked boasts of his heart's desire; he blesses the greedy and renounces the LORD" (Ps. 10:3).

8 Most Honorable

As believers, we can become more and more honorable as we pursue Christ and become more like Him. We know that He alone is the one who is worthy of honor and praise. "Salvation and glory and honor and power belong to the Lord our God!" (Rev. 19:1).

public meetings, to make their plea. What was the first thing they assured the men of the city about?

4. a. Describe the steps Shechem and Hamor presented in the process of becoming "one people" with Jacob's family.

   b. Do you think this was God's will for Israel? What makes you say that?

5. How would the people of Shechem ultimately benefit from this process?

6. What do you think would happen to the Israelites if this plan succeeded?

7. How did the men respond to their leader's reasoning?

LIVE OUT ...

8. Shechem was considered "more honorable" than people in his community because of his social stature. Read 2 Timothy 2:20–23 to discover how to be truly honorable.

   a. How is an honorable person like a gold or silver vessel?

   b. How is a dishonorable person like a wooden or clay vessel?

   c. When we're cleansed, what purpose do we serve?

   d. Describe how to become a vessel of honor.

   e. What do you need to do to become more honorable?

9. a. Hamor tried to integrate Israel into his people by marriage. According to John 1:12–13, how is it possible to become a child of God?

    b. How do you know that you are one of God's people?

10. a. What did Paul warn against in 1 Timothy 6:10?

    b. How have you found this to be true in your faith walk?

○ ○ ● ○ ○

LEARN ABOUT …

9 God's People

We become children of God through the new birth. When Nicodemus came to Jesus and asked Him about spiritual matters, Jesus told him, "Unless one is born again, he cannot see the kingdom of God" (John 3:3). Through the new birth, all people can be adopted into God's family.

Hamor and Shechem used the lure of riches to get the people to consent to a faux religious ritual. How grateful we should be that Moses did not gloss over Dinah's disgrace. He exposed men's maneuvering and allowed us to learn the difficult lessons about human nature. We've seen how lust, revenge, and now greed can control those who are not controlled by God.

Remember the story of King Midas, who was offered anything he wished from Dionysus? Foolishly, Midas asked that everything he touched be turned to gold. Though he was warned against making this wish, he didn't listen. At first he was thrilled with the gift. But soon, the gift turned into a curse. He turned his daughter into gold, his food and drink into gold. In despair he began to hate his wealth and splendor.

Paul warned that in the end times, deception will be worse than ever. He wrote, "Men will be lovers of themselves, *lovers of money*, boasters, proud, blasphemers, disobedient to parents, unthankful, unholy, unloving, unforgiving, slanderers, without self-control, brutal, despisers of good, traitors, headstrong, haughty, lovers of pleasure rather than lovers of God, having a form of godliness but denying its power. And from such people turn away!" (2 Tim. 3:2–5).

As believers, let's follow Paul's warning and turn away from the love of money and turn toward the love of God. The days are growing more evil, not less.

Listen to ...

He who seeks more than he needs hinders himself from enjoying what he has.

—Hebrew Proverb

DAY 5

Too Much to Ask

The *Brit Milah,* or circumcision, takes place eight days after the birth of a Jewish son to celebrate the boy's place in the family tree. Many people believe circumcision is performed on the eighth day because the blood begins to coagulate and the boy feels the least amount of pain. Truly this is within God's character to be merciful to children.

Rabbi Moshe Schapiro describes another theory regarding circumcision on the eighth day. He wrote: "As long as there would be human beings in the world, God assured Abraham, there would always be Jews. This covenant or pact between God and Abraham was sealed through the act of circumcision. Today, by performing the act of circumcision, Jews perpetuate the covenant and make their children a part of that eternal promise. The fact that the *Brit Milah* is performed on the eighth day after a boy is born hints to this idea of eternal Jewish continuity."

According to Schapiro, in the Torah, all references to numbers have great significance. The seventh day, or Sabbath, is spiritual in nature but is observed within the physical realm. On the other hand, eight is a transcendent number, signifying a higher dimension or supernatural reality.

Thus, the *Brit Milah*, which is performed on the eighth day, might be seen as a reminder that the Jewish covenant with God and their supernatural survival throughout the ages is not a natural phenomenon, but a supernatural one. Jewish endurance defies reason. The mark of circumcision was made on the reproductive organ to represent the idea that the Jewish people's seed would never be destroyed.[9] To ask Hamor's people to endure this painful rite was like asking them to become a part of this supernatural tribe. But Hamor took it lightly, and Jacob's people used it for their own reasons rather than to bring about the conversion of the Canaanites.

LIFT UP ...

Lord, please keep me from having a vengeful spirit that will only lead to bondage and sin. Because of Your Son, I can show grace and mercy to those who've hurt me. Amen.

LOOK AT ...

Shechem and Hamor convinced their men to undergo the painful rite of circumcision. The townspeople believed that it would profit their people to absorb Jacob and his family into their culture. For Jews, circumcision was a religious rite. For the Canaanites, it seemed to be an inconvenience to endure until they got what they wanted—Dinah for Shechem and the Israelites' possessions for themselves.

Today we see that two of Jacob's sons had a plan to take matters into their own hands and seek revenge for their sister's rape. They felt that forgiveness was too much to ask. When Jacob returned from Haran after wrestling with God, "he erected an altar there and called it El Elohe Israel" (Gen. 33:20). This proclaimed to all people his faith in the God of Israel. However, his sons' actions would speak louder than their father's words. Warren Wiersbe said, "By their deception and ruthless destruction, they ruined Jacob's testimony before the people of the land. What good was it for Jacob to build an altar and worship the true God before his pagan neighbors if his children were going to act like pagans?"[10] It's a lesson for us all: Does our walk match our talk?

READ GENESIS 34:25–31.

Now it came to pass on the third day, when they were in pain, that two of the sons of Jacob, Simeon and Levi, Dinah's brothers, each took his sword and came boldly upon the city and killed all the males. And they killed Hamor and Shechem his son with the edge of the sword, and took Dinah from Shechem's house, and went out. The sons of Jacob came upon the slain, and plundered the city, because their sister had been defiled. They took their sheep, their oxen, and their donkeys, what was in the city and what was in the field, and all their wealth. All their little ones and their wives they took captive; and they plundered even all that was in the houses. Then Jacob said to Simeon and Levi, "You have troubled me by making me obnoxious among the inhabitants of the land, among the Canaanites and the Perizzites; and since I am few in number, they will gather themselves together against me and kill me. I shall be destroyed, my household and I." But they said, "Should he treat our sister like a harlot?"
Genesis 34:25–31

1. a. Describe what Simeon and Levi did to the men of the city.

   b. Why do you think these two brothers were the ones who took action?

2. Describe what happened at Shechem's house.

3. Who came along afterward as their accomplices and why?

4. Recount what the sons took as plunder.

5. Whose reputation was Jacob worried about?

6. a. What did Jacob fear?

   b. What do you think he should have feared?

7. a. How did the sons respond?

   b. Do you think this was justified? Please explain.

LIVE OUT ...

8. a. Dinah's brothers outwardly agreed to peace but inwardly plotted revenge. Read Romans 12:19–20. Who is the one to repay vengeance?

   b. How are we to treat our enemies?

   c. What happens when we treat them this way?

   d. Have you ever experienced this? If so, explain.

LEARN ABOUT ...

2 Dinah's Deliverers

It's unclear whether Dinah had been held hostage, or whether she had been taken to Shechem's house to prepare for the wedding. Whatever the case, she was at Shechem's house when her brothers came seeking revenge. Simeon and Levi, her full brothers, "took" her. John Phillips wrote that she was "seized and dragged back home."[11]

4 People Plundered

The viciousness of the attack was described using words similar to an unjust war. The punishment they inflicted was far in excess of the crime, especially because they had agreed to a settlement. In addition, the innocent suffered along with the guilty. Women and children were taken captive, and property was plundered.

7 Justifying Judgment

Jacob's sons did not regret their revenge. They justified their cruelty by exaggerating that their sister was treated like a prostitute. Using God's ritual of circumcision to weaken their victims, they sought revenge on people they pretended to make peace with. Jacob's weak rebuke brought a weak response. The massacre was unjustifiable.

LEARN ABOUT …

8 Restrain Revenge

Revenge means to inflict harm or punishment to pay back for an insult or injury. God reserves vengeance for His domain. There are times He gives men the right to take vengeance as the hand of His authority. He told Moses, "Take vengeance on the Midianites" (Num. 31:2). Personal vengeance is forbidden.

---

9 Dinah's Days

Dinah's tragic story brought her grief and her brothers, Simeon and Levi, great shame. Most likely she never married. She traveled to Egypt with Jacob's clan because of a famine. Genesis 46:27 tells us that Jacob took seventy people with him to Egypt, including children and grandchildren. This move would solidify the Israelites as a unified people group.

9. We last saw Dinah being taken from Shechem's house by her brothers. Read Genesis 46:8–15. What do you learn about Dinah's future?

10. Has God ever moved you from one place to another (physically, emotionally, or spiritually) to draw you closer to Him and His people? If so, describe your journey and how God accompanied you.

○ ○ ● ○ ○

In her book *Startling Beauty: My Journey from Rape to Restoration,* Heather Gemmen tells how she endured a rape and found strength through the Spirit of God for hope and healing. While her children were asleep, a man broke into her home, tied her up, and raped her. In an interview she recalled, "There were a few moments where I simply thought, I'm going to die. It was like it wasn't real. I didn't really believe this was happening." She struggled with guilt and shame. "Any way I could blame myself, I did. Even though logically I knew it wasn't my fault."

Then she discovered she was pregnant, "That's when God began to just soften my heart and work in me because I finally just turned myself over to Him. [I] said, 'I can't do anything, and I let go of this desire for control.'" But it wasn't easy. People would try to comfort her with spiritual platitudes. She said, "There are times that people would quote Scripture to me, [like] Romans 8:28. God will make all things good for those of us who love Him and are called according to His purpose. And it sounds so beautiful but when you're in the midst of despair, frankly you want to hit people with the Bible because it doesn't feel true."

After giving birth to her baby, Rachel, Heather began to see that the attack could be transformed into something for her good. She made the choice to forgive her rapist. She said, "Who am I to say to

God this person doesn't deserve to be forgiven? I realized I needed to forgive him even though I had no way of knowing if he was sorry or not. I just had to forgive him."[12]

LISTEN TO ...

As we practice the work of forgiveness we discover more and more that forgiveness and healing are one.

—Agnes Sanford

Tamar—A Woman Scorned

Genesis 38

"Hell hath no fury like a woman scorned" is a proverb adapted from *The Mourning Bride* by playwright William Congreve. It means that no one is angrier than a woman who has been rejected in love.[1] This week we'll look at the life of Tamar, who suffered unrequited love over and over again. Her pain prompted her to attempt desperate measures to stand by the men in the line of Judah.

Recently we've witnessed a parade of despondent wives standing beside their politician husbands who apologize publicly for misdeeds or scandals. Silda Wall Spitzer appeared sphinxlike as her cheating husband, New York governor Eliot Spitzer, resigned after being exposed as "Client Nine" of a high-end prostitution ring. Before her, Dina Matos McGreevey stood by her husband, the former New Jersey governor, while he admitted that he was "a gay American." In 2007 we saw Suzanne Craig wearing oversized sunglasses, standing with her husband, US Senator Larry Craig, as he admitted to soliciting sex in an airport bathroom. Then there was Detroit mayor Kwame Kilpatrick, who brought his wife to stand beside him as he explained about the suggestive text messages he had sent to his chief of staff. And most notably, then-first lady Hillary Clinton stood by her husband's side as he denied sexual relations with White House intern Monica Lewinsky, a denial that later led to impeachment proceedings.[2]

Houston psychologist Sally Porter Ross says smart political spouses may have complicated reasons for supporting their husbands. "From that point on, she's in charge, she's got the power," Ross says. "She is absolutely on top."[3] Eventually, Tamar will be on top as her name is placed in the Messiah's genealogy.

Day 1: Genesis 38:1–5 — MY THREE SONS

Day 2: Genesis 38:6–11 — THE NEXT OF KIN

Day 3: Genesis 38:12–19 — SETTING A TRAP

Day 4: Genesis 38:20–24 — IN THE FAMILY WAY

Day 5: Genesis 38:25–30 — YOUR SINS WILL FIND YOU OUT

DAY 1
My Three Sons

LIFT UP ...

Lord, I know that sin can keep me from the blessings You have for me. Help me to confess my sin regularly so that I can abide in Your presence. Amen.

LOOK AT ...

Judah's tryst with Tamar is sandwiched within the life and times of Joseph, Judah's youngest brother. It's as though Moses placed brilliant bookends on either side of this dark story filled with distasteful details and declining morals. On one side, we recall Joseph as he developed into a stellar child with God-inspired dreams of the future. On the other end, we see Joseph as he adroitly served the pharaoh as second in command. We're reminded that his wisdom rescued not only the Egyptians but also his own family from famine.

It's important to note that before Judah's move to Canaan, he had collaborated with his brothers in selling Joseph to Midianite traders for a few pieces of silver. To cover up their deed, they killed a kid goat and stained Joseph's many-colored coat with blood to make their father believe the boy had encountered a wild beast. Jacob was inconsolable, and the conspiratorial brothers must have felt a great deal of guilt and shame. The Bible is honest about its characters, willing to expose them as they are: both flawed and faithful. That God chooses and uses fallible human beings to accomplish His work enhances His goodness and grace. It offers comfort to you and me. We too are imperfect. Therefore, we rejoice that God can redeem our past and replace it with a future and a hope.

Learn About ...

2 Determined

Reuben prevented his brothers from killing Joseph, pleading that he be placed in a pit. Later, he intended to rescue the child. But Judah talked his brothers into selling Joseph for profit. All agreed that Judah bore the greater guilt. "Let those be turned back and brought to confusion who plot my hurt" (Ps. 35:4).

4 Developed

Judah became friends with a Canaanite named Hirah. He would participate in Judah's downfall in several ways: (1) introducing him to an unbelieving wife; (2) inviting him to a pagan party after his wife's death; (3) encouraging him to visit a prostitute. "Friendship with the world is enmity with God" (James 4:4).

5 Detoured

Judah must have known about his father's and grandfather's arranged marriages. Their brides were chosen from among their own people as God commanded. However, Judah went in the opposite direction and married a Canaanite of his own choosing. Eventually Judah returned to his father's house. Although not the firstborn, he served as leader (see 1 Chron. 5:2).

READ GENESIS 38:1–5.

It came to pass at that time that Judah departed from his brothers, and visited a certain Adullamite whose name was Hirah. And Judah saw there a daughter of a certain Canaanite whose name was Shua, and he married her and went in to her. So she conceived and bore a son, and he called his name Er. She conceived again and bore a son, and she called his name Onan. And she conceived yet again and bore a son, and called his name Shelah. He was at Chezib when she bore him. Genesis 38:1–5

1. To what context does "at that time" refer? (Briefly skim through Genesis 37:12–36.)

2. a. Who is the main character of our story?

   b. What was his role in the events of Genesis 37:12–36?

3. a. Describe Judah's leave-taking in Genesis 38:1–5.

   b. What do you think was the spiritual significance of his departure?

4. What two key relationships did Judah develop while he was away from his family?

5. a. How did his path differ from that of his father and grandfather?

   b. What impact do you expect this would have on his future?

6. Underline the word *conceived* in our text, and list the names of Judah and Shua's three sons.

7. a. Where did the couple dwell?

b. Does it seem that Judah was putting down roots among the Canaanites? What makes you say that?

LIVE OUT ...

8. a. Judah's misdeeds stood in stark contrast to Joseph's shining example. Read Luke 11:33–36. What should a person do and not do with a lamp and why (v. 33)?

    b. What part of the human anatomy did Jesus liken to a lamp (v. 34)?

    c. Explain how seeing affects shining (v. 34).

    d. How are the spiritual qualities of light and dark mutually exclusive (vv. 35–36)?

    e. What things do you participate in that make sure you feed the light?

    f. How do you shine the light to those in darkness?

9. Judah's friendship with an unbeliever brought dire consequences. Journal about a time when an unbeliever caused you to compromise your faith. How could you have influenced that person instead?

10. Instead of following the example of his godly family members, Judah followed the ways of the world. Place a check in the appropriate box to indicate influences you have followed.

    ❑ "follow intoxicating drink" (Isa. 5:11)
    ❑ "follow after righteousness" (Isa. 51:1)

LEARN ABOUT ...

8 Doused

Judah was a son of the promises. Like John the Baptist, he could have brought the light of God's presence to a dark place. "This man came for a witness, to bear witness of the Light, that all through him might believe" (John 1:7). Instead he was swallowed up by the darkness.

10 Decided

Jesus made it clear that we have a choice whether to follow Him or not. We will walk either the narrow path that leads to life or the broad path whose end is destruction. Don't be fooled into thinking you can do both. He said, "He who is not with Me is against Me" (Matt. 12:30).

❑ "follow those who believe" (Mark 16:17)
❑ "follow the dictates of my heart" (Deut. 29:19)
❑ "follow a crowd" (Ex. 23:2)
❑ "follow His [Jesus'] steps" (1 Peter 2:21)

o o • o o

My Three Sons was one of television's longest running and most influential domestic comedies airing from 1960 to 1972. It centered on widower and aerospace consultant Steve Douglas as he raised his three motherless sons: eighteen-year-old Mike, fourteen-year-old Robbie, and seven-year-old Chip. "While initial director Peter Tewksbury called the premise a truly depressing one, producers Tibbles and Fedderson chose to ignore the potential for pathos and flung themselves wholeheartedly into the comedic consequences of a male-only household."[4] It took a serious but often lighthearted look at generational and gender conflicts. Prior to this groundbreaking sitcom, most family comedies were centered on strictly nuclear groupings—mom, dad, and biological children.

In Judah's home, there were conflicts that began from an unequally yoked marriage that could not be ignored, nor could they be turned into a domestic comedy. There seemed to be few lighthearted situations in the household. The family started off on the wrong foot and never regained its balance. In rapid-fire succession the couple conceived and bore three sons. Some commentators believe that Judah deferred child rearing to his wife, allowing her to raise his sons with pagan influences. Perhaps the names they were given tell their story. Firstborn Er's name means "the watcher." There is no doubt that he watched his parents awkwardly struggle with their unequally yoked relationship. Perhaps he observed his mother's indifference toward Judah's mysterious God and his father's neglect of spiritual things. Next came Onan, whose name means "strength." We see this child grow in his mother's willful dominance, eventually developing a strong wickedness. Third came Shelah. His name means "he that breaks," perhaps indicating Judah's surrender of headship in the home.[5] The three sons of Steve Douglas grew up to be good and moral men. Sadly, that was not the fate of Judah's three sons.

LISTEN TO ...

It is a great deal better to live a holy life than to talk about it. Lighthouses do not ring bells and fire cannon to call attention to their shining—they just shine.

—Dwight L. Moody

DAY 2
The Next of Kin

The "next of kin" in our legal system describes a right granted to a relative regarding inheritance or substitute decision making if a person becomes incapacitated for medical or psychological reasons. If no clear instructions have been provided in a will or legal document and the person is unmarried, the closest and most senior relative is given legal authority to execute the estate or make vital decisions. Usually the next of kin is a parent or a sibling, but it can also be an adult child or first cousin, aunt, or uncle.

In Bible times the next of kin, or kinsman-redeemer, had more responsibilities than his modern counterparts. The term meant "coming to the help or rescue." It was bestowed upon the nearest living male blood relative. His first duty was to be the blood avenger to punish a crime committed against a family member. The kinsman also served as redeemer in three other ways: (1) to buy back a relative who had been sold into slavery; (2) to redeem the paternal estate that might have been sold through poverty; (3) to marry the widow of a deceased relative to carry on the lineage and inheritance.

Ruth and Boaz beautifully depicted this role. After the death of Ruth's husband and the loss of the family property through famine, Boaz rescued Ruth from poverty and redeemed her through marriage and an heir. One day the Messiah would descend from this marriage. Today we'll see that Tamar, too, needed a kinsman to carry on the name of her deceased husband. Sadly, she did not inherit Ruth's happy ending.

LIFT UP ...

Father, when times of sorrow and grief surround me, I take comfort in knowing that You will never give me more than I can handle. Thank You for being my strength in times of suffering. Amen.

LOOK AT ...

It is believed that Judah was just a teenager when he moved from his father's tent to dwell among the Canaanites. The language used in our text is very telling: "Judah departed from his brothers." Reuben tried to act righteously during Joseph's betrayal, but Judah declined his counsel and sold him into slavery to the Ishmaelites. The most natural step was to physically move where he had already gone spiritually. He withdrew himself from his family's counsel and company. Young and impetuous, Judah made a downhill move.

Next, Judah journeyed away from his father's and his heavenly Father's influence. He decided to marry a Canaanite woman, breaking with the time-honored tradition of letting his father choose an acceptable bride. Instead, he allowed his unbelieving friend to do the matchmaking. Matthew Henry wrote, "Let young people be admonished by this to take their good parents for their best friends, and to be advised by them, and not by flatterers, who wheedle them, to make a prey of them."[6] Today we'll see that Judah moved even further away from the Lord as he arranged a marriage between his firstborn son and a Gentile bride.

LEARN ABOUT ...

I Tamar

Tamar was a Canaanite whose name meant "palm tree." This suggests her beauty, stature, and grace. Although she too made a mistake in how she handled the situation, she behaved more nobly than the heirs of God's covenant. Perhaps she was aware of the messianic hope. Her name was later included in Matthew's genealogy of Jesus. "Judah begot Perez and Zerah by Tamar" (Matt. 1:3).

READ GENESIS 38:6–11.

Then Judah took a wife for Er his firstborn, and her name was Tamar. But Er, Judah's firstborn, was wicked in the sight of the LORD, and the LORD killed him. And Judah said to Onan, "Go in to your brother's wife and marry her, and raise up an heir to your brother." But Onan knew that the heir would not be his; and it came to pass, when he went in to his brother's wife, that he emitted on the ground, lest he should give an heir to his brother. And the thing which he did displeased the LORD; therefore He killed him also. Then Judah said to Tamar his daughter-in-law, "Remain a widow in your father's house till my son Shelah is grown." For he said, "Lest he also die like his brothers." And Tamar went and dwelt in her father's house. Genesis 38:6–11

1. a. "Then" connects this text to the previous portion of Scripture. Look back at yesterday's text; "then" describe what Judah did next.

   b. Was this a godly idea? Please explain.

LEARN ABOUT ...

3 Tradition

We don't know Er's deadly sin. But Onan sinned by refusing to raise up an heir to perpetuate his brother's name. This tradition is known as a Levirate marriage, from the Latin word *levir* that means "brother-in-law." Onan knew his firstborn would be a foster child and financially compromise his estate.

---

5 Terrible

The redeemer's three qualifications were to be ready, willing, and able. Onan was *able* to produce an heir, since the text reveals his fertility. But he was not *ready* or *willing*, as he withheld his seed from Tamar. Shamefully, whenever Onan had intercourse with Tamar, he interrupted the act so that she couldn't conceive. His sin was lethal.

---

8 True Redeemer

Jesus possessed the qualities to be our kinsman-redeemer. He was *ready* by becoming our blood relative at the incarnation, *willing* at Gethsemane as He yielded His will to the Father, and *able* to pay the price for our sin because of His sinless life. We are His redeemed bride, called to produce more heirs through His promises.

2. Describe Er in your own words; then explain what happened to him.

3. a. What did Judah command Onan to do?

   b. How might this make the couple feel?

4. How did what Onan knew influence what he did? Do you think that Tamar was aware of his reasoning?

5. a. What were the consequences of his actions?

   b. How do you think this made Tamar feel?

6. a. What advice did Judah give Tamar concerning his third son?

   b. Why did he say this?

7. a. How did Tamar respond?

   b. What does this tell you about her character?

LIVE OUT ...

8. Tamar's kinsman-redeemer was unwilling to fulfill his duties. However, we know that our Redeemer lives! Fill in the chart to discover His qualities.

SCRIPTURE	OUR REDEEMER
Job 19:25	
Galatians 3:13–14	
1 Peter 1:18–19	
Revelation 5:9–10	

9. a. Tamar suffered the loss of her first husband, the shame of her second, and the scorn of her father-in-law. Although she behaved rightly, the men behaved badly. In the appropriate columns, record some situations in which you were good but others treated you poorly.

You Were Right	They Were Wrong

LEARN ABOUT …

10 Transgressions

The Bible reveals that there are several sins that have deadly consequences. David's assistants were struck dead for handling the ark inappropriately (2 Sam. 6). Ananias and Sapphira dropped dead because they lied to the Holy Spirit (Acts 5). In truth, all sins are deadly: "For the wages of sin is death" (Rom. 6:23).

b. Did you respond spiritually, or in the flesh? Knowing what you know now, what would you do differently?

10. Today we learned that sin has deadly consequences. But Jesus our Redeemer has bought us back from the consequences of sin. Rewrite the following verse into a personal prayer of praise to your Kinsman-Redeemer.

> Do not fear, for you will not be ashamed;
> Neither be disgraced, for you will not be put to
>   shame;
> For you will forget the shame of your youth,
> And will not remember the reproach of your widow-
>   hood anymore.
> For your Maker is your husband,
> The Lord of hosts is His name;
> And your Redeemer is the Holy One of Israel.
>   Isaiah 54:4–5

o o ● o o

Most of us have heard Samuel Medley's hymn "I Know That My Redeemer Lives," but few of us know the story behind it. As a young man, Medley joined the British Royal Navy, becoming a midshipman in 1755. He was wounded in battle off Port Lagos in 1759. Medley recalls that the surgeon examining his leg said, "I am afraid that amputation is the only thing that will save your life. I can confirm tomorrow morning."

Although Medley had lived a decadent life in the navy, that night he prayed fervently. The next morning, while reexamining his leg, the surgeon exclaimed, "This is little short of a miracle." He had found the patient so much better that he couldn't believe his eyes. God heard Medley's prayer for physical healing, but spiritual healing would come during his convalescence. His grandfather read him a sermon by Isaac Watts that led to his conversion.[7] Eventually he penned these stanzas to the famous hymn:

> I know that my Redeemer lives;
> What comfort this sweet sentence gives!
> He lives, He lives, who once was dead;
> He lives, my ever living Head.
>
> He lives triumphant from the grave,
> He lives eternally to save,
> He lives all glorious in the sky,
> He lives exalted there on high.
>
> He lives and grants me daily breath;
> He lives, and I shall conquer death:
> He lives my mansion to prepare;
> He lives to bring me safely there.

Tamar witnessed death and deception everywhere around her. The man who was intended to be her kinsman-redeemer had died. But one day through her bloodline, the true Redeemer of all humanity would live.

LISTEN TO ...

Noble fathers have noble children.

—Euripides

DAY 3

Setting a Trap

Have you heard about a tricky method used by monkey hunters? The trappers place a small cage in the jungle with a bunch of bananas locked inside. When a greedy monkey comes along and spots the bananas, it reaches its paw through the narrow rungs of the cage and grabs a banana. But it can't get the paw back out of the rungs, no matter how hard it tries, because it's hanging on to the banana. Even while the treacherous trappers close in on their prey, the stubborn primate won't let go of the banana. The trappers merely have to grab the unrelenting monkey. If you were standing in the jungle watching this happen, you'd want to urge the monkey, "Drop the banana!"

As you read about the elaborate trap Tamar set for Judah, you might want to shout, "Look out, it's a trap!" But to catch Judah, a banana wouldn't do the trick. Somehow Tamar discovered the perfect bait. Her trap was not in the jungle but along the road to Timnah. Perhaps you remember this city from the story of another man who fell into a trap there. Samson saw a beautiful woman in Timnah who was the beginning of his end.

James warned, "Each one is tempted when he is drawn away by his own desires and enticed" (James 1:14). To *draw away* means to bait a trap, and *enticed* refers to baiting a hook. The probing question is "What's your bait?" Eventually Satan will try to lure you with something you'll find very enticing.

LIFT UP ...

God, I know that Your will and Your timing are perfect. Forgive me for the times when I try to force Your will into my timetable. Help me to wait patiently on You. Amen.

LOOK AT ...

After the untimely death of Tamar's two husbands, we saw the widow relegated to her father's tent. It's as if Judah commanded her, "Go to your room!" Likely her reputation was tarnished. The text hints that Judah thought, "Tamar is a black widow. Everyone she marries ends up dead. I'd better hide Shelah." The prospects of Tamar finding another husband under these

Learn About …

1 Comforted

Death brings grief, which is a powerful emotion. It can bring people to their knees in prayer or force them to their feet, pursuing pleasure. Judah didn't turn to God but to unbelieving friends and a pagan festival at Timnah. Paul wrote, "Blessed be the God … of all comfort, who comforts us in all our tribulation" (2 Cor. 1:3–4).

3 Concealed

Throughout Genesis we've seen God's people utilize clothing to conceal and deceive. Jacob used a furry coat to mislead his father, Isaac, and steal Esau's birthright. Judah and his brothers used Joseph's blood-soaked garment to trick Jacob. And now we see Tamar dress like a temple prostitute to deceive Judah.

circumstances were slim. If Judah did not offer Shelah as the rightful kinsman, Tamar's future was bleak. Not only that, Judah's line would end. While Judah's feelings are understandable, they are unacceptable.

Thankfully, widows hold a very special place in God's heart. In the Old Testament, widows were believed to be under Yahweh's special care. The psalmist called God "a defender of widows" (Ps. 68:5). And Solomon said, "He protects the property of widows" (Prov. 15:25 NLT). By New Testament times sympathetic regard for widows became a sign of true godliness (James 1:27). Although Judah neglected Tamar, God was watching out for her. Unfortunately, Tamar took her fate into her own hands.

READ GENESIS 38:12–19.

Now in the process of time the daughter of Shua, Judah's wife, died; and Judah was comforted, and went up to his sheepshearers at Timnah, he and his friend Hirah the Adullamite. And it was told Tamar, saying, "Look, your father-in-law is going up to Timnah to shear his sheep." So she took off her widow's garments, covered herself with a veil and wrapped herself, and sat in an open place which was on the way to Timnah; for she saw that Shelah was grown, and she was not given to him as a wife. When Judah saw her, he thought she was a harlot, because she had covered her face. Then he turned to her by the way, and said, "Please let me come in to you"; for he did not know that she was his daughter-in-law. So she said, "What will you give me, that you may come in to me?" And he said, "I will send a young goat from the flock." So she said, "Will you give me a pledge till you send it?" Then he said, "What pledge shall I give you?" So she said, "Your signet and cord, and your staff that is in your hand." Then he gave them to her, and went in to her, and she conceived by him. So she arose and went away, and laid aside her veil and put on the garments of her widowhood. Genesis 38:12–19

1. a. What event occurred in Judah's life, and where did he seek comfort?

b. What might this reveal about his faith? Why?

2. a. Who was told about Judah's journey, and how did this person respond?

   b. What might this reveal about her faith?

3. Explain what circumstances prompted Tamar's decision.

4. Describe what Judah saw, thought, and did.

5. In your own words, recount the details of the bartering between Judah and Tamar.

6. What occurred because of this encounter?

7. a. What final action did Tamar take?

   b. Why do you believe this action was significant?

LIVE OUT ...

8. Judah had a choice to seek comfort from God or man. He chose poorly. Complete the following sentences:

   I felt grief when ...

   I found comfort by ...

   I discovered that ...

9. Today we saw Tamar change her clothes twice, back and forth between a widow and a woman of ill repute. Paul exhorted the

---

LEARN ABOUT ...

5 Conspired

The price of Judah's indiscretion was much more than a goat. Knowing that Judah would have to pay at a future date, Tamar demanded three pieces for surety: (1) a signet ring that represented his *person*; (2) bracelets that portrayed his *possessions*; and (3) a staff symbolic of his *position*. He sold his reputation.

---

8 Consoled

The Greek word usually translated as "comfort" comes from two Greek roots: *para*, which means next to, and *kaleo*, meaning to call. As comforter, God is called next to us to comfort, entreat, or encourage. God spoke through Isaiah, "As one whom his mother comforts, so I will comfort you; and you shall be comforted" (Isa. 66:13).

---

9 Converted

The Bible teaches that "all our righteousnesses are like filthy rags" (see Isa. 64:6). We may try to cover ourselves with good deeds, but in reality they are threadbare. Instead, we must be stripped of all human effort to be clothed in the Lord's righteousness. "He has covered me with the robe of righteousness" (Isa. 61:10).

Ephesians to "put off" the former ways and to "put on" the new in Christ. Fill in the columns with things you've put on or off.

PUT ON   PUT OFF

10. Judah was willing to sacrifice so much for so little in return. Who are the prodigals in your life? Do you know people who have discarded their robes of righteousness for filthy rags? Write a prayer for their redemption and restoration.

· · • · ·

The human body was created with amazing adaptability. Normally when climbing into a hot tub you have to lower yourself in one body part at a time. But once you are submerged, the water becomes pleasant. Or turning on a light in a dimly lit room irritates us. But within seconds it seems normal. All five senses possess the ability to adjust.

How do we so easily get used to things? Scientists call this striking phenomenon neuro-adaptation, because it involves *nerves* and *adaptation*. We assume that our nerves accurately portray the stimulation that surrounds us. Surprisingly, this is not the case. Our bodies can get used to things that are life threatening. Remember the frog? If it is placed in a pan of room temperature water, it just sits there. But if the pan is heated, ever so slowly, the frog may never notice the temperature change. It will get used to the increasing heat, sitting in the pan until it boils to death.

In a sense, humans also possess soul adaptation. Living in a heated spiritual environment can change us. If we're continually exposed to bad language, eventually unsavory words aren't as distasteful. Or they roll more readily off our tongues. Perhaps the debauched environment in Canaan had tainted both Judah and Tamar. They no longer bristled at sin. And before they knew it, they were lowering their personal standards too. Sadly, they adapted to their pagan environment. Paul warned, "Do not be conformed to this world, but be transformed by the renewing of your mind" (Rom. 12:2).

LISTEN TO ...

Once conform, once do what others do because they do it, and a kind of lethargy steals over all the finer senses of the soul.

—Michel de Montaigne

DAY 4
In the Family Way

Incest is sexual relations with a near kin. In the Hebrew it expresses the idea of mixing unnatural elements. For ancient Egyptians, marriage between brothers and sisters was generally accepted. A Spartan was allowed to marry the daughter of his father. Athenians encouraged marriage to the daughter of a mother. And the nuptials between an uncle and niece were applauded as a happy union of the dearest relations. However, the people of God were called to a higher code of sexual behavior than the pagan people they encountered. The law of Moses strictly condemned this perversion. Leviticus forbids a man from having intercourse with his mother, stepmother, sister, granddaughter, stepsister, aunt, daughter-in-law, sister-in-law, or stepdaughter. (Abraham and Sarah were brought out of a pagan land before the Levitical law.)

Without condoning Tamar's behavior, some commentators offer her grace, which means the unearned favor of God. Herbert Lockyer wrote, "Although we have no evidence of Tamar's faith in Jehovah, she must have had some conception of the important Messianic significance of the line of Judah, for denied Shelah, she was determined, though in an incestuous way, to save from extinction the family and tribe from which the Messiah was to spring"[8] However shocking Tamar's illicit behavior was, because she sought to perpetuate Judah's bloodline, a faithful heir arose. It's astounding that without approving of sin, God can "overcome evil with good" (Rom. 12:21). No matter what dark secret lies buried in your past, Jesus can cover it with His blood and make you whiter than snow. Of another harlot Jesus said, "I say to you, her sins, which are many, are forgiven, for she loved much. But to whom little is forgiven, the same loves little" (Luke 7:47).

LIFT UP ...

Father, it is only by Your grace that I am saved. Thank You for Your unconditional love, which covers my sin. Amen.

Look at ...

To understand Tamar's thoughts toward childbearing, we must study the chief goddess of the Canaanites, Ashtoreth. Her name means "to be fertile." She was identified with the planet Venus and was known as the goddess of sensual love, maternity, and fertility. A tall, straight wooden pole was erected in the places associated with worship of Ashtoreth. Those who followed her involved themselves in licentious conduct to honor her. Her priests and priestesses served as temple prostitutes. As patrons committed the act of sex, they believed fertility of flock, field, and family would be increased. Her cult polluted early Israel. "They forsook the Lord and served Baal and the Ashtoreths. And the anger of the Lord was hot against Israel" (Judg. 2:13–14). Eventually even King Solomon succumbed to her worship (see 1 Kings 11:5). No doubt Judah thought that the prostitute in Timnah was one of Ashtoreth's prostitutes.

Learn About ...

2 Harlot
The harlot's identity was unknown because it was customary for them to cover their faces, not because they were ashamed, but so they could appear innocent. *Harlot* here refers to a woman sacred to Ashtoreth who served the goddess by prostitution. This role was the most respectable designation for public prostitutes in Canaan.

Read Genesis 38:20–24.

And Judah sent the young goat by the hand of his friend the Adullamite, to receive his pledge from the woman's hand, but he did not find her. Then he asked the men of that place, saying, "Where is the harlot who was openly by the roadside?" And they said, "There was no harlot in this place." So he returned to Judah and said, "I cannot find her. Also, the men of the place said there was no harlot in this place." Then Judah said, "Let her take them for herself, lest we be shamed; for I sent this young goat and you have not found her." And it came to pass, about three months after, that Judah was told, saying, "Tamar your daughter-in-law has played the harlot; furthermore she is with child by harlotry." So Judah said, "Bring her out and let her be burned!" Genesis 38:20–24

1. How did Judah attempt to fulfill his pledge and why?

2. Describe the extent of Hirah the Adullamite's search and the result.

LEARN ABOUT ...

4 Helpless

Matthew Henry writes, "Lest he should be laughed at as a fool for trusting a strumpet with his signet and his bracelets. He expresses no concern about the sin, to get that pardoned, only about the shame, to prevent that."[9] The pledges were unquestionably of more value than a young goat.

---

6 Hostile

In the eyes of the law, Tamar was Shelah's legal wife, although Judah had no intention of allowing the union to be consummated. His suggestion to have her burned likely referred to branding of the face as a punishment for adultery. Perhaps he was overly zealous against her sin because he had a guilty conscience.

---

8 Hired Hand

The Septuagint and Vulgate both describe Hirah as Judah's shepherd. By sending a hired hand to care for his indiscretion reveals either that Judah was too great a man to take care of this menial task or that he was concerned about his identity and reputation. Hirah was involved in many of Judah's compromises.

3. a. Review yesterday's lesson; then list the items that Judah ultimately lost when Hirah came home empty-handed.

   b. How do you think he was feeling?

4. How did Judah respond when Hirah was unable to locate her?

5. Underline and record the time reference in this text. What does this reveal about Judah's level of concern at not finding the harlot?

6. a. What did Judah learn about Tamar, and how did he respond?

   b. How might you explain the intensity of his response?

7. Imagine being Tamar and not hearing from your father-in-law for months after he made a promise of a husband. What do you think her frame of mind was in performing this reckless act?

LIVE OUT ...

8. Judah asked Hirah to do his dirty work. Perhaps Hirah hoped to enjoy the harlot's company himself. Solomon warned of keeping company with harlots. Read Proverbs 7:6–26.

   a. Describe the characteristics of a man enticed by a harlot (vv. 7–9).

   b. List the attributes, charms, and enticements of the harlot (vv. 10–21).

   c. Describe the painful results of engaging in this behavior (vv. 22–26).

9. Judah enlisted others in his sin. Jesus said, "It is impossible that no offenses should come, but woe to him through whom they do come!" (Luke 17:1). Journal about a time you included another person in your sin. Ask God to forgive you. Then talk to Him about how you can right this wrong.

10. Judah was guiltier than Tamar in his actions. Yet he would have cried for mercy rather than demanding judgment as he did for her. Take the time to recite the Lord's Prayer regarding those you may have judged harshly:

> Our Father in heaven,
> Hallowed be Your name.
> Your kingdom come.
> Your will be done
> On earth as it is in heaven.
> Give us this day our daily bread.
> And forgive us our debts,
> As we forgive our debtors.
> And do not lead us into temptation,
> But deliver us from the evil one.
> For Yours is the kingdom and the power and the
>   glory forever. Amen. Matthew 6:9–13

LEARN ABOUT …

10 Harsh

Like Judah, we usually vent our harshest feelings toward others who are most like us. Counselors call this projecting, which describes placing our feelings onto others. When you're guilty of something, it's silly to assume everyone else is too. Jesus said, "Judge not, that you be not judged" (Matt. 7:1).

o o ● o o

Many attribute the prayer for peace to the thirteenth-century St. Francis of Assisi. However, the prayer in its present form cannot be traced back any further than 1912, when it was printed in France in a little inspiration magazine called *La Clochette*. It became popular in the United States during World War II when Cardinal Francis Spellman distributed millions of copies.

Since that time a variety of versions of this prayer have been publicized. Margaret Thatcher paraphrased it on the doorstep of 10 Downing Street to an audience of journalists to frame her tenure as England's prime minister. Mother Teresa and the Missionaries of Charity began each day by reciting its words. Even movies like *Rambo* have loosely quoted it.[10] Wouldn't it have been lovely if Judah had had a copy of this prayerful poem? Perhaps he could have learned its lesson of humility and charity rather than hostility and revenge. May we all be able to pray this prayer, wherever it originated:

> Lord, make me an instrument of Thy peace;
> where there is hatred, let me sow love;
> where there is injury, pardon;
> where there is doubt, faith;
> where there is despair, hope;
> where there is darkness, light;
> and where there is sadness, joy.
> O Divine Master,
> grant that I may not so much seek to be consoled as to console;
> to be understood, as to understand;
> to be loved, as to love;
> for it is in giving that we receive,
> it is in pardoning that we are pardoned,
> and it is in dying that we are born to Eternal Life. Amen.

LISTEN TO ...

Grace is love that cares and stoops and rescues.

—*John R. W. Stott*

DAY 5

Your Sins Will Find You Out

Unbelievably, the Northumbria police in England fingered a crook with one of his own fingers—no, not a finger*print*, *a finger*. Officers traced a motorcycle thief after discovering one of his fingers at the crime scene. The severed digit was found at a building site when workers called the police to report a motorcycle theft. In his hasty getaway, the thief had an accident in which detectives believe he was forced to rip his finger off after it became trapped under the crashed motorcycle.

Officers took the finger to the South Tyneside Hospital, where they found a man without a finger waiting in the accident and emergency department. Inspector Simon Charlton said, "I am sure it must be very painful for an offender to have ripped a finger from his hand, but it … left the police a good clue to go on." The man was transferred to the University of North Durham Hospital to have the finger reattached. A Northumbria Police spokesman said: "He is still undergoing surgery and he will be questioned by us in due course."[11]

Like the dim-witted thief, Judah left a trail of evidence that led straight to him. There would be no denying his part in the crime. Moses warned the children of Israel that if "you have sinned against the LORD … be sure your sin will find you out" (Num. 32:23). It's too bad that Judah never heard this piece of advice. Instead he would have to raise his hand and admit he was guilty. It was a hard lesson to learn.

LIFT UP …

Lord, thank You for working good out of difficult situations. When I am ashamed, help me to lift my eyes to You. Amen.

LOOK AT …

Foolishly, Judah demanded to have Tamar burned for committing adultery against his son Shelah. He didn't mention his promise to provide that son as her husband or his failure to keep his promise. Today we see that before Tamar would be publicly burned she lit a fire of her own. She unveiled evidence to reveal the identity of the man with whom she had sinned

LEARN ABOUT ...

1 Request

Our legal system demands that a person is innocent until proven guilty. Tamar's request for an audience with Judah was to prove her innocence. Previously her father-in-law had acted as prosecutor, judge, and jury. But now she would have her day in court. Little did Judah know that the evidence would point the signet finger directly at him.

2 Righteous?

As Judah passed premature judgment upon Tamar, judgment fell squarely upon him. The term "more righteous" is arbitrary. Both parties committed sin. That one was worse than the other did not justify either. Paul said, "When they measure themselves by themselves and compare themselves with themselves, they are not wise" (2 Cor. 10:12 niv).

and presented it openly for all to examine. Humbled, Judah realized that his poor choices brought him public disgrace. You cannot hide anything from the Creator of the universe. Whether now or later He will right all wrongs. Paul describes this getting what you deserve as reaping what you've sown. Paul wrote, "Do not be deceived, God is not mocked; for whatever a man sows, that he will also reap. For he who sows to his flesh will of the flesh reap corruption, but he who sows to the Spirit will of the Spirit reap everlasting life" (Gal. 6:7–8).

READ GENESIS 38:25–30.

When she was brought out, she sent to her father-in-law, saying, "By the man to whom these belong, I am with child." And she said, "Please determine whose these are—the signet and cord, and staff." So Judah acknowledged them and said, "She has been more righteous than I, because I did not give her to Shelah my son." And he never knew her again. Now it came to pass, at the time for giving birth, that behold, twins were in her womb. And so it was, when she was giving birth, that the one put out his hand; and the midwife took a scarlet thread and bound it on his hand, saying, "This one came out first." Then it happened, as he drew back his hand, that his brother came out unexpectedly; and she said, "How did you break through? This breach be upon you!" Therefore his name was called Perez. Afterward his brother came out who had the scarlet thread on his hand. And his name was called Zerah. Genesis 38:25–30

1. a. When Tamar was brought out for public condemnation, what did she bring, and what was her request?

   b. How do you think the crowd responded to her?

2. Describe Judah's response and how you think he felt.

3. As Tamar faced her accuser, do you think she felt vindicated for what she had done? Why or why not?

4. What kind of relationship do you expect the couple would have in the future?

5. In your own words, describe the unusual sequence of events during the birth of Tamar's twins.

6. What names were given to the boys?

LIVE OUT ...

7. a. It is interesting that Judah demanded judgment upon Tamar without seeking her equally guilty partner. A similar circumstance was brought to Jesus. Read John 8:1–11. Describe the case the Pharisees brought to Jesus to adjudicate (vv. 1–5).

   b. How did Jesus respond to their request?

   c. How did they respond (vv. 6–9)?

   d. Explain why you think this was the result.

   e. Recount the conversation between Jesus and the adulteress (vv. 10–11).

   f. How do you think she felt?

8. The text indicates that Judah would not have given Tamar an audience had she not requested it and shown evidence to clear her guilt. What about you? Do you ever judge others before hearing their sides? Journal about a time you thought that somebody was guilty of something, but eventually that person was proved innocent.

LEARN ABOUT ...

5 Red Thread

The scarlet thread tied upon the boy's hand points to the Messiah, whose shed blood redeems us all. That Judah was a Jew and Tamar a Gentile and that one of their sons would one day be included in the Lord's genealogy foreshadowed the truth that both Jews and Gentiles would share in the blessings of the gospel.

7 Ranked?

Humanity's view of righteousness differs drastically from God's. To Him sin is sin—none is lesser or greater than the other. Adulterers and gossips will meet the same fate. Peter wisely noted, "In truth I perceive that God shows no partiality" (Acts 10:34). Do you rank sins as mortal or venial? God doesn't.

9 Recorded

Jesus' genealogy includes Tamar, who played the harlot, and Rahab, the harlot from Jericho. Ruth the Moabitess, a people God deplored, is also included. Bathsheba, "the wife of Uriah" with whom David had an extramarital affair, shares a place. Jesus died for sinners that we may be included in His family too.

9. Judah's lineage would continue through Perez and Zerah. Fill in the following chart to follow their family tree.

SCRIPTURE	LINEAGE OF PEREZ
Numbers 26:20–22	
Ruth 4:12–22	
Nehemiah 11:4–6	
Matthew 1:2–3	

o o ● o o

God's redeeming Tamar's indiscretion by placing her within the Lord's genealogy gives hope to women with a tainted past. There's a new phenomenon happening in the adult industry—prostitutes who are getting saved. Annie Lobert sold her body for the first time trying to raise money to visit her Air Force boyfriend. Before she knew it, she signed up with an escort service and eventually moved to Sin City—Las Vegas, Nevada. But as with most women in the industry, one thing led to another, and she found herself using drugs, working for a pimp, and being physically abused. One day, Lobert overdosed on cocaine and had a heart attack. Convinced she was going to die, Lobert called to Jesus. She remembers a feeling of peace coming over her, as though God was so close that His face was inches away from hers. The striking blonde fully surrendered.

She started reading her Bible, watched Christian TV, and even joined a church. She eventually came to the realization that God wanted her to tell prostitutes, pimps, and others in the sex industry of His love for them. Now, through hookersforjesus.net, she ministers to others who were just like her. "I don't care if you're a prostitute, a pimp, a stripper, a porn star, or if you're just a regular person or a woman who's been sexually abused, or a man who's been sexually abused, or anyone who's been rejected in their life," Lobert says. "The message is the same across the board, because it's a message of redemption and love."[12]

LISTEN TO ...

If you are right, take the humble side—you will help the other fellow. If you are wrong, take the humble side—and you will help yourself.

—*Unknown*

Potiphar's Wife—The Desperate Housewife

Genesis 39

We've met amazing women in our study through Genesis. We saw the first and most perfect woman, Eve, who proved to be imperfect in her decision to eat forbidden fruit. We know now that if Eve hadn't done it, we would have. There was Sarah, who was protected by God when Abraham asked her to lie about her identity. In faith, she trusted God to give her a child in old age. Finally she gave birth to Isaac, the son of promise. We met Hagar, who ran to the desert but came face-to-face with God. Through her, we came face-to-face with God too. We read the love story of Rebekah and Isaac and remembered God's love for us. We engaged with the complicated love triangle of Rachel, Leah, and Jacob. We saw the sisters offer Bilhah and Zilpah to Jacob as mothers for their children. These women taught us that God is able to override our lack of faith, promote His plan, and restore all to faith.

We were devastated by Dinah's rape and her brothers' retaliation by wiping out an entire town. Through Dinah we learned that forgiveness, though difficult, is the path to healing. We've also met unnamed women like Noah's wife and Lot's wife. How noble was Noah's wife to have faith in God when everyone else doubted His word! And how faithless was Lot's wife in turning back to gaze upon a city doomed to destruction. Now we meet another nameless woman as we conclude our study in Genesis.

Interestingly, she was not in the Promised Land but in Egypt. We're calling Mrs. Potiphar "the Desperate Housewife." If she were a movie character, she might be Mrs. Robinson from *The Graduate*. Like Dustin Hoffman's character Ben Braddock, our hero Joseph could have said, "Mrs. Potiphar, you're trying to seduce me." She was a woman with too much money, too much time, and too little loyalty to her husband.

Day 1: Genesis 39:1–6   **HANDSOME HELPER**

Day 2: Genesis 39:7–10   **INDECENT PROPOSAL**

Day 3: Genesis 39:11–15   **ESCAPE ARTIST**

Day 4: Genesis 39:16–20   **FALSE WITNESS**

Day 5: Genesis 39:21–23   **FINDING GOD'S FAVOR**

DAY 1
Handsome Helper

LIFT UP ...

Lord, I know that You are with me wherever I go. Thank You for blessing me and those around me. Help me to see that all good things come from You. Amen.

LOOK AT ...

This week, we find Joseph a slave in Egypt in Potiphar's house. How did Joseph get to Egypt? Joseph's older brothers were extremely jealous of him. It could be because they saw Joseph as a tattletale. He "brought a bad report" (Gen. 37:2) about Bilhah's and Zilpah's sons. Though they must have been doing something truly wicked, the sons carried a grudge against Joseph. Maybe they were jealous because Joseph described his prophetic dreams. In these dreams wheat, stars, the sun, and the moon bowed to him (see Gen. 37:5–9). In addition, Jacob gave Joseph a coat of many colors, which may have indicated that Joseph would be Jacob's heir. So Joseph's brothers hatched a plot to kill the favored son. However, Reuben would not agree. To make a long story short, they threw Joseph into a pit, and while Reuben was away, Judah suggested they sell him into slavery. Ultimately Joseph was taken to Egypt, and the boys went home and reported to Jacob that Joseph was dead. This week we'll see how Joseph, one of the most righteous men in the Bible, dealt with a temptress in the house of his master.

READ GENESIS 39:1–6.

Now Joseph had been taken down to Egypt. And Potiphar, an officer of Pharaoh, captain of the guard, an Egyptian, bought him from the Ishmaelites who had taken him down there. The LORD was with Joseph, and he was a successful man; and he was in the house of his master the Egyptian. And his master saw that the LORD was with him and that the LORD made all he did to prosper in his hand. So Joseph found favor in his sight, and served him. Then he made him

LEARN ABOUT ...

I Bought

Potiphar was an Egyptian who most likely protected Pharaoh. The word *officer* comes from the root word *cayric*. It could mean a eunuch or a high chamberlain or courtier. Adam Clarke said, "It is not uncommon in the east for eunuchs to have wives."[1]

---

3 Believe

Joseph succeeded because of his faith in the Lord. Here "Lord" refers to Jehovah or Yahweh. This is one of the most important names of God in Scripture. God revealed Himself to Abraham, Isaac, and Jacob as Jehovah. At the burning bush, God revealed Himself more fully to Moses as Jehovah—I AM WHO I AM (Ex. 3).

---

5 Blessed

Twice in our study, two masters acknowledged that they were blessed because a child of God lived with them. Laban said to Jacob, "I have learned by experience that the Lord has blessed me for your sake" (Gen. 30:27). Here we find that Potiphar prospered because of Joseph's presence.

overseer of his house, and all that he had he put under his authority. So it was, from the time that he had made him overseer of his house and all that he had, that the Lord blessed the Egyptian's house for Joseph's sake; and the blessing of the Lord was on all that he had in the house and in the field. Thus he left all that he had in Joseph's hand, and he did not know what he had except for the bread which he ate. Now Joseph was handsome in form and appearance. Genesis 39:1–6

1. We know that Joseph was taken down to Egypt. Describe the man who bought him from the Ishmaelites.

2. a. How many times is the Lord named in this passage?

   b. What do you think this reveals about Joseph?

3. Let's dissect the phrase "the Lord was with Joseph" to understand how God's presence affected Joseph in Egypt. Two times we read the phrase "the Lord was with Joseph." What was the result of this?

4. "So" what did Potiphar do after he learned that "the Lord made all he did to prosper"?

5. We read that the Lord blessed the Egyptian's house. Describe the blessing God placed upon his house and why God blessed it.

6. To what extent did Potiphar trust Joseph?

7. How was Joseph described?

LIVE OUT ...

8. We saw that the Lord was with Jacob. In the book of Exodus, God told Moses, "I am the LORD. I appeared to Abraham, to Isaac, and to Jacob, as God Almighty, but by My name LORD I was not known to them" (Ex. 6:2–3). In what ways do you feel that God has revealed Himself as Jehovah, the Lord God Almightly, more fully through the study of the women of Genesis?

9. Both Potiphar and Laban experienced God's blessing because a believer was nearby.

 a. How do you think Jacob and Joseph blessed their masters in practical ways?

 b. How is it possible to bless others in spiritual ways?

 c. Why do you think God blessed the unbelieving masters?

10. Both Joseph and his mother, Rachel, were described as beautiful. Solomon wrote that God "has made everything beautiful in its time. Also He has put eternity in their hearts" (Eccl. 3:11). Use this Scripture as a starting point to pray for a beauty that is pleasing to the Lord. Thank Him for showing you just how beautiful you are in His sight.

∘ ∘ ● ∘ ∘

Egyptologists tell us that when Joseph was sold to Potiphar, slavery was a luxury and privilege for the ruling elite. Slaves were usually taken captive in war; native Egyptians became slaves when, poverty stricken, they sold

LEARN ABOUT ...

7 Beautiful

"Handsome in form and appearance" could be translated "beautiful in his person and beautiful in his countenance." In other words, he had a nice frame and fine-looking face. Apparently he got his looks from his mother, Rachel, who was also described as "beautiful of form and appearance" (Gen. 29:17).

8 Become

The Great I AM wants us to become more and more like Him. We are called "to be conformed to the image of His Son, that He might be the firstborn among many brethren" (Rom. 8:29). While salvation is immediate when we accept Christ as Lord, transformation takes a lifetime.

9 Be a Blessing

Even in tough situations, God blesses His own. But He also delights in blessing His people, because it is a witness to those who do not believe. His hand of blessing is open wide so that those who do not yet know Him can take His hand and follow Him. "God shall bless us, and all the ends of the earth shall fear Him" (Ps. 67:7).

LEARN ABOUT ...

10 Beyond Beautiful

God sees you as "beautiful." In His eyes you are fair, lovely, beyond duplication. You are one of a kind, made in His image. From Eve in the garden through all the women in the Bible, there is no one like *you!* The joys and trials in life have molded and shaped you into the woman God intended you to be. Celebrate your beauty!

themselves on the market. Thus, the foreign slaves were considered more valuable than natives because they were of higher rank.

It's no wonder Joseph rose to such a prominent position in Potiphar's household. Groomed to be Jacob's heir, he had every tool needed to prosper. No doubt Joseph had learned many valuable lessons both spiritually and practically from his father. When he put the principles to work in Potiphar's house and fields, he prospered.

Bible students see Joseph as foreshadowing Jesus, the true Servant. Jesus said, "Whoever desires to become great among you, let him be your servant. And whoever desires to be first among you, let him be your slave—just as the Son of Man did not come to be served, but to serve, and to give His life a ransom for many" (Matt. 20:26–28). The parallels are striking: Joseph was sold into slavery by his brothers for silver just as Jesus was sold out to the cross by Judas for thirty pieces of silver. Joseph became a slave so that his family could one day be nourished. Jesus became a servant so that the world could partake of the "bread of life" and never hunger again (see John 6:35). Everywhere Joseph went, the people were blessed. Jesus pronounced blessing after blessing, the greatest of which is eternal life. Have you received this blessing from Jesus?

LISTEN TO ...

Once it was the blessing, now it is the Lord.

—Albert Simpson

DAY 2

Indecent Proposal

The story is told about woman who absolutely loved apples. Her neighbor had a few apple trees that always produced sweet and crunchy apples. Occasionally she would creep into her neighbor's yard and pluck some apples to enjoy. She would look in the driveway to make sure the owner wasn't home. She would look left and right to make sure no one was around. She wanted to make sure no one was watching.

Every year, the woman looked forward to the apple season. She believed her little secret was safe. Soon she married and used the fresh apples to bake apple pies. But she never told where she got the apples. The couple had a baby girl who grew to be precious toddler. And the woman continued her little secret of taking the apples, always making sure no one was watching. One day she said, "Honey, I'm going for a walk with our darling daughter." So off she went, but she couldn't resist the delicious apples. So she looked in the driveway. She looked left and she looked right. She was ready to pick the delicious fruit when her small daughter said, "Mommy, you didn't look up. Don't you know that God is watching?"[2]

We're all tempted by something. Whether it's a desire for glittering gold, handsome hunks, or tasty treats, remember that God is watching all you do. Don't settle for sneaking around in the shadows when He is the one who "gives us richly all things to enjoy" (1 Tim. 6:17).

LIFT UP ...

Father, I know You never allow a temptation without providing a way of escape. Please help me to recognize when I am being tempted, and teach me how to answer the temptation with a godly response. Amen.

LOOK AT ...

The Lord was with Joseph and raised him to a position of prominence in Potiphar's household. Through Joseph's stewardship, everything prospered. It's amazing to think that Joseph could work so selflessly, knowing that he would not benefit personally. It's a lesson for all

LEARN ABOUT ...

I Longing

Potiphar's wife looked at Joseph with a burning desire. The word *cast* literally means she felt the weight of her power; in other words, she exalted herself. She looked at Joseph through proud, possessive eyes and expected him to yield. "There is a generation—oh, how lofty are their eyes! And their eyelids are lifted up" (Prov. 30:13).

3 Listing

Though a slave, Joseph was not silent. He cataloged his reasons for staying faithful: (1) He was committed to Potiphar; (2) she was committed to Potiphar; (3) he was committed to God. Believers should "always be ready to give a defense to everyone who asks you a reason for the hope that is in you" (I Peter 3:15).

of us. The Bible tells us that we should work "not with eyeservice, as men-pleasers, but as bondservants of Christ, doing the will of God from the heart" (Eph. 6:6). Clearly, Joseph was wholehearted in his service to his master.

Today we'll see that Potiphar's wife placed Joseph in a compromising position. We know that the world today is full of temptations at home, at work, and at play. Joseph is a good and godly example of how to deal with the temptations that come our way. Being tempted is not a sin. However, giving in to temptation *is* a sin. Let's see how Joseph did the decent thing when Mrs. Potiphar made an indecent proposal.

READ GENESIS 39:7–10.

And it came to pass after these things that his master's wife cast longing eyes on Joseph, and she said, "Lie with me." But he refused and said to his master's wife, "Look, my master does not know what is with me in the house, and he has committed all that he has to my hand. There is no one greater in this house than I, nor has he kept back anything from me but you, because you are his wife. How then can I do this great wickedness, and sin against God?" So it was, as she spoke to Joseph day by day, that he did not heed her, to lie with her or to be with her. Genesis 39:7–10

1. How did Potiphar's wife begin to look at Joseph?

2. What did she demand?

3. Joseph refused Mrs. Potiphar for a number of righteous reasons. Which phrase reveals that he refused because his master trusted him?

4. How did Joseph try to protect Potiphar's marriage?

5. What was Joseph's final reason for refusing Mrs. Potiphar's advances?

6. Describe how often Joseph was tempted and how he resisted.

LIVE OUT ...

7. Potiphar's wife looked at Joseph with longing. Read 1 John 2:16, and talk about how today's story can be connected to this passage. (For instance, how do you see Joseph working out the will of God?)

8. Consider what you look at with longing—whatever that may be that is not of God. Now journal an "exchange prayer" asking God to exchange that ungodly longing with a godly longing. Thank Him for satisfying you with good things instead.

> Oh, that men would give thanks to the LORD for His
> goodness,
> And for His wonderful works to the children of men!
> For He satisfies the longing soul,
> And fills the hungry soul with goodness. Psalm 107:8–9

9. Read James 1:12, and describe the outcome of resisting temptation. How have you experienced this in your life?

o o ● o o

In our first lesson, we saw Eve being tempted to eat the forbidden fruit. Now in our last lesson, we encounter Potiphar's wife, who serves as the temptress. You might call this the devolution of womanhood. Sin takes its toll, and temptation is everywhere.

LEARN ABOUT ...

6 Long Lasting

Mrs. Potiphar was persistent. She came to Joseph day after day with the same objective. Joseph was adamant in his refusal to give in to temptation. He put his obedience to Potiphar first. The word *heed* means that he didn't listen to or obey her. Wisely he tried to avoid being in the same place as the seductress.

7 Lusting

Lust is a desire for what is forbidden, an obsessive sexual craving. Lust refers to the desire for things that are contrary to the will of God. Christians are able to crucify the flesh through the power of the Holy Spirit (see Gal. 5:24). The flesh, with its passions and lusts, is to be denied (see Titus 2:12).

9 Life

When we're tempted, we're being lured to disobey or sin against God with the implied promise of pleasure. God does not tempt us, but he does allow the temptation to test our faith. Jesus promises great blessings to those who resist temptation. Jesus instructed us to pray, "Lead us not into temptation" (Luke 11:4 NIV).

James records the downward spiral that leads to temptation: "But each one is tempted when he is drawn away by his own desires and enticed. Then, when desire has conceived, it gives birth to sin; and sin, when it is full-grown, brings forth death" (James 1:14–15). What causes temptation? Our desires that run rampant. Mrs. Potiphar desired Joseph. He was young. He was handsome. He was available. But she wasn't.

We can't gaze into the Potiphar home and determine why Mrs. Potiphar wanted to cheat on her man. Social scientists tell us that women cheat for a variety of reasons. Some cheat out of boredom, loneliness, jealousy, or desire for revenge. Some do it to from low self-esteem or because they feel unloved. There are unknown and unknowable reasons for infidelity. The Bible tells us that the "heart is deceitful above all things" (Jer. 17:9).

It's evident that Potiphar's wife deceived herself into thinking her flesh could satisfy her spiritual cravings. Oh, that she could have known the love of God of Abraham, Isaac, and Jacob rather than seeking the love of man. She could have learned about the unconditional, eternal love of the Great I AM, the God Joseph served. She could have realized the true desires of her heart.

Listen to …

Holiness is not freedom from temptation, but power to overcome temptation.

—*G. Campbell Morgan*

DAY 3

Escape Artist

Christian author Dave Jackson and a friend of his were on a train to Kansas City when an attractive woman came and sat beside Jackson. He thought his friend (sitting several seats behind) was the "lucky guy" because he kept an empty seat beside him. Soon Jackson and the woman began a conversation, and he learned she was going home to see her mother after having had "some spats" with her husband. After a while, they both dropped off to sleep, and Jackson was shocked to find the woman's head on his shoulder.

Jackson wrote,

> She cuddled closer. I wondered what she really wanted—or would allow. At first I couldn't believe what I was thinking. But then it was her fault. She knew exactly what she was doing. I might as well enjoy it. After all, what could happen on a train full of people? Nothing, nothing really … except what Jesus warned about happening in the heart.
>
> Finally, I excused myself so I could go back and talk with my friend— the "lucky" one with the empty seat beside him. Or maybe I was the lucky one since that extra space was still available. I only knew I didn't need to stay where I had been.
>
> Perhaps it wasn't luck at all. Maybe that was the "way of escape" that 1 Corinthians 10:13 talks about, which God had provided from the beginning.[3]

People from all walks of life are tempted. The question isn't whether we're tempted, but rather how we respond to the temptation. Will we give in, or will we find the way of escape? God has promised to provide a way out—our job is to look for the escape hatch.

LIFT UP …

Lord God, please give me the wisdom to recognize temptations. Help me to run away as fast and as far as possible from the things that tempt me. And when I run, let me run to You. Amen.

LOOK AT ...

We've seen that Potiphar's wife tried to seduce Joseph into having an adulterous affair with her. He refused out of loyalty to his master, because he believed in the sanctity of marriage, and because it would have been a sin against God. Joseph tried to remove himself from the situation, but Mrs. Potiphar was relentless.

Today we'll see that he found himself alone with her and that she continued her sexual harassment. Now the temptation, which Joseph continued to resist, turned into a severe trial. Often, the trials in our lives are temptations that become adversities. Prolonged, they test whether our faith is true or false. For Joseph, facing a temptation landed him in the trial of prison. Could he believe that God was good when he resisted sexual temptation yet still faced imprisonment? For some of us, our trials are different. Perhaps we face the trial of physical suffering, marital discord, or emotional pain. It's been said that Satan tempts us so that we might sin, but God allows trials so that we might shine forth as pure gold. In today's passage we see that Joseph passed the test of his trial and won the gold medal. His faith was proved pure as gold.

READ GENESIS 39:11–15.

But it happened about this time, when Joseph went into the house to do his work, and none of the men of the house was inside, that she caught him by his garment, saying, "Lie with me." But he left his garment in her hand, and fled and ran outside. And so it was, when she saw that he had left his garment in her hand and fled outside, that she called to the men of her house and spoke to them, saying, "See, he has brought in to us a Hebrew to mock us. He came in to me to lie with me, and I cried out with a loud voice. And it happened, when he heard that I lifted my voice and cried out, that he left his garment with me, and fled and went outside." Genesis 39:11–15

1. a. What "happened" concerning Joseph's working conditions?

    b. Do you think this was accidental? Why or why not?

2. What proposition did Potiphar's wife extend again?

3. What occurred as Joseph fled?

4. When Potiphar's wife cried out to the other slaves, who did she first blame for the situation?

5. Why did Mrs. Potiphar say her husband brought Joseph into the household? What does this tell you about her?

6. According to Mrs. Potiphar, who initiated the encounter?

7. a. Based on her account, why did he flee?

   b. Do you think the other slaves would have believed this account? Why or why not?

LIVE OUT ...

8. a. Today we saw Joseph flee Potiphar's wife. Fill in the following chart to discover the things we as believers are encouraged to flee from.

SCRIPTURE	FLEE FROM
1 Corinthians 6:18	
1 Corinthians 10:14	
1 Timothy 6:10–11	

   b. Which of the above do you think Mrs. Potiphar was using to tempt Joseph?

LEARN ABOUT ...

3 Exposing

This is the second time Joseph lost a garment. The first time, his brothers took his coat of many colors when they threw him into the pit. This time, he was willing to be exposed and shed his garment to protect his purity. It's been said, "Joseph lost his coat but kept his character."

4 Mocking

Potiphar's wife enlisted other witnesses to boost her support among the household slaves. She believed that because they were native Egyptians they would be jealous of the Hebrew Joseph and his position. But there is a more subtle mockery. She also mocked her husband and his choice of bringing Joseph into the house.

7 Lying

We know that Joseph ran because he was righteous. But Mrs. Potiphar lied and told the servants he ran because he was guilty. She had the evidence in her hands and used it with a vengeance. The Bible tells us, "You shall not steal, nor deal falsely, nor lie to one another" (Lev. 19:11).

8 Submitting

The best way to flee from temptation is to submit to God. It may seem contradictory, because submission means to yield or give in to God, but when we surrender to God, we find the strength to resist Satan's enticements. James 4:7 says, "Submit to God. Resist the devil and he will flee from you." There is victory in surrender.

---

9 Loving

There is a way the world can know we are Christians. "By this all will know that you are My disciples, if you have love for one another" (John 13:35). For Joseph, the loving thing was to run from Potiphar's house. For us, the loving thing is to share the gospel message. Will you live love and share Christ?

c. Which do you need to flee from? Journal a prayer asking God to help you flee from this particular temptation.

9. When Mrs. Potiphar didn't get her way, she subtly mocked her husband and his choice of a Hebrew servant. Perhaps it was to draw attention away from her actions. Journal about a time you've felt like an outsider in an environment (work, school, or socially, etc.) because of your faith. How did you respond?

10. a. Mrs. Potiphar lied in order to falsely accuse Joseph. Talk about some of the people in this study who lied to get their way. How did God overcome their deception and work it out for good?

b. Does that make lying right? Please explain.

c. Now talk about a time you lied to get your way.

d. How will you try to walk in the truth, knowing that Jesus is "the way, the truth, and the life" (John 14:6)?

○ ○ ● ○ ○

Though the term is not in the Bible, what happened to Joseph was sexual harassment. The US Equal Employment Opportunity Commission (EEOC) states, "Unwelcome sexual advances, requests for sexual favors, and other verbal or physical conduct of a sexual nature constitutes sexual harassment when submission to or rejection of this conduct explicitly or implicitly affects an individual's employment, unreasonably interferes with an individual's work performance or creates an intimidating, hostile or offensive work environment."[4]

The EEOC acknowledges that sexual harassment can happen to either men or women. In our society sexual harassment occurs more often to women than men. However, adolescent males are more prone to experience sexual harassment than adult males. The EEOC goes on to say that any conduct that is unwelcome or of a sexual nature is harassment. This includes coarse jesting and inappropriate touching as well as acts of seduction.

The EEOC believes education is the best tool to prevent harassment. As mothers, we can educate our sons about the kind of behavior that is predatory. As women in the workplace, we can take measures to stand against men who treat women as sexual objects. We can make it clear we will not tolerate sexual harassment. As Paul wrote to the Corinthian church, which had been embroiled in a scandal of its own, "Watch, stand fast in the faith, be brave, be strong. Let all that you do be done with love" (1 Cor. 16:13–14).

LISTEN TO ...

Flee temptation and don't leave a forwarding address.

—Unknown

DAY 4
False Witness

It's no secret that powerful people sometimes have affairs with subordinates. Corporate America is full of these stories. In big cases, this leads to headlines and lawsuits. One such instance was the case of Adelyn Lee, who sued her boss and former boyfriend, Larry Ellison, chief executive of Oracle, for sexual harassment. Lee won $100,000 in round one of the lawsuits when she claimed she was fired for refusing to have sex with Ellison after their breakup. Her evidence was an e-mail supposedly sent to Ellison by her supervisor that said, "I have terminated Adelyn per your request."

But in a soap opera–like twist, Lee was brought up on charges of forging the e-mail. Ellison proved she committed perjury and falsified evidence by using data archives to prove his innocence. The jury agreed and found her guilty. Prosecutor Paul Wasserman said, "You cannot lie with impunity in a civil lawsuit and expect to get away with it." But no one came out smelling like a rose in this tabloid trial.[5]

Potiphar's wife was willing to bear false witness so Joseph would suffer. But Joseph never spoke a word against his accuser, nor did he reveal her treachery to her husband. Instead, he went to prison. Joseph, like Jesus, was sentenced without having done anything wrong.

LIFT UP ...

Father, I pray that You will help me to distinguish the truth from lies. Help me to keep my emotions under control so I can understand what is truly happening with the people around me and how to respond in a godly manner. Amen.

LOOK AT ...

Mrs. Potiphar continued harassing Joseph day after day, tempting him to lie with her and sin sexually. Joseph refused and resisted the temptation. The temptation became a trial when the woman of the house began crying wolf to the servants. Bringing the Egyptian servants in to corroborate her story of attempted rape, Potiphar's wife told a twisted version of the story, claiming that he instigated the relationship and fled when she cried out in protest.

We know Mrs. Potiphar was guilty of trying to commit adultery. We can rephrase Christ's words to fit a female situation: "You have heard that it was said to those of old, 'You shall not commit adultery.' But I say to you that whoever looks at a [man] to lust for [him] has already committed adultery with [him] in [her] heart" (Matt. 5:27–28). God also commands us not to bear false witness against our neighbors. How low was she willing to go?

Learn About …

I Incriminating

Joseph was probably wearing Egyptian clothing, as seen on ancient statues and cuneiform tablets. Herodotus said, "They wear tunics made of linen with fringes hanging about the legs, called *calasiris*, and loose white woolen cloaks over these." Men wore kiltlike loincloths. Women wore tunic dresses with straps.[6]

---

2 Intolerance

Throughout history, the Jewish people have faced prejudice. Satan has helped feed this powerful misperception because God promised that the Messiah would come from the chosen people and free all from sin's power. Joseph would rise to save his family from famine. No doubt, there were forces at work trying to take him out of the picture.

---

7 Indicted

Joseph foreshadowed Jesus, who was persecuted for righteousness' sake. Joseph was shackled and chained. Christ's captors "treated Him with contempt and mocked Him" (Luke 23:11). As believers, we can expect to be treated the same way. "If they persecuted Me, they will also persecute you" (John 15:20).

READ GENESIS 39:16–20.

So she kept his garment with her until his master came home. Then she spoke to him with words like these, saying, "The Hebrew servant whom you brought to us came in to me to mock me; so it happened, as I lifted my voice and cried out, that he left his garment with me and fled outside." So it was, when his master heard the words which his wife spoke to him, saying, "Your servant did to me after this manner," that his anger was aroused. Then Joseph's master took him and put him into the prison, a place where the king's prisoners were confined. And he was there in the prison. Genesis 39:16–20

1. What did Potiphar's wife do with Joseph's garment?

2. In her version of the incident, how did she reveal a prejudice against the Jews?

3. How did she try to make her husband feel guilty?

4. What words aroused Potiphar's anger?

5. Where was Joseph imprisoned?

6. Read Psalm 105:16–18, and describe how Joseph was treated at first in prison.

LIVE OUT …

7. Though he was without fault, Joseph was imprisoned based on the garment in Mrs. Potiphar's hands. If Christianity were a crime, would the world find you guilty? What evidence would they use against you in a court of law?

8. a. Potiphar's wife resorted to using prejudice to fuel the fire of her anger. Describe some instances of prejudice against Jewish people that you are aware of either historically or currently. Do you believe the prejudice is personal, political, or spiritual in nature? Please explain.

   b. Check the boxes below to indicate other types of prejudice you may have witnessed or encountered.

   ❏ Racial   ❏ Economic   ❏ Social
   ❏ Religious   ❏ Gender   ❏ Other _____

   c. How should knowing Jesus set us free from prejudice?

∘ ∘ ● ∘ ∘

Joseph suffered in prison, having his ankles fettered with chains and his neck bound in iron. Why would God allow this good man to suffer such harsh persecution? We can't always understand God's ways. But we do know that Joseph endured persecution and prospered. In fact, persecution put him in place to promote the safety of Egypt and of his family.

The same was true for Christ's disciples after His death and resurrection. They were persecuted for righteousness' sake in order to spread the gospel message throughout the world. According to *Foxe's Book of Martyrs,* James the brother of John was beheaded. Thomas went to the Parthians, Medes, and Persians and was slain with a lance or dart in India. Simon the Zealot traveled to Britain and was crucified. Bartholomew went to Armenia, where he was beaten, crucified, then beheaded. Matthew wrote the gospel, went to Egypt, and supposedly converted their king Hircanus. It is said he was run through with a sword. Philip journeyed to Phrygia (modern Turkey) and was crucified and stoned to death.

Peter was crucified upside down because he believed he wasn't worthy to die in the same manner as his Lord. John, author of our gospel, was boiled in oil and eventually died on the island of Patmos. Andrew (Peter's brother) went to Ethiopia and when threatened with crucifixion said, "O cross, most welcome and long looked for; with a willing mind, joyfully and desirously, I come to thee, being the scholar of Him which did hang on thee; because I have always been thy lover, and have coveted to embrace thee."[7] Persecution can bring passion that saves lives. If you're being persecuted for righteousness' sake, ask God to give you the strength to find joy in the trial and glorify Him through your suffering.

LISTEN TO ...

Wherever you see persecution, there is more than a probability that truth is on the persecuted side.

—Hugh Latimer

DAY 5

Finding God's Favor

When my (Penny's) oldest daughter graduated from high school, a Disneyland Imagineer gave the commencement address. I settled back to listen, thinking he might give the kids a few comments about higher education or how they too could make it in the big world. Then his words began to inspire me. I quickly asked my husband for a pen and scribbled down his incredible message.

The Imagineer acknowledged he had heard these words at a graduation he attended, but they are well worth remembering:

> People are unreasonable, illogical, and self-centered. Love them anyway.
>
> If you do good, people will accuse you of selfish ulterior motives. Do good anyway.
>
> If you are successful, you will win false friends and true enemies. Succeed anyway.
>
> Honesty and frankness make you vulnerable. Be honest and frank anyway.
>
> The good you do today will be forgotten tomorrow. Do good anyway.
>
> The biggest people with the biggest ideas can be shot down by the smallest people with the smallest minds. Think big anyway.
>
> People favor underdogs but follow only top dogs. Fight for some underdogs anyway.
>
> What you spend years building may be destroyed overnight. Build anyway.

Joseph decided he would do good and succeed despite what small-minded and selfish people had done to him. His ability to think big allowed him to have the vision to help Egypt and the surrounding nations survive famine. Amazingly, Joseph the underdog became the top dog in a foreign land. He was restored to his family. Most importantly, he found favor with God. What a true success story!

Lift up ...

Lord, thank You for offering me favor even in unexpected places. Help me to honor You regardless of the position You place me in, knowing that I am really serving You. Amen.

Look at ...

Wrongly imprisoned, Joseph found himself in circumstances beyond his control. He was now in the king's prison, under the rule of the prison keeper. He was probably around eighteen years old when he entered Potiphar's service. Some estimate that he was around twenty years old when the prison doors slammed shut behind him. When he began to serve as Pharaoh's vizier, he was thirty. Later, he married and had two sons named Ephraim and Manasseh. The biblical record states that he lived to be 110 years old (see Gen. 50:26). After four hundred years, his descendants carried his mummified remains to the Promised Land to be buried as he had requested.

What was the secret to Joseph's success? How did he find favor with people and God? Surely, it can only be explained because Joseph was a man of remarkable faith. Through problems and prosperity he stayed true to the Lord. Can the same be said of you?

Learn About ...

2 Found Favor

Favor speaks of a superior offering goodwill to a person in an inferior or subordinate position. Most often it speaks of God offering His blessing to people. In this case, God opened the eyes of the prison keeper to see Joseph in his true light—as a noble and good man.

Read Genesis 39:21–23.

But the LORD was with Joseph and showed him mercy, and He gave him favor in the sight of the keeper of the prison. And the keeper of the prison committed to Joseph's hand all the prisoners who were in the prison; whatever they did there, it was his doing. The keeper of the prison did not look into anything that was under Joseph's authority, because the LORD was with him; and whatever he did, the LORD made it prosper. Genesis 39:21–23

1. a. In prison, how was the Lord with Joseph personally?

b. Why do you think this passage begins with the word *But?*

2. What did the Lord give Joseph in the eyes of the prison keeper?

3. a. Who did Joseph have responsibility over?

b. How do you imagine he treated these people?

4. Explain why the prison keeper was comfortable with Joseph's leadership.

5. How did the Lord reward Joseph?

6. Do you think this means Joseph prospered financially? Why or why not?

LIVE OUT ...

7. As we close our study of Joseph and the women in Genesis, let's spend some time reflecting on the lessons we've learned. We know that Joseph found favor in the prison keeper's eyes. How has this study helped you look at people or circumstances through God's eyes?

8. We saw how God extended mercy and allowed Joseph to prosper in prison. We believe that in turn Joseph extended mercy to the prisoners in his care.

a. Review the list of the women we've studied and describe how God was merciful and/or allowed each of them to prosper.

Eve:

Noah's wife:

Sarah:

Hagar:

Lot's wife:

Rebekah:

Rachel:

Leah:

Bilhah and Zilpah:

Dinah:

Tamar:

Potiphar's wife:

b. Now journal about how God has been merciful to you during this study. How has He allowed you to prosper physically, emotionally, or spiritually in the true sense of the word?

○ ○ ● ○ ○

LEARN ABOUT ...

8 Personal Prosperity

The psalmist describes the person who prospers as a healthy tree planted by a river. A godly woman will be blessed when she delights in God's Word and meditates on the meaning of Scripture. "[S]he shall be like a tree ... whose leaf also shall not wither; and whatever [s]he does shall prosper" (Ps. 1:3). Does this portray you?

When the story of your life is recorded, will your descendants say that the Lord was with you? From the outside looking in, anyone looking at Joseph's early life might not have really believed that the Lord was with him. But one phrase remained constant through Joseph's life: "The Lord was with him."

Pastor Chuck Smith described what *did not happen* as a result of the Lord's presence with Joseph:

It *did not* prevent his brothers from hating him.

It *did not* prevent him from being sold into slavery.

It *did not* prevent him from being tempted by Potiphar's wife.

It *did not* prevent him from being falsely accused.

It *did not* prevent him from imprisonment.

But there were also blessings from God's presence. Here is a list of what God's presence *did do.*

It kept him from sin.

It gave him success.

It propelled him to a new position.[8]

When Jacob died, Joseph went home to bury his father. After returning to Egypt, he met with his brothers, who trembled at the thought that he would exact revenge for the evil they had done to him. Joseph's words have echoed through time as God's standard for anyone dealing with trials: "You meant evil against me; but God meant it for good" (Gen. 50:20).

We pray that you will see that God will turn all things for good when you love Him. May your life be filled with beautiful relationships, especially the most important relationship—a personal relationship with Jesus Christ, the Lord and Savior.

notes

Definitions are taken from Biblesoft PC Study Bible, Version 4.2b, © 1988–2004: *The New Unger's Bible Dictionary, Nelson's Bible Dictionary, Vine's Expository Dictionary of New Testament Words, Vine's Expository Dictionary of Biblical Words,* and *Strong's Greek/Hebrew Definitions.*

INTRODUCTION

1 Herbert Lockyer, *All the Women of the Bible* (Grand Rapids, MI: Zondervan, 1967), 13.

LESSON 1: EVE—TROUBLE IN PARADISE

1 Warren W. Wiersbe, *Be Basic* (Colorado Springs, CO: David C. Cook, 1998), 42.

2 *Matthew Henry's Commentary on the Whole Bible: New Modern Edition,* Electronic Database (Peabody, MA: Hendrickson Publishers, Inc., 1991).

3 John Morris, "People's self-esteem is more tied to appearances than to 'what's inside': UW study," University of Waterloo, July 31, 2007, http://newsrelease.uwaterloo.ca/news.php?id=4890 (accessed January 7, 2008).

4 *Nelson's Illustrated Bible Dictionary,* in PC Study Bible, version 4.2b (Seattle: Biblesoft, 2004), adapted.

5 *The New Unger's Bible Dictionary* (Chicago: Moody Press, 1988), adapted.

6 David Wallechinsky and Irving Wallace, "Biography of Gangsters: Arizona Clark 'Ma' Barker," www.trivia-library.com/c/biography-of-gangsters-arizona-clark-ma-barker.htm (accessed January 11, 2008), adapted.

7 *Matthew Henry's Commentary on the Whole Bible:* "Genesis 3:16," *Bible Illustrator for Windows Version,* version 3.0F (Parsons Technology, 1998), adapted.

8 John H. Gerstner, "The Language of the Battlefield," *Our Savior God: Studies on Man, Christ and the Atonement,* ed. James M. Boice (Grand Rapids, MI: Baker, 1980), 159–60.

9 Warren Wiersbe, *Be Basic* (Colorado Springs, CO: David C. Cook, 1998), 69.

10 *Matthew Henry's Commentary on the Whole Bible: New Modern Edition,* Electronic Database (Peabody, MA: Hendrickson Publishers, Inc., 1991).

11 *International Standard Bible Encyclopaedia,* Electronic Database (Seattle: Biblesoft, 1996).

12 W. Marc Whitford, "Breakthroughs in Science, Toad Flavored Sheep," *Clarkson Integrator*, September 26, 1972, adapted.

LESSON 2: NOAH'S WIFE—BEHIND EVERY GREAT MAN

1 Wolfgang Mieder, Steward A. Kingsbury, and Kelsie B. Harder, eds., *Dictionary of American Proverbs* (New York: Oxford University Press, 1992).

2 Author unknown, "First Ladies: Political Role and Public Image," www.sites.si.edu (accessed January 15, 2008).

3 *Nelson's Illustrated Bible Dictionary*, in PC Study Bible, version 4.2b (Seattle: Biblesoft, 2004), adapted.

4 James Montgomery Boice, *Genesis, Volume I: Creation and Fall (Genesis 1–11)* (Grand Rapids, MI: Baker, 1998), 291.

5 *The New Unger's Bible Dictionary* (Chicago: Moody Press, 1988), adapted.

6 Ana Marie Cox, "The Myth about Girls Going Wild," March 23, 2006, http://www.time.com/time/nation/article/0,8599,1176483,00.html?iid=fb_share (accessed January 13, 2006).

7 Author unknown, "Family Values," www.wikipedia.com (accessed January 17, 2008).

8 John Phillips, *Exploring Genesis: An Expository Commentary* (Chicago: Moody Press, 1980), 81.

9 *The New Unger's Bible Dictionary* (Chicago: Moody Press, 1988), adapted.

10 Dr. Andrew Kennedy Hutchison Boyd, *The Recreations of a Country Parson* (Boston: Ticknor and Fields, 1861), 189.

11 *The New Unger's Bible Dictionary* (Chicago: Moody Press, 1988), adapted.

12 *Easton's Bible Dictionary,* in PC Study Bible, version 4.2b (Seattle: Biblesoft, 2004), adapted.

13 James Patterson and Peter Kim, *The Day America Told the Truth* (New York: Prentice Hall Trade, 1991), quoted in William Willimon, "Don't Think for Yourself," *Preach-*

ing Today (Copyright © 2008 FindEx.com, Inc., and its licensors, used by permission), adapted.

14 Jennifer Stawarz, "Infant snoring linked to parental snoring," November 4, 2006, http://www.innovations-report.com/html/reports/studies/report-57836.html (accessed February 3, 2008).

15 Author unknown, "It's All in the Family: Mental Health Link between Parents and Children," http://family.samhsa.gov/be/family.aspx (accessed January 23, 2008), adapted.

16 *Nelson's Bible Dictionary,* in PC Study Bible, version 4.2b (Seattle: Biblesoft, 2004), adapted.

17 "Topic: Obedience," Index #2614-2619 (Copyright © 2008 FindEx.com, Inc., and its licensors, used by permission), adapted.

18 *Adam Clarke's Commentary,* "Genesis 7:16," in PC Study Bible, version 4.2b (Seattle: Biblesoft, 2004), adapted.

LESSON 3: SARAH—STAND BY YOUR MAN

1 Denise Noe, "Thoughts on Stand by Your Man," October 21, 2007, http://mensnews-daily.com/2007/10/21/thoughts-on-stand-by-your-man/ (accessed January 26, 2008).

2 Following Stephen's precedent in Acts 7:2, we will call the couple Sarah and Abraham throughout the study, although they were initially named Sarai and Abram, respectively.

3 *The New Unger's Bible Dictionary* (Chicago: Moody Press, 1988), adapted.

4 *Nelson's Bible Dictionary,* in PC Study Bible, version 4.2b (Seattle: Biblesoft, 2004), adapted.

5 Dr. Greg Smalley and Dr. Michael Smalley, "How Do You Leave and Cleave?" http://www.crosswalk.com/marriage/677998/ (accessed January 24, 2008).

6 "Relating: Dealing with Little White Lies," www.theknot.com (accessed January 25, 2008), adapted.

7 Warren Wiersbe, *Be Obedient: Learning the Secret of Living By Faith* (Colorado Springs, CO: David C. Cook, 2004), 22.

8 *Fausset's Bible Dictionary,* Electronic Database (Seattle: Biblesoft, 1998).

9 "Dishonesty: Sin of Dishonesty," Index #575–577 (Copyright © 2008 FindEx.com, Inc., and its licensors, used by permission), adapted.

10 Jacqueline Beals, PhD, "Lower Dopamine Receptor Density Reduces Ability to Learn from Mistakes," December 6, 2007, *Medscape Today*, www.medscape.com (accessed January 28, 2008).

11 Thomas Robinson, *The Bible Timeline* (London: Murdoch Books, 1992).

12 *Nelson's Illustrated Bible Dictionary* in PC Study Bible, version 4.2b (Seattle: Biblesoft, 2004), adapted.

13 Paul Johnson, *The Spectator*, June 8, 1996, quoted in *Christianity Today*, October 7, 1996.

14 "Angels: Cloud Lane," Index 143–149 (Copyright © 2008 FindEx.com, Inc., and its licensors, used by permission), adapted.

15 John Phillips, *Exploring Genesis: An Expository Commentary* (Chicago: Moody Press, 1980), 168.

16 James S. Hewett, ed., *Illustrations Unlimited* (Wheaton, IL: Tyndale House, 1988), 411.

17 David B. Bohl, "The Essence of All Growth in Life," *Dumb Little Man: Tips for Life*, February 2, 2008, www.dumblittleman.com/2008/02/essence-of-all-growth-in-life.html (accessed February 3, 2008).

18 Ibid.

LESSON 4: HAGAR—WHERE DO I FIT IN?

1 Author unknown, "History of English Society," www.wikipedia.com (accessed January 30, 2008).

2 *McClintock and Strong's Encyclopedia*, Electronic Database (Seattle: Biblesoft, 2000), adapted.

3 James S. Hewett, ed., *Illustrations Unlimited* (Wheaton, IL: Tyndale House, 1988), 219–220.

4 *Nelson's Illustrated Bible Dictionary,* in PC Study Bible, version 4.2b (Seattle: Biblesoft, 2004).

5 Carl T. Hall, "Living in Pain—Affliction: For chronic pain sufferers, even hope can hurt," *San Francisco Chronicle*, April 5, 1999, http://www.sfgate.com/cgi-bin/article.cgi?file=/chronicle/archive/1999/04/05/MN37A1P.DTL (February 1, 2008), adapted.

6 Warren Wiersbe, *Be Obedient: Learning the Secret of Living by Faith* (Colorado Springs, CO: David C. Cook, 2004), 58.

7 *The New Unger's Bible Dictionary* (Chicago: Moody Press, 1988), adapted.

8 Darrell G. Young, "The Roots of the Israeli-Arab Conflict," *Focus on Jerusalem Prophecy Ministry*, August 2005, www.focusonjerusalem.com/TheRootsoftheIsraeli-ArabConflict. htm (accessed February 2, 2008).

9 *Nelson's Illustrated Bible Dictionary*, in PC Study Bible, version 4.2b (Seattle: Biblesoft, 2004), adapted.

10 Howard F. Vos, *Genesis* (Chicago: Moody Press, 1999), 98.

11 David Van Biema, "The Legacy of Abraham," *Time*, September 30, 2002, www.time.com (accessed February 5, 2008).

12 Ibid.

LESSON 5: LOT'S WIFE—LIVING IN THE PAST

1 T. Young, "Stop Living in the Past," *EZine Articles*, August 22, 2006, EZineArticles.com (accessed February 26, 2008).

2 *Nelson's Bible Dictionary*, in PC Study Bible, version 4.2b (Seattle: Biblesoft, 2004), adapted.

3 Jay Jones, "For Gays in Las Vegas, the Welcome Mat is Out," *Los Angeles Times*, October 3, 2007, www.latimes.com/entertainment (accessed February 25, 2008).

4 Author unknown, "Knock-Knock Jokes," www.wikipedia.com (accessed January 20, 2009).

5 *Matthew Henry's Commentary*, in PC Study Bible, version 4.2b (Seattle: Biblesoft, 2004), adapted.

6 *Nelson's Illustrated Bible Dictionary*, in PC Study Bible, version 4.2b (Seattle: Biblesoft, 2004), adapted.

7 C. S. Lewis, *Mere Christianity* (New York: HarperCollins, 2001), 117.

8 Aesop, "The Town Mouse and the Country Mouse," ed. D. L. Ashliman, 2000, www. pitt.edu/~dash/type0112.html#aesop (accessed February 28, 2008), adapted.

9 *Nelson's Illustrated Bible Dictionary*, in PC Study Bible, version 4.2b (Seattle: Biblesoft, 2004), adapted.

10 "Pursued by the Atoning Love," QuickVerse SermonBuilder (Copyright © 2008 FindEx. com, Inc., and its licensors, used by permission).

11 Reuters, "The Long Journey of a Homesick Cat," October 11, 1999, http://www.blakjak. demon.co.uk/stz_ljhc.htm (accessed February 28, 2008), adapted.

12 *Strong's Greek/Hebrew Dictionary*, in PC Study Bible, version 4.2b (Seattle: Biblesoft, 2004), adapted.

13 Tino Wallenda, "The Flying Wallendas," www.wallenda.com/history.html (accessed February 4, 2008).

LESSON 6: REBEKAH—A FAIRY-TALE ROMANCE

1 *The Wycliffe Bible Commentary*, Electronic Database (Chicago: Moody Press, 1962).

2 *Nelson's Illustrated Bible Dictionary*, in PC Study Bible, version 4.2b (Seattle: Biblesoft, 2004), adapted.

3 *McClintock and Strong's Encyclopedia*, Electronic Database (Seattle: Biblesoft, 2000).

4 Lenya Heitzig, *Holy Moments* (Ventura, CA: Regal, 2006), 21–22.

5 John Phillips, *Exploring Genesis: An Expository Commentary* (Chicago: Moody Press, 1980), 191.

6 Herbert Lockyer, *All the Women of the Bible* (Grand Rapids, MI: Zondervan, 1967), 135.

7 Rich Deem, *Scientific Evidence for Answered Prayer and the Existence of God*, March 18, 2007, www.godandscience.org/apologetics/prayer.html (accessed March 1, 2008), adapted.

8 *Responsibility of Being Best Man and Maid of Honor*, January 2007, www.static.cnhi.zope. net (accessed March 1, 2008).

9 John Phillips, *Exploring Genesis: An Expository Commentary* (Chicago: Moody Press, 1980), 192.

10 *Matthew Henry's Commentary on the Whole Bible: New Modern Edition*, Electronic Database (Peabody, MA: Hendrickson Publishers, Inc., 1991).

11 *Nelson's Illustrated Bible Dictionary*, in PC Study Bible, version 4.2b (Seattle: Biblesoft, 2004), adapted.

12 *Nelson's Illustrated Bible Dictionary*, in PC Study Bible, version 4.2b (Seattle: Biblesoft, 2004), adapted.

13 *The New Unger's Bible Dictionary* (Chicago: Moody Press, 1988), adapted.

14 *Nelson's Illustrated Bible Dictionary*, in PC Study Bible, version 4.2b (Seattle: Biblesoft, 2004), adapted.

15 Herbert Lockyer, *All the Women of the Bible* (Grand Rapids, MI: Zondervan, 1967), 135.

16 *The New Unger's Bible Dictionary* (Chicago: Moody Press, 1988), adapted.

17 Donna Lea Simpson, "What Defines a Romance Novel?" November 12, 2007, http://romancefiction.suite101.com/article.cfm/what_defines_a_romance_novel (accessed February 7, 2008).

LESSON 7: RACHEL AND LEAH—HE LOVES ME, HE LOVES ME NOT

1 Warren Wiersbe, *Be Authentic: Exhibiting Real Faith in the Real World* (Colorado Springs, CO: David C. Cook, 1997), 38.

2 Ivan Berger, "He Loves Me Not, Digitally," *New York Times,* February 12, 2004, http://www.nytimes.com/2004/02/12/technology/circuits/12love.html (accessed March 9, 2008).

3 Reuters, "Love at First Sight or in Half a Second," September 18, 2007, http://www.reuters.com/article/lifestyleMolt/idUSN1844443620070918 (accessed March 9, 2008).

4 James Montgomery Boice, *Genesis: Volume 2* (Grand Rapids, MI: Baker Books, 1998), 781.

5 Barry L. Ross, PhD, "The Patriarchs and Hurrian Social and Legal Customs," Anderson University School of Theology, facultyweb.anderson.edu/~blross/Lec.Cultural%20Background%20of%20the%20Patriarchs.doc (accessed March 11, 2008).

6 *Nelson's Illustrated Bible Dictionary*, in PC Study Bible, version 4.2b (Seattle: Biblesoft, 2004), adapted.

7 Dr. Wolfgang Ziegler, "Is It the Truth?" December 8, 2005, www.digaria.com (accessed March 11, 2008).

8 Herbert Lockyer, *All the Women of the Bible* (Grand Rapids, MI: Zondervan, 1967), 83.

9 *Nelson's Illustrated Bible Dictionary*, in PC Study Bible, version 4.2b (Seattle: Biblesoft, 2004), adapted.

LESSON 8: DINAH—TRUE LOVE WAITS

1 Kelli Mahoney, "Answers to Christian Teens' Questions about Date Rape," 2008, http://christianteens.about.com/od/advice/a/DateRapeFAQs.htm (accessed March 29, 2008).

2 *Strong's Greek/Hebrew Definitions*, in PC Study Bible, version 4.2b (Seattle: Biblesoft, 2004), adapted.

3 "'Roofies': The Date Rape Drug," *Newsweek,* February 26, 1996, http://www.newsweek.com/id/101568 (accessed March 29, 2008).

4 Nancy Gibbs, "When Is It Rape?" *Time,* June 24, 2001, http://www.time.com/time/magazine/article/0,9171,1101910603-157165,00.html (accessed March 31, 2008).

5 Warren Wiersbe, *Be Authentic* (Colorado Springs, CO: David C. Cook, 1997), 63.

6 John Phillips, *Exploring Genesis: An Expository Commentary* (Chicago: Moody Press, 1980), 270.

7 Norman Vincent Peale, *This Incredible Century* (Chicago: Tyndale, 1991), quoted in *Men of Integrity* (Copyright © 2008 FindEx.com, Inc., and its licensors, used by permission), adapted.

8 "Ending Violence against Women and Girls," United Nations Population Fund, http://www.unfpa.org/swp/2000/english/ch03.html (accessed January 22, 2009).

9 Rabbi Moshe Schapiro, "What Is Circumcision?" *Jewish Literacy*, January 18, 2000, http://www.aish.com/literacy/lifecycle/What_is_Circumcision$.asp (accessed April 3, 2008).

10 Warren Wiersbe, *Be Authentic* (Colorado Springs, CO: David C. Cook, 1997), 64–65.

11 John Phillips, *Exploring Genesis: An Expository Commentary* (Chicago: Moody Press, 1980), 271.

12 Zsa Zsa Palagyi, "Heather Gemmen: Finding 'Beauty' after Rape," http://www.cbn.com/700club/features/Amazing/Heather_Gemmen022406.aspx (accessed April 3, 2008), adapted.

LESSON 9: TAMAR—A WOMAN SCORNED

1 *The New Dictionary of Cultural Literacy, Third Edition,* ed. E. D. Hirsch Jr., Joseph F. Kett, and James Trefil (New York: Houghton Mifflin, 2002), adapted.

2 Andy Granias, "Why do political wives stand by?" Badger Herald, March, 13, 2008, www.badgerherald.com (accessed March 26, 2008), adapted.

3 Claudia Feldman, "United we stand," Houston Chronicle, March 11, 2008, www.chron.com (accessed March 26, 2008).

4 My Three Sons, http://www.museum.tv/archives/etv/M/htmlM/mythreesons/mythreesons.htm (accessed March 26, 2008).

5 John Phillips, Exploring Genesis: An Expository Commentary (Chicago: Moody Press, 1980), 304.

6 Matthew Henry's Commentary on the Whole Bible: New Modern Edition, Electronic Database (Peabody, MA: Hendrickson Publishers, Inc., 1991).

7 "Samuel Medley, 1738–1799," Stem Publishing, www.stempublishing.com/hymns/biographies/medley.html (accessed March 28, 2008).

8 Herbert Lockyer, *All the Women of the Bible* (Grand Rapids, MI: Zondervan, 1967), 163.

9 Matthew Henry's Commentary on the Whole Bible: New Modern Edition, Electronic Database (Peabody, MA: Hendrickson Publishers, Inc., 1991).

10 Author unknown, "The Prayer of St. Francis," www.wikipedia.com (accessed January 22, 2009).

11 "Lost finger leads police to thief," BBC News, http://news.bbc.co.uk/2/hi/uk_news/england/tyne/6937570.stm (accessed January 22, 2009).

12 John Przybys, "Hookers for Jesus: Reaching Out," Las Vegas Review-Journal, February 19, 2008, http://www.lvrj.com/living/15760547.html (accessed March 30, 2008).

LESSON 10: POTIPHAR'S WIFE—THE DESPERATE HOUSEWIFE

1 *Adam Clarke's Commentary,* "Genesis 39:1," in PC Study Bible, version 4.2b (Seattle: Biblesoft, 2004), adapted.

2 "Temptation," QuickVerse SermonBuilder (Copyright © 2008 FindEx.com, Inc., and its licensors, used by permission).

3 Dave Jackson, "Escape," *Leadership,* January 1, 1988, www.ctlibrary.com/le/1988/winter/88/1052.html (accessed April 14, 2008), adapted.

4 "Facts about Sexual Harassment," US Equal Employment Opportunity Commission, June 27, 2002, www.eeoc.gov/facts/fs-sex.html (accessed April 16, 2008), adapted.

5 Benjamin Pimentel, "Woman Who Accused Oracle Chief Guilty of Perjury," January 29, 1997, http://www.sfgate.com/cgi-bin/article/comments/view?f=/c/a/1997/01/29/MN32281.DTL (accessed April 17, 2008), adapted.

6 André Dollinger, "Articles of Dress," http://nefertiti.iwebland.com/religion/body_and_soul.htm (accessed April 17, 2008), adapted.

7 W. Grinton Berry, ed., *Foxe's Book of Martyrs* (Grand Rapids, MI: Baker Books, 1978), 6–18, adapted.

8 Chuck Smith, "Genesis 39 Study Notes," www.calvarychapelcostamesa.com (accessed April 17, 2008).